OUT OF ASHES

OUT OF ASHES
THE BOERS' STRUGGLE FOR FREEDOM THROUGH THE ENGLISH WAR 1899-1902

By

DANIEL J. THERON
B.A., B.D., M.A.,Th.D./Ph.D.

ISBN 1-58721-152-1

1stBooks – Rev. 7/27/00

ABOUT THE BOOK

The book, as indicated by the title, deals with the struggle for freedom and self-determination of the Boers in South Africa. It had its beginning when the author's mother had penned her memoirs about her family's experiences during that war, fleeing in ox wagons to escape the concentration camps. He also well remembers many stories about the war told by his father, a Cape rebel, who took up arms under Jan Smuts. The book intertwines these recollections with the course of a bitter war for the gold fields of Johannesburg. It tells the compelling story of the holocaust of home and hearth in a scorched earth policy to bring the courageous Boers to their knees and to surrender their freedom. It gives a moving account of the concentration camps in which thousands of children, women, and old men had perished. The last two chapters recount how the Boers, like a phoenix, miraculously revived from the ashes, and deal with the political developments of the twentieth century in South Africa until 1999.

DEDICATED IN DEEP REVERENCE
TO THE MEMORY OF

MY MATERNAL GREAT-GRANDPARENTS

DAWID STEPHANUS AND
MAGDALENA JOHANNA [LOUW] DE VILLIERS

MY GRANDPARENTS

DANIEL JOHANNES JACOBUS AND
MARIA JOHANNA [HUGO] THERON

JACOB AND MAGDALENA JOHANNA [DE VILLIERS]
STORM

MY PARENTS

DANIEL JOHANNES JACOBUS AND
NEELTJE JOHANNA ELIZABETH [STORM] THERON

THE BOERS UNDER ARMS WHO FELL IN BATTLE OR
DIED AS A RESULT OF THE WAR

AND TO

THE THOUSANDS OF INNOCENT CHILDREN, WOMEN,
AND OLD MEN

WHO HAD DIED

IN THE CONCENTRATION CAMPS

TABLE OF CONTENTS

PREFACE AND ACKNOWLEDGMENTS

Genocide and religiocide are two inescapable blots on the history of mankind, even to this day, and will without doubt continue to repeat their repulsive manifestation in history to come. The twentieth century, the bloodiest in the chronicles of mankind, in spite of so much that are worthy of pride, is pock-marked by instances of both genocide and religiocide. The century began with the near extinction of the Boers in the two republics of the Transvaal and Orange Free State during the English War of 1899-1902.

This book had its beginning when the author's mother, Neëlte Johanna Elizabeth Theron (nee Storm), committed her recollections of this war to writing. She was a young child, not quite seven years old, when this devastating war broke out. She was fortunate to have survived the war, for a very large percentage of her contemporaries became victims of the concentration camps' scourge inflicted upon the Boer women and children. Her survival, as well as that of the rest of her family, can directly be attributed to her mother and her maternal grandfather, Dawid de Villiers', courageous decision to become refugees with a *kapplekommando* (a convoy of women, children, and old men), fleeing in ox wagons almost constantly for more than a year, escaping capture and internment in the deadly concentration camps created by overwhelming British forces.

In addition to his mother's recollections, just mentioned, a good deal of information the author's father, Daniël Johannes Jacobus Theron, who was a Cape rebel, had supplied to him as he grew up. Other members of his family, his grandmother, Lenie Johanna Storm, great aunt, Sannie de Villiers Fourie, and a second cousin, Henry J. Storm, as well as the late Pieter Hermanus de Jaeger, who lived in Vrede, O.F.S, also supplied valuable information, which would otherwise have been lost (personal interview, 1977). As this book was being started in 1976, Sannie Fourie celebrated her 92nd birthday on September 11, 1975, and was living with her daughter in Viljoenskroon, O.F.S. (personal interview), Henry J. Storm was 93 on June 13, 1975, living in Kroonstad, and Nellie Theron was 83 on

December 2, 1975, living in Vrede, O.F.S. Henry Storm had shortly before summarized his recollections in a radio talk on the South African Broadcasting Corporation. In a series of letters the author's mother, Nellie Theron, had answered questions put to her to clarify certain facts.

Other standard sources about the war have been consulted to coordinate the material covered. Some of these are mentioned and discussed in the Bibliography.

The original purpose of the book was to relate the experiences of a few families, out of thousands during the war, following the scorched earth war policy by British invaders of the Transvaal and Orange Free State Republics. Their homes were torched and their livestock killed or stolen. Their hardship and suffering will intertwine with the course of the war, and some of the hardships that many endured afterwards in their struggle to get back on their feet again will also be covered in a subsequent chapter.

In 1999 when finishing touches, as well as the last chapter, are being added to the manuscript, thoughts go to the centennial of the outbreak of that war which will be recalled during this year, and this book is being slightly revised to put more emphasis on the long and bitter struggle of the Boer volk during that infamous conflict and afterwards. All of the eyewitnesses, mentioned above, who have supplied oral as well as written information have now gone to their eternal rest.

An expression of gratitude is due members of the family who helped to supply photos incorporated in the book, as well as acknowledging the artist Eileen Fabian of Brevard, NC, USA who painted the author's portrait.

History is an eminent teacher and a most distinguished professor. If we would but preserve it and learn from it, this beautiful planet of ours would be a much better place of habitation.

The Author
West Simsbury, Connecticut
February 27, 1976
Hendersonville, North Carolina
December 12, 1999

BIBLIOGRAPHY

Many volumes have been written about the Second English War, and the author has made extensive use of these. Some of the books are recollections of people who were involved in the war themselves, like Christiaan R. de Wet, *Die Stryd Tussen Boer en Brit* , Tafelberg Uitgewers, Kaapstad, 1959 (This book was originally written by de Wet in Dutch, and translated in Afrikaans by J. J. Human), Deneys Reitz, *Commando,* Charles Boni Paper Books, New York, 1930, and by historians who followed later, like Rayne Kruger, *Good-bye Dolly Gray*, J. B. Lippincott Company, Philadelphia and New York, 1960, Stuart Cloete, *Rags of Glory*, Doubleday and Company, Garden City, New York, 1963, J. C. Scheepers Strydom, *Ruitervuur*, Tafelberg-Uitgewers Beperk, Kaapstad en Johannesburg, 1970, Thomas Pakenham, *The Boer War*, Random House, New York, Copyrighted 1979.

A few observations about Pakenham's book: Of course, he writes from the British point of view, and a preponderance of his sources comes from British reports written either in South Africa by military men, or by journalists in British news papers, both of which are well laced with propaganda, just like their reports during World Wars I and II were liberally doused with the same.

With the title of his book, *The Boer War*, the author makes a statement and expresses an opinion both of which are not supported by the facts of history.

The title, *The Boer War*, almost makes one think that the Boers had sent an armada to invade and attack England. Of course, the facts of history speak quite differently. We need not repeat here how England continually harassed the Boers ever since the inception of its meddling in Southern Africa, beginning in 1795 already, for these facts of history will be covered in Chapter I. A brief reminder of the events preceding the inception of the war in 1899 will suffice: The Jameson incursion into the Transvaal in 1896, the amassing of troops on the western and eastern borders of the Transvaal in 1899, and the involvement of Cecil Rhodes supply adequate evidence to justify naming the conflict The English War, or the The Second War for Freedom. This was what the Boers, who were involved in the war themselves, as well as the Afrikaaners later called it. To talk about the Boer War is adding insult to injury.

Pakenham claims to have mastered both Dutch and Afrikaans to attain access to original sources, but how well he mastered these two languages is questionable judging from some slips that occur in his work. He claims that Afrikaans is almost all English. How uninformed! Afrikaans originated from Dutch as spoken during the seventeenth century. It is part of the Indo-European family of languages. As a consequence, many words do have the same stems as found in English, Dutch, German, French, Italian, etc., all of which share a common ancestry with the Classical languages, long before English was spoken in South Africa.

Sometimes the historian, so called, lapses into fiction, and makes one wonder how accurate his claim to historical facts really is, e. g. growing subtropical jakaranda trees in Bloemfontein in the heart of the cold high veld where jakarandas would not survive. Today Pretoria is called the Jakaranda City, and it is glorious in its jakaranda garb in the spring, but at the time of English War II when he wrote of jakarandas in Pretoria, as if they were common, there were most likely only two small jakaranda trees, planted in the city about 1896!

Pakenham's statistics of the war are most unreliable as given on page xix—twenty-two thousand British casualties and twenty-five thousand Boer casualties. As one lumbers through the book and tallies the Boer casualties of various battles and skirmishes one wonders where he obtained the Boer, or the African native casualty figures from. Of course, if one includes the some twenty-six thousand women, children, and old men who had perished in the concentration camps, twenty-five thousand for the Boers is low by about six thousand. On the other hand, if one should included the number of British soldiers who died due to poor medical care, the figure of twenty-two thousand is most likely far too low as well. According to an authority on English War II, Dr. Fransjohan Pretorius of the University of Pretoria, only about 6,200 Boers lost their lives, including battle field casualties, accidents, illness, and deaths in prisoner of war camps.

Pakenham sets out and sticks with the idea of blaming the purpose of the whole, unfortunate war on Milner's vision of the British Empire and his determination of expanding it. Where were the British parliament and their monarch? They raised taxes 50% to provide the money, and so provided everything to wage the war.

One could go on and on. Suffice it to say that the book contains a voluminous collection of official reports and surmises by the author himself as to what went on in the minds of Milner and British generals. All this makes it boring reading to plow through to say the least. However, it does serve the purpose of indicating how dragged out the war in reality had been.

One of the major shortcomings of the book, its claim to historicity notwithstanding, is the complete omission—as if it had never taken place—of the terms of peace at Vereniging which had finally brought the war to an honorable conclusion for the courageous Boers.

CHAPTER I

THE FUSE

As the driver cracked the whip over the short team of oxen, they swayed rhythmically to the left and then again to the right, straining vigorously at the yokes, unearthing topsoil with a single-shared plow behind them. They seemed to have gotten the message from the driver that they were racing against time. They ripped the share faster and faster through the soil throwing it in a neat, crumbly bank to the right. In the fresh furrow, behind the plow, Jacob Storm, walking in the newly created furrow, steadied its course, pressing on the two handles with both hands to keep the sharp-nosed share deep enough under the soil.

It was the end of September 1899. He was plowing to sow maize. It was early to sow maize. October 15 might have been a better time to do so. Frost might kill the young plants, if they should come up too soon. But he had to sow early this spring, or perhaps, not at all. He might be called to war—any day now.

To make things worse, welcome as it usually is, the weather had been threatening all afternoon and was just about to break loose over the area. They hurried the team along to the end of the field to get them unyoked before the storm would strike. Nearby lightning flashes were already freely playing in short-lived, but massive networks all over the face of the deepening storm, rapidly thundering in from the west in a clearly defined phalanx, stretching from south to north as far as the eye could see.

Jacob would have liked to finish the section, usually called an acre regardless of its size, which he was plowing. Time was of the essence. But he had to stop. He had already overstayed and would be caught before he could get home. It was dangerous to have oxen yoked in a thunderstorm. The whole team could be struck and wiped out by a lightning bolt, traveling along the pull chains. In such a catastrophe, he, the driver, and *pickaninny* (a young black boy), in front of the team as leader, would most likely not survive either.

1

As soon as the oxen had been out spanned Jacob and his two helpers hurried home. The sky was now a deep, dark blue and the wind had picked up in a fury, tucking wildly at their clothes and whipping sand and stubbles into their faces. The two Basutos ducked into the barn, but Jacob rushed home a little distance farther. In closely spaced convulsions lightning and thunder shook the earth around him, and the rain began to gush down in torrents.

As his wife, Lenie, opened the Dutch kitchen door, a gust of wind and water swirled in with him. Drenched he stopped on a burlap bag spread out in the middle of the kitchen. It soaked up the water as it drained off his wet clothes and muddy shoes.

The kitchen is a hazardous place in a thunderstorm. The metal chimney pipe, leading from the roof into the stove, is a perfect conductor.

The children were quiet in their bedrooms or elsewhere in the house. Quiet during a thunder storm was always the rule, as if making undue noise would infuriate the elements and invite a strike. A hush had fallen over the house. This was no ordinary storm. It gusted, lashed, and clapped around the house. Wind-driven hailstones began to click off the window panes. Neither the rain, nor the hail could be heard in the house, for it had a thatched roof. A hard hailstorm would destroy the wheat that had been sowed in late autumn, and that would be harvested in the summer.

Jacob slipped off his shoes and walked out of the kitchen to their bedroom to get dry clothes. In the living room seven year old Nellie had been sitting quietly on a bench in awe of the storm. Hesitantly she got up to meet him, because she had a prize possession to show him—a new rag doll her mother had made for her earlier in the day. He saw the pleasant gleam in her dark brown eyes, sparkling like her mother's and she saw how wet he was. She held the doll out for him to see. He widened his eyes as if in great surprise and wonder, and put his hand on her long, black, straight hair. Without a word each knew what the other was saying. Then he pushed the curtain of the bedroom door aside and disappeared. He looked anxiously out the bedroom window to see how much hail the storm carried in its wings, but fortunately it was not threatening, for hailstorms usually do not materialize until late December and throughout the hot, summer months .

Jacob was one of the later pioneers of the Orange Free State. His parents were Hendrik and Katherina Storm, nee van Jaarsveld. Hendrik had been an officer in the Dutch army. Upon leaving the service, he had migrated to the Cape Colony, a British possession since 1806. His sons, however, thought that there were better opportunities among the Boers in the north. So around 1880 Jacob and two of his brothers, Willem and Stephanus, left the district of Ceres in the Cape Colony, where they were living. They were to cast their lot with the people of the young republic, pinched in a huge nutcracker formed by the Klip and Vaal Rivers to the north, and the Caledon and Orange Rivers to the south. To the east the majestic Malutu and part of the Dragon Mountains were wedged in between the rivers, as if spreading the yawning nutcracker apart at their origins.

In due time an attractive, dark haired young lady, Magdalena Johanna de Villiers, endowed with lively dark eyes, characteristic of her French Huguenot descent, became the wife of Jacob Storm. They settled down on a large farm, Helderfontein, about eighteen miles from the town of Ficksburg, in the eastern part of the republic, near the boundary of Basutoland (Lesotho). The farm belonged to David de Villiers, his father-in-law, who was still farming there himself.

Jacob lead a busy life. He had a large family. To feed and clothe them was a major task even in those days. A frugal, practical, and deeply religious man, he devoted himself unstintingly to his family. He cultivated an extensive vegetable garden from which they ate in the summer. Lenie canned and dried green beans and other vegetables for winter consumption. Many an hour was spent on rainy days and in the evenings as he fashioned shoes for the children on wooden forms that more or less matched the sizes of their feet. Hand-me-downs were common.

By 1899 their household had grown to seven children, two boys and five girls. They made up a carefree and happy family in which Jacob and Lenie, as her name was abbreviated, enjoyed undisputed authority, love, and respect. Frugal as they were, they had made good headway in accumulating enough possessions to look forward to the day when Jacob could buy his own farm and be independent, were it not that the course of history shattered that dream for good, and turned life into a nightmare and hell beyond the power of their imagination.

Tension had been building up for several years between England and the *Zuid Afrikaansche Republiek* north of the Vaal River, under the presidency of the legendary Paul Kruger, Oom Paul, Uncle Paul, as he was affectionately called. Such tension in itself was nothing new. Almost the entire nineteenth century, was marred by friction, if not outright animosity, between the British and the Cape colonists who were of Dutch, some German, and French Huguenot descent.

In 1795, in the course of hostilities and upheaval with France, aftermath of the French Revolution, England took the Cape Colony into so-called protective custody, under the pretense that France might occupy it. The Cape Colony had been a Dutch midway station since 1652, and later developed into a colony. England's pretense was a sham. France did not have a navy anywhere near strong enough to venture into the southern hemisphere to launch a successful conquest of the Cape Colony. In fact, the French navy was no match for the British navy. As it turned out the British navy was able to destroy it at Aboukir in 1798 in the course of an ill-fated Egyptian campaign.

The Dutch settlement came about by accident. In 1647 a Dutch vessel, the Haerlem, ran aground in Table Bay, in a fierce storm. The surviving crew that got ashore spent many months anxiously waiting for rescue by a passing ship, either to or from India. They began to garden with seeds and other necessities salvaged from the ship. So long was their waiting that their plantings eventually began to provide for them. They found the climate quite balmy, delightful, and excellent for gardening. After many months, they were finally picked up by a passing vessel and returned to Holland. Out of their experience came a recommendation for a halfway station at the Cape to provide ships, plying the route to and from India, with fresh provisions. The idea appealed to the Gentlemen Seventeen who ran the

Dutch East Indian Company. It would help combat scurvy, which plagued the crews who lived mainly on salted, dry fish during their long voyages to India and back, and took many lives.

But it was not until 1652 that three ships arrived under Jan van Riebeeck, a naval surgeon, at the site where Cape Town would later cling precariously to the lower slopes of Table Mountain, jutting out heavenward for all of three thousand feet over the tempestuous south Atlantic, standing sentinel over the vast continent of Africa to the north. Here they founded the halfway station and Cape Town. But with the passage of time many of the immigrants moved inland away from Cape Town and became independent farmers.

In 1803 England, like a good neighbor and ally during the wars against France, returned the Cape to the Dutch, but in 1806 the British came back and retook it forcefully from the Dutch. After a few skirmishes it was all over, or so it seemed. Yet, it set in motion a struggle that would mar the entire nineteenth century in Southern Africa. Magnanimously England paid Holland a consolation price for her vast and valuable colony. It was a convenient and timely substitute for the loss of a large part of the British colonial empire on the North American continent, two and a half decades earlier.

When white people set foot at the Cape in 1652 there were Hottentots and Bushmen in the area. By 1779, it is reported, some of the colonists had gotten a first glimpse of a black man deep in the interior. Negro tribes were migrating southward while the whites in much smaller numbers were pushing northward. So began another monumental and vexing, racial problem. Eventually, friction developed on the eastern frontier of the colony with the Xhosa tribe. It became a dangerous area to homestead and the colonists looked to their government to provide protection and to stabilize the boundary, but in vain. As new British governors came and went, frontier policy was marked by vacillation, appeasement, and worthless agreements. The Xhosas soon learned to exploit the wishy-washy policy at the expense of the frontier *Boeren* (farmers), murdering and plundering with impunity.

The colonists were stern people. They firmly believed in the old adage, "spare the rod and spoil the child". Corporal punishment of their own children was very common and also applied to their slaves and servants. But while stern, and at times severe, they were deeply religious people of the Calvinist persuasion, holding to the Old Testament concept that man was created in the image of God, and consequently, human life, regardless of color, was respected and held sacred. They could never say, "The only good, black man is a dead, black man". That some of them were at times excessive in meting out punishment can not be denied. In this respect they were in all likelihood not much different from the rest of the contemporary world. Treatment of their slaves and servants quickly provided their detractors, among whom several missionaries numbered, ample ammunition, and in the eyes of the world it gave England the pretense of a cause to justify grabbing the Dutch colony.

A long docket of cases against some very prominent colonists came into being, alleging mistreatment of Hottentot servants. They were tried before a circuit court. It evolved into a much-a-do about nothing. Many allegations were presented. Hardly anything could be proved, but the accused were nevertheless maligned and slandered by innuendo and hear-say. The circuit court of 1812 soon was dubbed "The Black Circuit", and its memory lived on in infamy for generations.

A certain farmer, F.C. Bezuidenhout, failed to answer a summons about mistreatment of servants. He opened fire upon an arresting party. He was killed in the shootout and it touched off what became known as the Slagtersnek Rebellion. The abortive uprising ended with the arrest of about sixty farmers, who had sided with him, and the hanging of five leaders.

Many of the colonists were independent *boeren* (farmers), far away from Cape Town now, after a century and a half since the first settlement. They were soon at loggerheads with their new government.

In 1820 four thousand British settlers had come to the eastern Cape. England was determined to Anglicize the Cape Colony. Dutch was abolished as official language and English substituted in its place. This meant that the overwhelming

6

majority of the white colonists, who had never had any reason to learn English, were hopelessly lost in official business, courts, and politics. It was a blow to the hearts of the colonists that evoked deep resentment. They were now aliens in their own country.

In the nineteenth century the inhumanity of slavery had finally, and irrevocably caught up with the conscience of the western world. In 1833 the British Parliament passed the emancipation act by which slaves in the colonies would be set free. There was to be a period of apprenticeship and full liberty would come in 1838.

Unfortunately, adequate preparations for the consequences of such a major social change in the Cape were lacking. The mission stations, which had already become an aggravation as havens for loafers and hangers-on, would soon become more so as liberated slaves would leave their former masters to find lodging and food.

The colonists, some of whom had large amounts invested in their slaves, were to be compensated by the British government, although at a rather small fraction of the original cost. The last straw, in an already badly bungled operation, was the apparent insincerity of the British government. £20,000,000 were voted for compensation to former slave owners in the Empire, but the colonists had to collect in England, and could not do so in the colony! But it is claimed with adequate documentation that the liberation of the slaves itself was not a major cause of friction with the British government, but rather the way in which it was done. E. g., by far most of the slaves in the Cape Colony were concentrated in the southwestern part where intensive farming was done, but the overwhelming number of colonists who had left the Cape Colony during the Great Trek came from the eastern part where there were few slaves and where farmers engaged mainly in raising livestock.

Unfortunately, the missionaries that came with British rule, and who had the sanction of the British, were fat on the fire. Some of them espoused the theory of the natural goodness of man, made popular by certain French philosophers of that era. The unadulterated, unspoiled child of nature, could do no wrong, theft, murder, and raids notwithstanding. The colonists, on the other hand, as Calvinists, believed firmly in the natural depravity of man, including their own. For them man was continually involved in a titanic struggle against evil, and, but for the grace of God and spiritual rebirth, there was no salvation.

It was soon apparent that a yawning chasm in philosophy of life, attitude, and practice separated colonists and government on irreconcilable mountains. Disenchantment, utter dissatisfaction, and animosity climaxed in the Great Trek between 1835 and 1838. (Some pioneers had left as early as 1833.) About twelve thousand colonists, men, women, and children, packed their covered wagons and lumbered northeastward into the uncharted, wild interior of Southern Africa in search for independence and self-determination. It is noteworthy that even a few British settlers, sharing indignation at the authorities over border harassment, went along.

Not to be landlocked, many of them having rolled with their wagons across the endless plains between the Orange, Klip, and Vaal Rivers, accomplished the near-impossible feat of crossing the rugged Dragon Mountains into the territory named Natal. So they thought they would gain an outlet to the Indian Ocean at Port Natal (Durban). (Vasco de Gama, the daring Portuguese explorer, with his ship, Saint Gabriel, had found himself off the coast of that part of Africa on Christmas Day, 1497, and conferred the name Terra Natalis on it.)

Fierce fighting between the pioneers and the Zulu tribe, that had moved southeastward into this area, followed. After much bloodshed on both sides, they came to amicable terms and the pioneers settled down. They established the Republic of Natalia and began to homestead. But in May 1842 a small British force came to Durban and occupied the port. The Boer pioneers called out a commando under Andries Pretorius. They were attacked by the British, but repulsed them, and bottled them up in the port. A certain Richard Smith got out. He undertook a grueling, Paul Revere-like ride over six hundred rugged miles, reaching Grahamstown, in the Cape Colony, in nine days, to summon help. It came by sea, and the British force was rescued. In 1843 Natal was annexed by England. So, to get away from British rule once again, the majority of pioneers abandoned the territory secured at great sacrifice, and struggled back over the Dragon Mountains. Some settled south of the Vaal River, others spread across it, joining pioneers who had already settled in these areas. But in 1848 the territory between the Orange, Klip, and Vaal Rivers was annexed by Great Britain as the Orange River Sovereignty.

In 1852 Great Britain acknowledged the independence of the Transvaal, and when a hot Basuto war threatened the Orange River Sovereignty, the British withdrew, generously granting it independence in 1854. In time two republics had emerged, the *Oranje Frij Staat*, south of the Vaal and Klip Rivers and the *Zuid Afrikaansche Republiek*, north of the Vaal River, which became known as the Transvaal.

Then came the shady Kimberley diamond deal. Diamonds had been discovered in the western part of the Orange Free State and Kimberley became the diamond mining Mecca of the world. It was indeed a gem and provided the small republic with a great deal of income. Kimberley rightfully appeared to have fallen within the boundaries of the Orange Free State, but Great Britain disputed the boundary. New boundary beacons were claimed by Great Britain and a due survey was made. But still Kimberley fell within the republic's jurisdiction. So the new boundary was also disputed and changed again. Might was right, and Kimberley finally ended up in British territory behind a zig-zag boundary line, still in existence to this day. Again, like when the Cape Colony was grabbed from Holland, a former ally, England magnanimously paid the Orange Free State a consolation price of £90,000 for the loss, a cheap soothing of conscience which nonetheless proved the Orange Free State's rightful claim to ownership. It would have been ridiculous for the Boers to have gone to war over the dispute, and President Brand accepted the indemnification from England with the remark: "Half an egg is better than an empty shell."

The Transvaal and the Orange Free State were completely landlocked, surrounded by British possessions on almost all sides, except the eastern border of the Transvaal, where it is separated by the Lembombo Mountain Range from the

9

Portuguese colony, Mozambique. The two republics traded through the Cape Colony and Natal, under British jurisdiction. Consequently, there appeared little reason for England to add them to her fold and spend money for their administration.

But the Transvaal held more than ordinary promise as a colony. In 1868 gold was discovered in the northern part. In 1875 Thomas Francois Burgers, President of the republic, secured a loan in Holland to build a railway from Pretoria, the capital, to Delgoa Bay in Mozambique, the Portuguese colony. Material began to arrive in the port for construction of the railway. Completion of the line would be a giant step for the Boer republic, and eventually for the Orange Free State as well—away from being held hostage by transportation connections provided by and running through the two adjacent British colonies, Natal and the Cape. But it would also mean a loss of considerable transportation revenue for these two colonies.

So, to forestall further moves towards independence, the Transvaal was annexed by Great Britain in 1877. The Boers wanted nothing of it. After fruitless efforts of negotiation for independence, war broke out against England in 1880. The task turned out more formidable and costly for the British than had been surmised or worth. In the end a British force was decisively defeated at Majuba, on February 27, 1881, on the Transvaal-Natal border. This brought to an end the short, First English War of 1880—1881. The Transvaal was left alone, except that England claimed jurisdiction over its foreign policy.

But in 1886 newspapers of the world carried the story of a fabulous gold discovery on the high veld of the Transvaal, some forty miles north of the Vaal River. Fortune seekers and entrepreneurs flocked to the glitter, and in a short while a bustling city had mushroomed into Johannesburg on what was formerly a peaceful, but rather poor farm among rocky hillocks, *kopjes* (little heads), as they were called in the Boer language. The massive influx of foreigners created an acute problem for the otherwise quiet, agrarian republic. Agitation of the newcomers, most of them British, for the franchise aroused the suspicion of the Paul Kruger government. Kruger had been elected president in 1883. His government feared too much power by migrant fortune seekers and adopted a non-compromising stance.

The railway from Pretoria to Delgoa Bay in Mozambique, planned in 1875 by Burgers, was completed by the Kruger government in 1894. The Transvaal and the Orange Free State were no longer solely dependent on transportation through the Cape Colony and Natal, under Great Britain. Coal burners were lustily belching their way from Pretoria, capital of the Transvaal, eastward through the mountains and opened up an outlet to the shipping lanes and powers of the world other than Great Britain. The two republics were no longer transportation captives. This probably more than anything else, made British empire builders realize that the coveted and invaluable prize of gold could be lost forever. Johannesburg could not be excised from the Transvaal, as was diamond bearing Kimberley, from the Orange Free State, by a mere border dispute. British statesman felt, right or wrong, probably the latter, that they had contributed so much to the Transvaal that they had a rightful claim to her riches. Joseph Chamberlain, Colonial Secretary, in his epoch making speech in the British House of Commons in the beginning of February 1901 spoke rather arrogantly of "the Transvaal, the country we created," to which Lloyd George appropriately retorted, "In the beginning Joseph Chamberlain created heaven and earth—including the Transvaal".

Agitation of the newcomers in the Transvaal, while stiffening the back of the Kruger government, gave England a seemingly valid pretext to bring the gold under her protection, and let its riches flow into its own coffers.

In 1896 Leander Starr Jameson, who had played a major role to help Cecil Rhodes subdue the native tribes in what would become Rhodesia, invaded the Transvaal with a small band from Pitsani near Mafeking, on the western border. He had counted on an uprising by the so-called Reformers in Johannesburg, the young, but vigorously burgeoning, gold mecca.

His men were ordered to cut the telegraph wires to Pretoria, but being New Years Day, the Boers joked that they were so drunk that they cut a farm fence instead. True or not, it was a good joke to much satisfaction of the Boers. Kruger learned of the caper almost instantly and dispatched General Piet Cronje to deal with it. The next day Jameson surrendered. Puny and abortive as his attempt was, it shattered all trust and goodwill, which was shaky at best, between Boer and British in South Africa. Disclaimers by Joseph Chamberlain on behalf of the British government were regarded as false. Cecil Rhodes, Prime Minister of the Cape Colony, who was evidently in on the plot (although he attempted to dissuade Jameson at the last minute), lost so much support among the Boers, a formidable block of constituents in the Cape, that he had to resign.

The Boers, as said before, made up of Dutch, French Huguenot, and some German descendants, had in reality long ceased to be colonists of a European mother country. As memories faded and as family ties were forgotten with the passage of time and the birth of new generations, Southern Africa became their home. For more than two centuries they had tamed, cultivated, come to love it, and tap-rooted deeply into its soil. As they were moving northward— first slowly, and then in a deliberate spurt between 1835 and 1838—Negro tribes were moving southward. At various points they encountered each other. Sometimes as in Natal, the encounters were less than friendly, to say the least. When hostilities did break out, they fought and paid with their lives for what they regarded as their own.

Descendants of Dutch, French, and German colonists had blended their customs into an undistinguishable unity. Slowly, but surely they had developed their own vernacular from Dutch as it was spoken in the seventeenth century. French and German had disappeared. All that remained was for this inescapable fact of nationhood to be generally realized and fully recognized before it would replace Dutch, which would long have disappeared from the scene, had it not been firmly entrenched in the Dutch Bible and anchored in their Dutch hymns, which occupied a prominent place, not only in their Church, but also in their homes where both were used for family devotions, or "taking books," as it was called.

Although not politically united throughout all of Southern

12

Africa, the Boers had grown into a nation that belonged geographically, that had developed its own language (although it had no legal standing), practised its own customs, and cherished its own national aspirations, the least of which by far was not liberty.

The flagrant, and at times arrogant, disregard by Great Britain throughout the nineteenth century for the evident ingredients of Boer nationhood and nationalism was not taken lightly by the Boers. A strong oral tradition about their past experiences with the British had fostered unfathomable resentment and hostility against England without which the long and desperate struggle of the English War of 1899—1902 can not be fully explained.

Since the two republics were bordering on British territory on all sides, except for the Portuguese colony east of the Transvaal, and since they had a long-standing, deep distrust of Great Britain's intentions with regard to their freedom, it was only natural that they became bound together by a treaty of mutual defense.

As Jacob and his neighbors sowed their wheat, harvested their maize in the winter of 1899, and plowed again in the spring, they realized that they did so under the threat of unmistakable thunderheads of war. They doubted that they would be around to gather in the harvest.

British troops had begun to amass on the western border of the Transvaal at Mafeking in the area from which Jameson had launched his futile invasion three years earlier. In addition troops were increasing in Natal on the eastern front, as well as in the lower Cape Colony. It was obvious that an attack on the Transvaal from two fronts could be unleashed at any time.

The spring of 1899 had barely begun to turn the winter gray of the rolling plains and the rock-strewn hills into a soft green when war broke out on October 11. The first shots rang out at Kraaipan near Mafeking.

The desire and will to enjoy freedom and to be masters of their own destiny were inbred in the Boers and deeply rooted in their European ancestry. Their Dutch ancestors had tirelessly fought what became known as the Eighty Years War against

Spain, defending their national, political liberty, and religious freedom. Their French Huguenot ancestry were persecuted for their religious beliefs and had fled for their own protection, leaving home hearth, kin, and a dear fatherland behind for liberty of conscience and beliefs. The love of freedom in many realms of life had for nearly a long century been suppressed and gnawed at by Great Britain. Therefore, it was small wonder indeed that the Boers, untrained as soldiers, and unprepared as they were for military action, were more than ready to shed their blood in protection of their homeland and their freedom, as best they could. This willingness to go to war, to suffer, and to sacrifice was firmly ingrained in all, man, woman, and child.

Two small, but brave republics had virtually no standing, professional armed forces. Instead, *burgers* could be summoned to arms and organized into commandos. Commanding officers were elected. As a consequence, discipline was rather poor. For all intents and purposes military training was nonexistent. Despite this state of unpreparedness, the experiences with Great Britain during the course of the century about to draw to a close, of which the loathsome Jameson debacle was uppermost in their minds, had so conditioned the Boers that there were few second thoughts about joining battle. They were psychologically more than prepared to have a showdown with Great Britain. In addition they did not have a high regard for the fighting ability of the British Tommy, as British soldiers were called.

Jacob Storm and his brothers, Willem and Stephanus, their sons who could carry a gun, as well as thousands of other Boers, both in the Orange Free State and the Transvaal Republic, were ready to do battle, and sacrifice their lives to preserve the liberty of their republics.

CHAPTER II

THE ROARING FIRE

As expected, the inevitable summons to join their commando had come to Jacob Storm, his brothers, other relatives, and his neighbors. It was a tearful but somewhat restrained departure for the sake of the children. He swung into the saddle of his own horse with his gun behind his back, some ammunition in his bandoleer, and provisions for about a week, together with other necessities, strapped to the saddle. Lenie and her seven children stood dumbfounded outside the thatched roof house as he disappeared over the horizon, most of the children, fortunately, too young to realize the gravity and danger of the war, or to be concerned about the utter unprepared state of the army their father was to join.

Mirabile dictu the two republics soon had commandeered armies totaling about sixty thousand men, many of them actually too old and many too young to make up an efficient fighting force, especially since they had no military training at all. Their toughness as farmers, their horsemanship, their familiarity with rifles and with the country they were defending, and above all their determination to resist British domination had to make up for training.

When dusk deepened into darkness around the hulk of the Storm family's farm house that evening, Lenie and her children huddled together around the dining room table after supper by the light of a flickering candle.

Lenie stood barely five feet six inches tall. Her jet black hair was tightly drawn to the back of her head over her ears and neatly rolled into a bolla secured by hairpins. Her dark brown eyes were lovely and lively. Her outward appearance seemed meek, but shielded a great inner strength and character.

She "took books," with the children around the dining room table, their customary family devotions. The home-made candle flickered in the draft and poured hot fat down on the side away from the draft into the candle holder. She had to take Jacob's place as head of the household as many other women had to do from that day on. Solemnly she read from the large, big-lettered, Dutch Bible. They knelt by their chairs as she said the family prayer. No matter how she tried to be brave, the words stuck with a lump in her throat, and when they rose from their knees, their sobs took the place of the usual evening hymn.

In spite of overwhelming odds, it was hoped that the conflict would soon come to an end and climax in victory for the Boers as did the First English War of 1880-1881. The initial successes of the Boers with their renowned and feared sharpshooting—they seldom wasted a bullet in either hunting or war, for ammunition was always scarce and precious—encouraged such hopes.

General Piet Cronje, said to be the only Boer General with military training, had his army near the border opposite Mafeking. They quickly crossed into British territory. Commandant Jacobus H. de la Rey, who turned out to be one of the ablest Boer leaders, captured an armored train, the *Mosquito*, near Mafeking. Soon the town was under siege. From here de la Rey moved quickly south for about three hundred miles along the railway line just west of the Transvaal border, capturing village after village without resistance. The British force was bottled up in Mafeking and a long siege ensued.

Kimberley, the bone of contention between the Orange Free State and Great Britain, not too many years earlier, had a population of about fifty thousand of which about thirteen thousand were whites. Realizing that frontal attacks are costly in terms of manpower, the Boers with their limited resources in this respect, preferred to achieve surrender of both Mafeking and Kimberley through siege with a minimum loss of manpower. It was no small satisfaction to them that they had a famous empire builder and antagonist almost in their grasp, none other than Cecil Rhodes, instigator of the Jameson fiasco, himself, and he frantically helped organize the defense of the stolen diamond Mecca.

The western front simmered down rather quickly with the main action around Mafeking and Kimberley, which the Boers hoped would surrender due to lack of food and ammunition.

The eastern front was only several hundred miles from the harbor of Durban where British troops could and did land, and from where a major attack would be launched.

The eastern front was difficult for invaders as well as for defenders, because it is mountainous terrain, and largely because of this, some of the toughest battles of the war would be fought here.

Even before the war broke out Transvaal Boer forces under commandant General Piet Joubert were amassing near the town of Volksrust close to the Natal border. Here Joubert had about fourteen thousand men. Further to the south near Van Reenen's Pass, a force of about six thousand from the Orange Free State encamped under their chief commandant, Martinus Prinsloo.

War had no sooner broken out, when Joubert's force moved unopposed into Natal. The British forces under Sir George White and General Penn Symons, numbering about twelve thousand were deeper into Natal, around Ladysmith and Dundee. The Boers found it hard to believe that they had met no resistance at the narrow approaches on the border. They were even more baffled that the railway line was left intact. Using it, they were soon right up to White and Symons' forces, and would join battle. On October 19 General Kock surprised a small settlement, Elandslaagte and took it. More important than occupying the small town were the capture of a train loaded with supplies, and effectively cutting communications between the two British generals and their forces, Symons at Dundee and White at Ladysmith.

Symons had recently been knighted. Whether this made him feel unusually superior and invulnerable, is hard to judge. He certainly acted that way. He openly boasted that no Boer force would dare attack an entire British brigade. Even when he was warned by a sergeant who had escaped when advancing Boers had captured a British patrol, he dismissed it as a minor incident. However, when day light and a rising fog exposed the surroundings of Dundee on Oct.20, the hills were teeming with Boers who had advanced during the night. Not until shells from Boer artillery began tearing up his camp below, was he goaded into action. British guns pounded the top of Talana Hill nearby.

As the British advanced the Boer fire was devastating. It was not "might-it-hit" volleys, but target shooting for which the Boers were famous as hunters. With foolhardy disdain of his enemy Symons stood in the wide open while commanding his troops—a perfect target. He was mortally wounded in the stomach and died a few days later. With great loss they finally dislodged the Boers who fled undisciplined down the other side. Then the impossible happened. When the British troops had reached the top of Talana Hill, the gunners below did not realize that the hill was won, and they continued to rake it with a thunderous bombardment, blasting off the top and killing many of their own.

Before being wounded, Symons had dispatched some cavalry to deal with the Boers should they retreat, but they fought back and split the cavalry in two. The larger company engaged men under General Erasmus on a hill called Impati to the left flank of Talana and were captured. The smaller company was able to return to camp.

The approach to Talana Hill was strewn with fallen khaki figures and the top was a miserable sight, a mixture of Boer and British dead and wounded. Symons' brigade had suffered over five hundred casualties dead and wounded; the Boers around one hundred and fifty.

The battle was reported in England with typical, public relations hyperbole as a glorious victory. But reports do not make facts. The position of Dundee was now more precarious. The Boer army was little hurt and Kock at Elandslaagte had been strengthened up to a thousand men dividing British forces.

Then it became White's turn to spring a surprise. Kock's men were having a great time at Elandslaagte partying and even fraternizing with British citizenry and prisoners. For this unwarlike celebration they paid dearly. General John French, who had lately arrived to take command of the cavalry under White, attacked at dawn. The Boers had sufficient presence of mind to flee helter-skelter to a better defense position in the nearby hills. The battle see-sawed until the afternoon with the British still seemingly at an advantage due to the surprise sprung on the partying Boers.

Then a reinforcement of about three thousand bolstered the

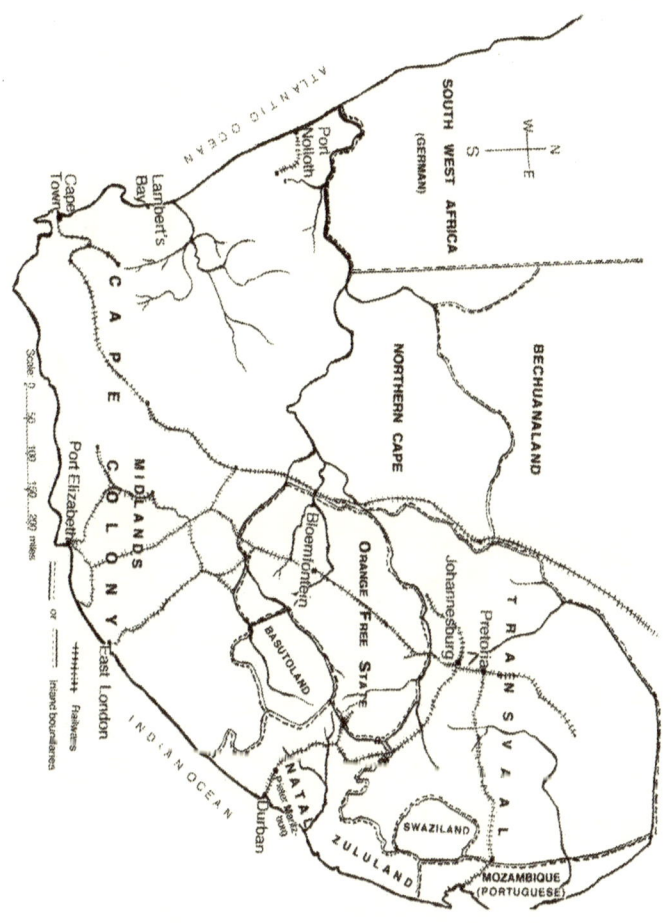

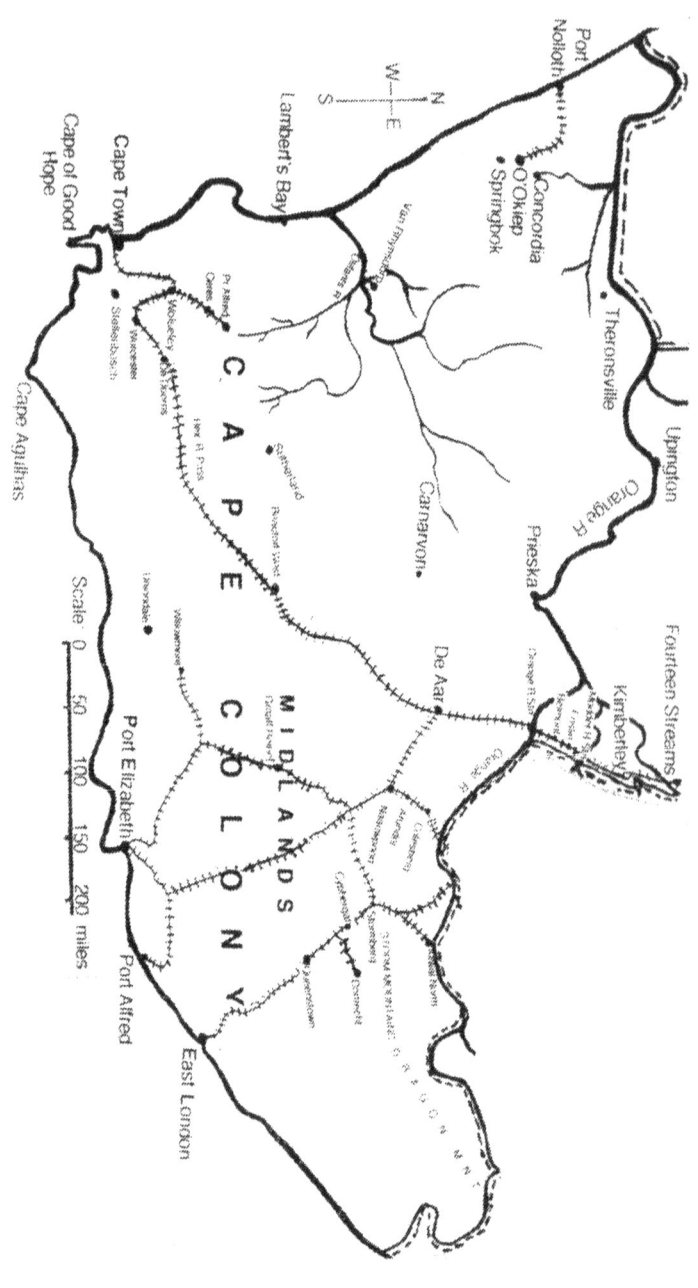

20

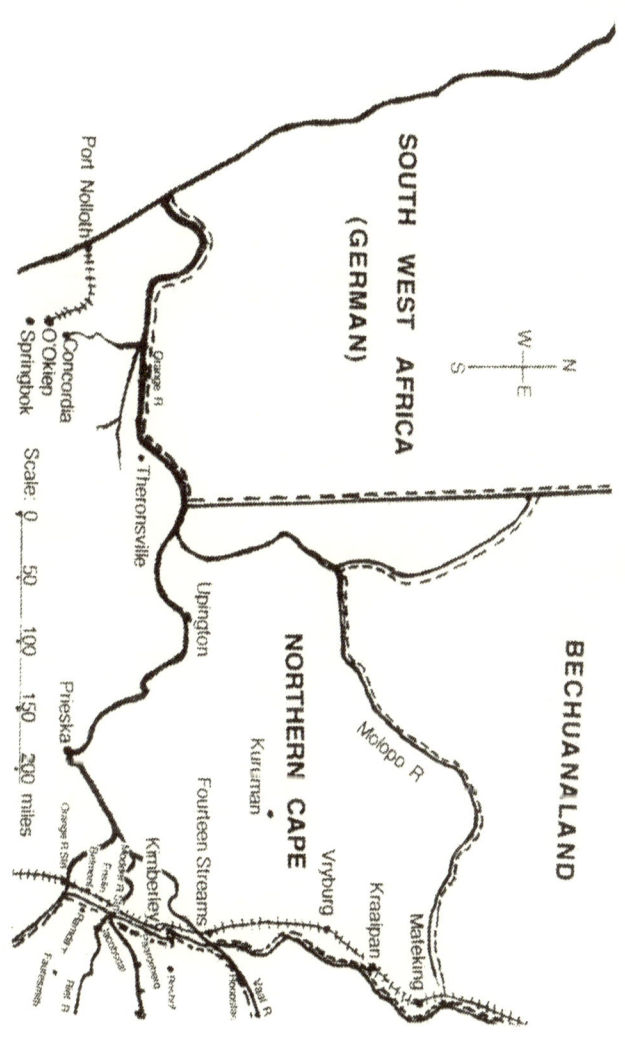

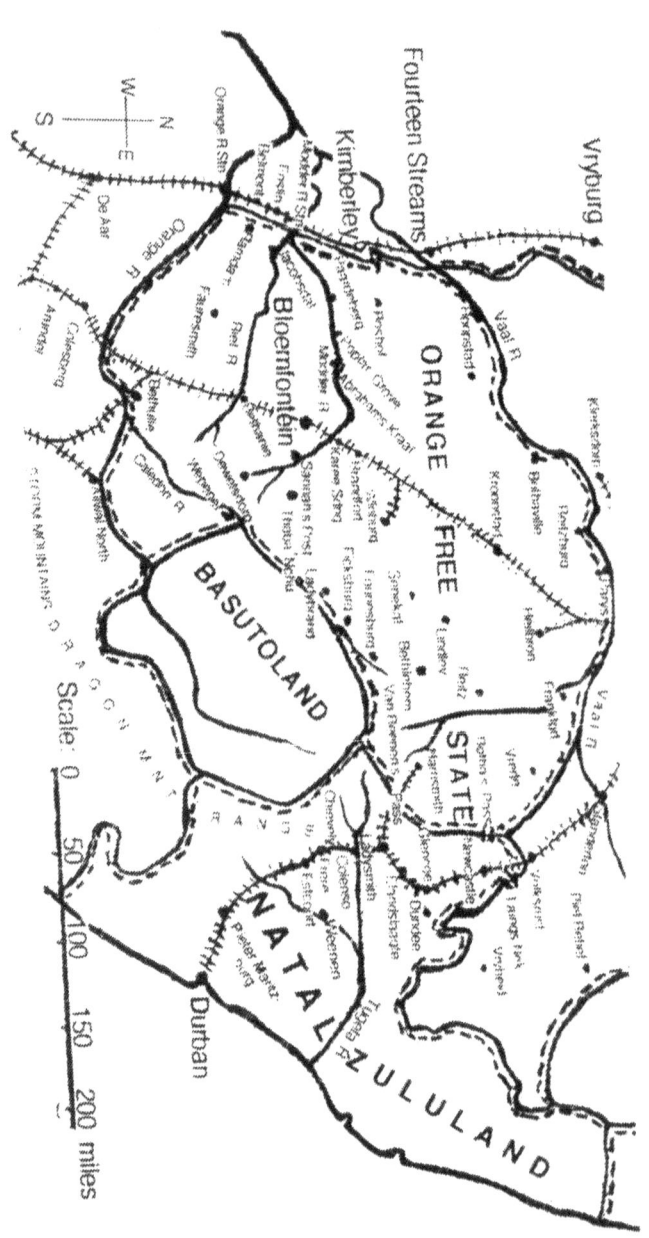

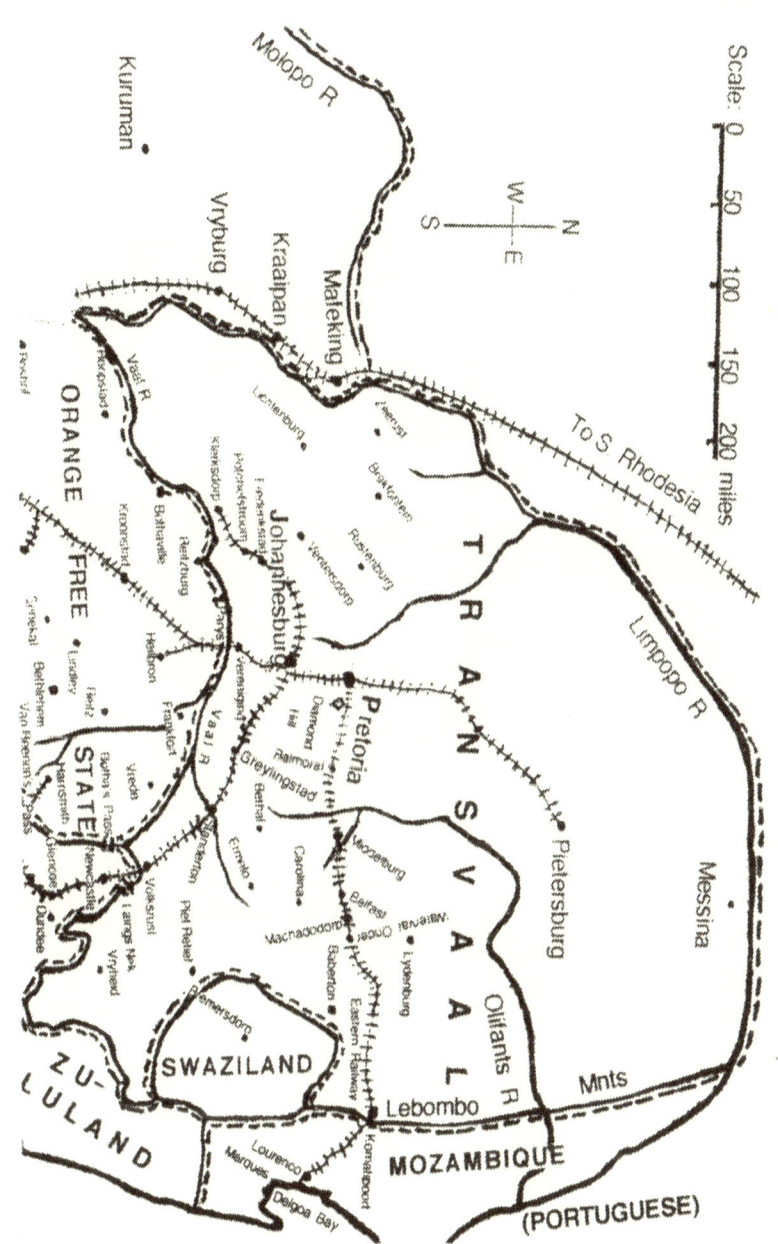

23

British attackers. They suffered heavy losses as they advanced on the Boers. Outnumbered and outgunned by far, the Boers retreated, many being captured with their equipment. They also lost General Kock. Communications between Dundee (now under the command of General Yule), and Ladysmith could evidently be restored. But that night rumors came that the Free State burgers were advancing with a superior force and that General Joubert was approaching too. Elandslaagte, liberated at great cost, was promptly evacuated. The retreating British troops abandoned material and prisoners of war in panic. With the Boers still on Impati at Dundee, Yule also slipped out of his camp leaving tents and equipment behind. All this came as a near shock to the Boers, because the rumors about the force from the Orange Free State and Joubert's advance were greatly premature!

The battle front now shifted further south to Ladysmith, an important railway junction linking Durban, the Transvaal, and the Orange Free State. The force of Freestaters that had been at Van Reenen's Pass converged upon Ladysmith with Joubert's army from the Transvaal. White had his work cut out for himself. During the last days of October the hills around the town were ablaze with gunfire and reverberated with artillery explosions as the two opposing forces joined in a desperate struggle.

Several younger Boer leaders made their debut and distinguished themselves most eminently. Louis Botha, who became one of the great generals of the war, took the place of Commandant Lucas Meyer, who had fallen ill. He led his men with unyielding determination against a certain Colonel Grimmwood and pinned him and his men down hopelessly on a ridge.

In another sector there came to the fore Vice-Commandant Christiaan Rudolph de Wet, an ubiquitous fox of the veld, from the Orange Free State and an unmitigated disciplinarian, so much needed by the Boers. He too was to become a legend of the war. He was pitched against a certain Colonel Carleton on a hill called Tchrengula. De Wet was always quick. Before Carleton could do it, he occupied a higher ridge with some of his men. He

24

was wounded himself but pressed the assault on Carleton's men from rock to rock stumbling over dead soldiers strewn at their feet. Carleton was in an untenable position, and after heavy losses, ultimately raised a make-shift white flag, signaling his surrender. De Wet took more than eight hundred prisoners.

Loose mules, used to haul the artillery pieces, wandered or stampeded towards Ladysmith, mingling with those who were bringing their mangled charges off the various battlefields. White saw the hopelessness of the situation, although he had not even learned about the fate that de Wet had visited upon Carleton. The order went out to retreat as convenient.

The Boers had wrested a major victory from their enemy. The British had suffered the loss of well over a thousand men; the Boers several hundred.

Great as the victory was, the mistake committed here by Joubert at this time was greater by far. Had he pressed his victory to its ultimate conclusion and ordered immediate pursuit of the disorganized British forces, he might well have driven them without much effort straight through Ladysmith and annihilated them completely.

It is useless to surmise about the possible consequences of such a bold course of action, but it might well have altered the entire war and lessened the tragic suffering which it inflicted on both sides. Joubert acted with the caution of an older man which seemed to have been reinforced by his training as a lawyer. He rejected the enthusiasm for pursuit of his younger, more energetic, and daring commandants.

This gave White and Yule time to fortify themselves in Ladysmith. The Boers could do no better than to encircle White with his twelve thousand troops in Ladysmith. They blocked the railway line south of the town and had the British force cut off from further supplies.

The day after White's defeat Sir Redvers Buller arrived in Cape Town to take charge of the war. He came with appropriate pomp and circumstance which he seemed to have relished as if his birthright. He discarded the original plan of the War Office to attack the Orange Free State from a staging area in the Cape Midlands. Instead he divided the Army Corps into three divisions. One would relieve Ladysmith, the other Kimberley, while the third would operate in the Cape Midlands. If he could relieve the two besieged towns, he would resume the original plan. Then he disappeared from Cape Town and arrived in Durban by ship a few days later to take personal charge of the liberation of Ladysmith.

Joubert's temporizing after the battle of Ladysmith and the inevitable siege of the town gave the British time to mobilize reinforcements. The British had been dealt the unbeatable trump card—the ace of numbers—unlimited. To add to the Boers' predicament in Natal Joubert became seriously ill, but still remained Commandant General. The Orange Free State needed their men to defend in the region of the Cape Midlands and this would substantially reduce their strength in Natal.

The situation was far from desperate for the Boers. Botha took a force south of Ladysmith, overran Colenso and despite upcoming British forces, got to within ten miles of Durban, the harbor of supply for the British.

The success at Ladysmith inspired a rather large number of Cape Boers either to cross into the Orange Free State to join the forces of President Martinus Theunis Steyn, or to attach themselves to operations in their own districts. Rebellion became such a threat that the Cape had to warn its citizens about the harsh consequences of treason. In some districts martial law had to be proclaimed. General James Barry Munnik Hertzog, a judge of the Orange Free State Supreme Court, penetrated deep into the Cape with a force as part of Steyn's tactic to harass the British.

*   *   *   *   *

On Helderfontein, where Jacob Storm had left his family, Lenie and her children managed as best they could. Initially they were helped by Basutos who had been living on the farm for a number of years. But as reports of war circulated, they were frightened and one by one moved with their families back over the border into Basutoland where they felt safer. Lenie's father, Dawid de Villiers, much too old and with a greatly disabled arm,

26

had remained behind when the other men went to war. His presence was invaluable, and he assisted as best he could.

Dawid was one of the early pioneers of the Orange Free State. In 1864 he and his wife, Lenie Louw, had come more than six hundred miles by wagon from the area of Swellendam and Bredasdorp in the Cape Colony and began to homestead near where the town of Ficksburg was founded. Their farm, named Omdraai, nestled in the shadows of the majestic Malutu Mountains of Basuto Land. They knew the privations and dangers of pioneering first hand. More than once Basutos would cross the Caledon River to plunder.

One day some strange Basutos came calling at the farm, saying that they were from the chief in Basuto Land. As a gesture of good will he sent a piece of meat to the chief along with his emissaries. But at dusk that evening Dawid was suddenly attacked outside his house. Before he fully realized what was happening, a shotgun blast shattered one of his arms at the elbow.

The Basutos were unaccustomed to firearms and were frightened of the big bang, even if they were using guns themselves. Many had the habit to aim and then close their eyes in anticipation of the blast before pulling the trigger. Consequently their aim was rather haphazard and they easily missed, even at short range. This probably saved his life. Wounded and bleeding profusely, he managed to reach the safety of the house before further shots could be fired. Here they stood vigil through the night to fend off any further attacks until dawn when help arrived. He survived the wound, but never regained full use of his arm. He later exchanged his farm Omdraai for the farm Helderfontein.

When the war broke out, he was too old to be commandeered. He was far more valuable as a counselor to the women and children on the farms around him than as a soldier.

Initially food was available in abundance. The summer was coming and the garden yielded its supply of vegetables as usual. Meat was to be had from sheep, hogs, or chickens. The supply of wheat and maize from the previous crops would last until the new crops were harvested.

27

As the Freestaters began moving from the Natal front to defend their own borders, Jacob came home for a few days. It was a joyous reunion. Then he left for the western front of the Orange Free State.

In the summer of 1899-1900 Lenie, now without any servants, harvested the wheat with the help of her children. The older ones would cut the stalks with sickles and bind it in sheaves. The younger ones would carry the sheaves out of the field to a spot cleared of the grass that grew there, and made it into a threshing floor. When they had gathered enough on the threshing floor, they would sit around a small mound of wheat and beat it endlessly with sticks to free the kernels. Then they would turn it over, beat it some more, repeat the process a few times, and finally winnow.

Without enough bags Lenie could not store the grain in the barn. So she emptied a room in the house, lined the dirt floor and partly up the walls with a few old burlap bags she had to keep dampness and dirt out. With buckets they carried the grain and stored it in the home-made "silo."

*   *   *   *   *

With a small army under Commandant J. Prinsloo Jacob was shifted to the southwestern border of the Orange Free State. Prinsloo was entrusted with the task of checking the march of Lord Methuen from Orange River Station in his attempt to relieve Kimberley, until General Piet Cronje would arrive with a larger force from the stalemated western front of the Transvaal. Methuen, in command of eight thousand men, viewed his objective as so easy indeed that he announced in advance when he could be expected at Kimberley, putting the fear of God into the opposing Boers on the way, as he expressed it.

Prinsloo's men made a valiant defense of a couple of hills near Belmont in the Cape Province territory, inflicting about three hundred casualties on the Tommies, while suffering about a third of that themselves. In the end they had to yield under pressure of superior numbers and they fell back to another defense position near Enslin. Meanwhile a forward contingent of

Cronje's army had arrived under the able leadership of Koos de la Rey, who also became one of the celebrated generals of the war. Prinsloo's leadership ability left something to be desired.

In addition to swelling the ranks of the Boers to about two thousand, de la Rey also provided some much needed leadership. Still they were no match for Methuen's forces of about four times their number. The result was another indecisive confrontation in the vicinity of Enslin (Graspan), and another retreat for the Boer force.

Some of the Freestaters were so disappointed with Prinsloo—they had to put the blame for their failure on someone—that they deserted. Jacob and his brothers were more responsible. The fact that their father had been an officer in the Dutch army gave them some appreciation for the necessity of military discipline.

The end result of it all was that de la Rey got the major say. The Boers had now retreated up against the Modder River near its confluence with the Riet River. Rather than crossing the Modder River and taking up positions on a few hills beyond, de la Rey made a momentous determination that was to have far-reaching results in the war itself as well as a decade and a half later in World War I. He reasoned that the effect of the Boers' firepower would be greatly enhanced if delivered horizontally rather than from an elevated position on a hill. A bullet fired over level ground could hit another target, if it should miss the first, whereas a bullet, fired from a hill, would bury itself harmlessly in the dirt, should it miss its intended target. Furthermore, he reasoned that the top of a hill, or mountain, would give the enemy's artillery a perfect silhouetted target to lob their shells.

He blew up the railway bridge across the river and deployed his men, now increased to about three thousand five hundred, along the southern banks of the Modder and Riet Rivers on either side of the tracks. Parallel with the rivers he had them dig shallow trenches in which, nervous with the new method of warfare, they ensconced themselves, lying in wait for Methuen.

On November 28—Methuen was supposed to have been in Kimberley the previous day—the British army began its fatal advance before dawn, hoping to breakfast beyond the Modder River, prior to yet another, and final assault on the Boers in the hills beyond. But before the day was over, in fact before breakfast, those hills, as well as breakfast, became only a distant dream.

If the swift, but silently flowing river with tree-lined banks gave the impression of a peaceful setting to the hungry Tommies, imagining visions of breakfast, it was soon to be belied as Boer guns unexpectedly wrought death and destruction among them from their trench just as de la Rey had figured. Their only protection was a prostrate position on the level ground in the open. An unobscured sun climbed in the sky and slowly turned the temperature up in excess of a blistering 100 degrees Fahrenheit, made unbearable by incessant firing and artillery shells bursting with great precision among them. Those who rose up ran the risk of immediately being riddled with bullets.

The battle raged on as the day got hotter and hotter. The greatly more effective firepower of the Boers and their superior protection, both due to de la Rey's trench tactic, made them more than a match for Methuen's overwhelming numbers.

The danger of the trench was outflanking. In the afternoon it did happen. Some of Methuen's men had crept up and skirted around one end of the trench. To make it worse, they succeeded in crossing the river, exposing the Boer flank as well as their rear. The Boers on that end fought a desperate battle and held advance at bay, hoping that darkness would come to their aid. But unexpected help was given by the enemy itself. As at Talana Hill in Natal, newly arrived British reinforcements unleashed a withering artillery attack on their own men across the river and undid their heroic achievement.

When darkness, after an interminable day, drew its curtain, as if in mercy, over the valley so tranquil, but beguiling at sunrise, it hid a sordid battlefield strewn with dead horses, wounded men, suffering unbelievable thirst, disfigured corpses, smoldering wagons, and once stately trees now reduced to ugly stumps extending a few bare branches to heaven like arms in supplication. Methuen himself was wounded. Five hundred of his men were either killed or wounded. Koos de la Rey mourned the death of his own son C. de la Rey, who was shot and killed beside him.

An epoch making battle of trench warfare had finally grinded to a halt.

When it was clear that the battle was over, Jacob staggered out of the trench, stiff and tired beyond endurance. With thousands of other Boers he made for the river to get a drink and to wash his face covered with dust, red and tender from the scorching heat. They ate what they had and bedded down under the stars. He thought of Lenie and his family. As his moving lips said a prayer known to him and God alone, exhaustion overcame him.

Despite their victory the Boer council of war decided to abandon their position. Should the British attack again, there would no longer be the important element of surprise which contributed greatly to their success. In addition they were still far outnumbered, they had been outflanked, and some of the Freestaters were again beginning to desert. Contrary to de la Rey's judgment, they retreated over the Modder River to the hills beyond where Methuen had thought them to be in the first place.

Although the Boers had decided to fall back, the mission which Prinsloo had set out to accomplish was completed by de la Rey. They had gained valuable time for the rest of their forces under Cronje to arrive, as well as to patch up differences between the Freestaters and the Transvaalers. But most important they had stemmed the rolling tide towards Kimberley.

The third month of the war was soon to begin with intense activity on all fronts. The Boers with their small and untrained numbers were still doing exceptionally well indeed. Overwhelming numbers notwithstanding, it was a marvel that the British armies were still held back beyond the borders of the two republics.

November 1899 had brought what became known as Mournful Monday to England with the news of the disastrous battle of Ladysmith, and made the somber winter mood of the northern hemisphere even gloomier. The worst was yet to come.

In the Cape Midlands near Stormberg, William Gatacre, a knighted major-general, a tough taskmaster indeed, commanded an army of about three thousand. It was from this region that the British originally had thought to march into the Orange Free State. His Boer opponent was General C. H. Olivier, commanding an army of about two thousand composed of Freestaters and many Cape rebels from the area.

On December 9 Gatacre got an early start before dawn in a move from Molteno to Stormberg Junction. Unfortunately, his path led between several hills. In the dark they got lost and ended up at a hill called Kissieberg, greatly surprising a Boer outpost, high on an escarpment, overlooking a valley. When day broke they saw the British column winding its way like a huge serpent below, thinking that they knew where they were going. Figuring that an offense was the best defense, they opened fire.

Valiantly the British charged the steep cliffs. To their credit some made it to the top despite the near impossible ascent and heavy Boer firing on them from the top. But here again, miraculously, the British gunners below obliged the hard pressed Boers and by mistake blasted their own men off the very hard gained summit. They fled in panic down the steep mountain side. An officer, without Gatacre's knowledge, ordered a retreat and he was unable to stop the rush.

So back to Molteno. Relatively little damage seemed to have been done. Then like a bolt from the clear blue sky came the real blow. Gatacre had left about six hundred men behind, and they were captured by the Boers under Olivier.

The Stormberg debacle was only the beginning of the December misadventures.

Methuen was now already two weeks behind in his schedule to relieve Kimberley. He had recovered from his wound and was about to resume his intention to instill the fear of God in the Boers. On December 9 he too was on the move on the southwestern front; this time with an army swelled to about thirteen thousand. Kimberley knew of his advance, and encouraged by the numbers of such an imposing army, trains were in readiness and refugees were packed to depart for Cape Town once the city was liberated.

What Methuen, Colonel R. G. Kekewich, in charge in Kimberley, and Cecil Rhodes, still in the beleaguered city, did not know, was that de la Rey, an uneducated farmer (*boer*), but nonetheless a brilliant strategist, stood squarely astride the path of celebration, if not in person, then certainly in spirit.

On December 10, a Sunday, when he probably thought the Boers might not fight for religious scruples, he began to soften up Magersfontein Hill, where the Boers were supposed to be, with a devastating bombardment, turning the hill inside out.

A night march and an attack at dawn the next day were planned. A newly arrived brigade of Highlanders under the popular Major-General Andrew J. Wauchope, was to spearhead the assault. On December 11 the march got under way shortly after midnight, and in the early dawn they were approaching the hilly area. Magersfontein Hill began to take shape in the dim light of the fast breaking day. If they were to surprise the Boers, they had to hurry before daylight would betray their presence. Wauchope began to deploy his men for an assault on the hill where the Boers were supposed to be. The only problem, as he found out in the short time of his life left to him, was that they were not on the hill at all to speak of.

Many miles to the north, a man on a heart breaking, personal mission, was on his way to visit his wife in the Transvaal. It was Koos de la Rey. He had made all preparations for the anticipated onslaught by Methuen's army. Cronje had arrived with reinforcements. President Steyn of the Orange Free State had visited the front, relieved Prinsloo of responsibilities, read the riot act to the disgruntled Freestaters, and helped to restore unity with his pleasant personality. With all preparations made, with General Cronje present, and in charge, de la Rey felt that he could take leave to break the news of their son's death to his wife personally.

Wauchope's Highlanders had no sooner begun fanning out, when the seemingly peaceful dawn erupted around then with a hail storm of lead flashing at short range in the dim light from the bores of the Boer Mausers. With sudden horror they realized that they had once again, as their comrades at the Modder River, marched right into the teeth of a deadly, unsuspected defense.

33

Thousands of Boer guns spewed a barrage of bullets at them almost point blank. Still closely bunched together as they had pressed their march to beat the dawn, they made careful aiming superfluous. Hundreds fell dead almost instantly, or wounded, and those who were not cut down by gunfire, prostrated themselves in the open begging, as it were, protection from the bare earth or such loose stones and flimsy vegetation as it had to offer, for up to a thousand yards from their trench the Boers had cleared the terrain.

In planning the deployment of his men for battle de la Rey had decided again not to defend from a hill, but to employ trench warfare which stood him in such good stead at Modder River. But he ran into trouble almost at once. General Piet Cronje, who had arrived, being his superior, had a final voice. Cronje belonged to the old school of defending from a hill or mountain. However, Steyn, competent, persuasive, and highly respected, supported de la Rey. Cronje was magnanimous enough to yield, although, no doubt, not convinced, and even likely a little miffed.

During the intervening days the Boers had readied themselves by digging a shallow and narrow trench two to four feet deep several hundred yards from the foot if the hill stretching more than ten miles! The length of the trench system, which in one direction reached almost to the Modder River, was to safeguard against outflanking by a much larger force, as had happened in the previous battle. The distance from the hill would enhance the element of surprise. The scooped out mound of dirt was camouflaged with brush and branches, and the front of the trenches obstructed with barbed wire This would be especially useful, if there should be a cavalry charge.

Wauchope perished. His Highlanders had little choice but to stay put where they were caught, flat on the ground. They had little choice. Getting up to retreat was suicide.

Again the sun rose to a scorching noon, blistering the backs of the Highlanders' bare legs. The Boers were not much more comfortable in their trench. At one point the attack made some headway. A gallant assault sliced a wedge through to the mountain. This could spell disaster. The trench would be exposed from the rear, and from higher ground the British troops could fire right into the Boer positions. Before long the trench would crumble. But Cronje and a few of his aids were on the hill at just about that point of the breech. (He had wandered off during the night, either because the trench would hamper his ability to exercise command, or because he was not convinced of the effectiveness of the trench—most likely the latter.) Hastily they moved into position, took shelter and opened a brisk volley of fire. Some of those that had broken through fell in the skirmish. The rest were captured. The Boers quickly reinforced and plugged the gap, or they would have been in serious trouble.

As the day piled frustration upon frustration, Methuen with large numbers at his disposal poured in a wave of men on the eastern flank where the Freestaters from Ficksburg were ensconced. Jacob Storm was cramped in the trench with his brothers Willem and Stephanus, and with his brother-in-law, Johannes de Villiers, and his nephew, Henry Storm. As new arrivals of British troops ventured near the trench, they fired desperately, the barrels of their guns already heated by the sun, getting almost too hot to touch. The dull thuds of bullets slamming into khaki uniforms and flesh were almost drowned out in the continuous roar of gunfire flashing from both sides, punctuated intermittently by the deafening roar of artillery shells bursting around them.

The tactic of the trench had one more unintentional benefit. It served as an instrument of discipline so needed by the Boers. They did not dare flee. It was do or die, and they had to choose the former.

The men from Ficksburg fought fiercely. As the dead and wounded began to pile up in front of the trench with no further advance, the British conceded, retreating as best they could while still under fire. The men from Ficksburg had caused a major retreat. Now the Boer artillery, which had waited patiently and silently while Methuen was tearing up the hill the previous day and while the battle was raging, briskly helped the British along in their flight.

The last sporadic reports of guns ceased. Now the moans of the wounded, their throats parched with thirst, were the only sounds of the onslaught remaining. Magersfontein Hill, its shoulders starkly silhouetted against the evening sky, its top utterly disheveled, looked down on the inhuman carnage. At its feet more than two hundred Boers were sprawled out, dead or wounded, and about four times as many British, over half of them Highlanders.

Methuen retreated. An armistice was granted the next day for him to gather his dead and to minister to the wounded who had survived. Since the Boer positions could be spied upon the workers were led blindfolded.

*   *   *   *   *

In Natal the battle front would soon heat up and create heart-rending scenes of death and suffering, in sharp contrast to the peaceful beauty that nature had bestowed upon that part of Southern Africa.

On the western border of Natal, ten to eleven thousand feet above sea level, up in the Dragon Mountains, a small waterfall cascades almost perpendicularly down a wind-swept, rocky facade to ravines far below. The splatter and rush of water infuses a delicate touch of life and music into the breath-taking scene that the slow chisel of time had ruggedly sculptured and the brush of nature had decorated with moss and trees through many, many millions of years.

Captivated by the splendor and majesty of creation, almost in ecstasy, one's eye can gaze or wander for hours at nature's matchless work of art framed in a rim all around where the mystic purple horizon reaches out to the clouds drifting in the blue heaven above.

In this spectacular setting begins the renowned Tugela River. Like a true offspring of its mother, the Dragon Mountains, it slinks its way, as if a young serpent itself, through green valleys, gorges, and mountain ranges to the distant Indian Ocean.

In sharp contrast to the beauty of its origin and the grandeur of the terrain of its journey, it together with its tributaries, would witness some of the saddest and most gruesome history of

36

Southern Africa's development during the 19th century, perpetrated by human beings intent to kill and to destroy.

Buller in Natal, the Commander-in-Chief, was by no means ignorant of the disasters that had befallen his troops on the other fronts. His local opponent was no longer cautious General Piet Joubert, but the younger, more daring Louis Botha, a respected leader and a formidable tactician. (Joubert had fallen ill and had departed for Pretoria.)

With an army of about eight thousand Botha blocked Buller's approach to Colenso and to beleaguered Ladysmith, further to the north. Although favored by a superior defense position along the Tugela River, Botha's problem was that Buller by now had assembled and mustered an army of just under twenty thousand. He was extremely well equipped with field guns and also naval guns, so heavy and huge, that each required a full team of twelve to fourteen oxen to pull it into emplacement. The array of his army was surpassed only by his own reputation.

The Boers did not have to be told twice that they were at a distinct disadvantage. Being only human, many requests for sick leave began to pour in, but they were refused.

Buller was fully aware that it would be an exacting task to dislodge Botha. However, with the devastating reverses on the other fronts, he seems to have decided that he would chance it in an all out effort to restore morale.

It is likely that Buller's timing was purposely calculated. December 16 was drawing near. It was a day of great historical as well as religious significance for the Boers, especially in the Orange Free State and the Transvaal.

When the Boer pioneers had struggled over the mountains into Natal in 1838 they obtained land from the Zulu Chief, or King, Dingaan. The pioneer leader, Pieter Retief, went to Dingaan's head *kraal*, Unkunugungluvu, with a party of sixty-six white men and a few black attendants, to finalize and sign the treaty. Dingaan was a cruel and illiterate man, and knew and recognized no court of law, or public opinion where a treaty could be tested, except the court of the sword. When Retief and his men were to depart on February 4, 1838, Dingaan invited them to a farewell party where his warriors would entertain them with war dances. As a gesture of good will he suggested that the Boers leave their guns outside the enclosure where the war dances would be staged. They accepted the suggestion and went in unarmed. The war dances began and got rowdy as the demonstration progressed. Then suddenly the fat king shouted, *Bulalani abapagati!*, kill the wizards. Retief and his men were overwhelmed, dragged out of the *kraal* to a hill, clubbed to death, and left to the vultures.

Retief's heart was cut out and buried on the way along which they had come in superstition that it would magically prevent their comrades to return for vengeance. (The treaty was later found in Retief's clothing).

While the other pioneers were still waiting at their leisure along a tributary of the Tugela River for the return of Retief, they were unexpectedly overpowered on the night of February 17, 1838 by Dingaan's *impis* (divisions). Forty men, fifty-six women, one hundred eighty-five children, and two hundred non-whites were slaughtered. Some escaped to warn others further up the river who were able to defend themselves or flee.

So gruesome were the scenes of these murders that those who returned to see what had happened wept openly. They named the place Weenen, which means crying.

Having lost an able leader, their numbers greatly reduced, and confronted by a cruel tyrant, who knew no mercy towards his own people, let alone others, and mindful of the horrors of the massacre, the men were ready to pack up and leave. But the women put their foot down, and prevailed. Dingaan had to be punished.

An appeal was made to a certain Andries Pretorius, in the Cape Colony to come to their aid and assume leadership. He accepted. In December 1838 he was ready to do battle with Dingaan. He set out with a commando of 460 men on horseback, accompanied by a wagon train of sixty wagons, which they pulled in a circle, or triangle, at night with their animals safeguarded inside the enclosure. Reconnaissance revealed that Dingaan had a huge force of *impis* in the field against them, numbering in the thousands. The small commando, armed with front-loaders, did not seem to have much of a chance at all against such an overwhelming force.

(It must be stated here that Thomas Pakenham in his voluminous book, *The Boer War* (718 pp.), is wrong, as he is in a number of places throughout, by assuming that there were women in Pretorius' *laager*. There was none. His assumption is most likely based on the legendary tradition that women did indeed on other occasions during the Great Trek and later assist their men in readying their front loaders.)

Fearful of their lives and of the rest of the pioneers left behind, they made a solemn vow to God in which they were led by Sarel Celliers, who accompanied them as chaplain. On December 9 Celliers read to them the vow that if granted success in battle, they would henceforth celebrate the day of victory as a "Sabbath" and instruct their offspring to do the same.

On the evening of December 15 they were sure that an attack would be launched the next day. Their *laager* was positioned on the banks of a river called Ngoma. The *laager* was possibly in the shape of a triangle which was easier to defend than a circle or quadrangle. Underneath and between the closely drawn wagons they obstructed openings with branches, preferably cut from thorn trees, if they could be found.

Early the next morning the attack did indeed come. In a semicircle, like the horns of a bull, as their successful custom was, thousands of warriors screaming their battle cry, descended upon the *laager*, wildly dancing, and gesticulating with their spears and cattle skin shields in the air. The tips of the horn formation pinned the *laager* against the Ngoma River. From the wagons the muzzle-loaders belched smoke and fire as fast as new charges could be pumped in. The clumsy, but deadly, round, lead balls took a heavy toll among the attackers and repulsed them. They retreated to regroup and stormed again for a second time. Again they were thrown back. The tips of the attacking horns tried to ford the river and were attempting an assault through the water. Impeded in the stream, so many perished under heavy fire that their blood colored the water red (Hence the name Blood River). The attackers retreated to regroup and to attack for a third time. The only cannon that the pioneers had, whenever the gun crew could get it ready, blasted swaths through the brave warriors with terrifying results. The third assault also failed to penetrate the *laager*. In the face of a devastating defense they finally turned and fled. Pretorius, lightly wounded in the hand by an *assegaai* (long spear) hurled into the *laager*, opened the gate, ordered his men to mount, and to charge in pursuit.

The battle had taken a staggering toll among Dingaan's men—about three thousand, approximately one third of the attackers, mislead by their leaders and witch doctors, were strewn around the outside perimeter of the wagons. It was hard to believe that Pretorius, alone, was slightly wounded.

The defeat of Dingaan's *impis* precipitated a civil war among the Zulus. Dingaan was murdered and his half brother, a more moderate man, became ruler.

Then peace came to Natal, and the pioneers settled down.

So Dingaan's Day, the 16th of December, became hallowed to the pioneers and to their descendants, the Boers. (It was later renamed Day of the Covenant.)

Perhaps Buller reasoned that, if the Boers would hold to their covenant to keep December 16 as a Sunday, he could wrest a major victory from them near, or better yet on Dingaan's Day itself. It would have a far-reaching, devastating effect on them. In addition such a victory could be used to enhance the relationship of the British with the Zulus, a relationship which had been rather shaky at best. Be that as it may, it was about December 12 when he began to move in the beautiful setting of the Tugela River.

With his impressive array of artillery, like Methuen at

Magersfontein Hill on the western front, he unleashed a large scale bombardment on the hills beyond the Tugela River where he thought the Boers were. For two days he pounded the area. In slowly rising columns of dust and lyddite, exploding bombs shook the hills and echoes reverberated for many miles around. Hard choked Ladysmith, now under siege for several months, heard it in the distance and took courage. It was indeed enough to instill the fear of God into the Boers, who maintained a meek silence in the display of such awesome power.

For White in Ladysmith, his siege now secured by only about six thousand Boers, the preliminaries to the actual assault by Buller's troops came a few days early. According to word that Buller was able to send through to him, he was supposed to attempt a breakout on December 17, which meant that Buller had indeed figured on dealing a decisive blow to the Boers on December 16. Confused, White just sat still and awaited developments. Buller kept his own counsel, perhaps for fear of revealing his plans. The town was full of spies. However, a bombardment such as he had staged could hardly be concealed, and would hardly be a mere exercise.

The advance on the center of the Boer positions was under a certain Colonel C. J. Long who was in charge of the Royal Artillery. He was to test a new tactic. With the dumb Boers as his opponents, why not? The heavy guns would be the vanguard rather than behind the infantry, as was usually the case. His idea seemed to have been to decimate the enemy at short range, blast an opening through their lines, and march his infantry through without much of a loss.

The lighter field guns were advanced to within a few hundred yards of the river. The ponderous naval guns were farther to the rear. With all this happening there was no sign or sound betraying the positions of the Boers. But then, before Long's guns could be wheeled around into firing position, suddenly a shot rang out from the river bank, signaling an abrupt end to the Boers' baffling, taciturn restraint during the two days of hellish, but nearly harmless bombardment. It was mostly way over their heads.

Botha had deployed his army over a front of about ten miles.

The length of the line, like at Magersfontein Hill, was to forestall outflanking by Buller's superior numbers. The key to Botha's defense was a hill, called Hlangwane, at the extreme north. If this hill should fall, it would expose his flank and enable the enemy to start rolling up his line from an elevated position. It was a difficult and dangerous position to defend. The Boers knew that those who were to defend Hlangwane Hill would certainly have to shoulder a heavy responsibility, endure concentrated attacks, and possibly suffer many casualties. Independent as they could be, many were unwilling to man the hill. Paul Kruger got word of it in Pretoria. He was always ready with either a quote or an example from the Bible. He did not fail this time either. He determined that the matter should be settled by drawing lots to indicate who would man the hill. In this arrangement the Boers acquiesced, and Hlangwane Hill was properly occupied for defense.

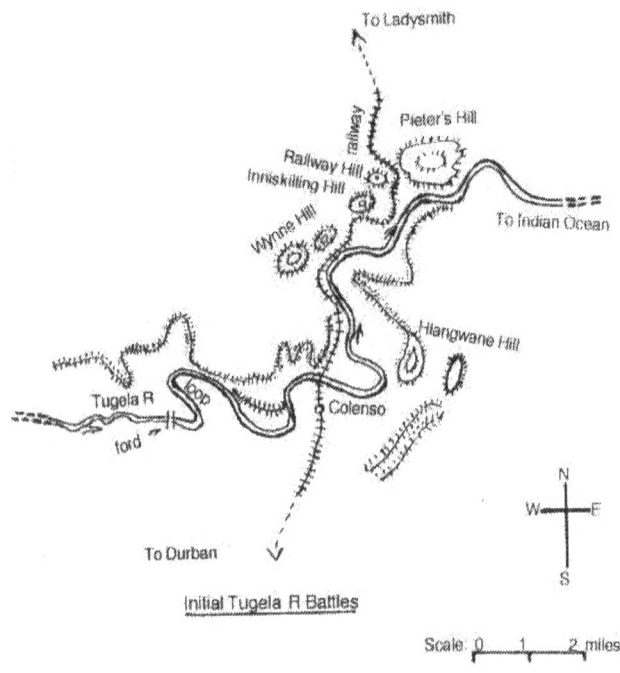

Initial Tugela R Battles

Scale: 0   1   2 miles

42

A barrage of bullets from the Boers on the bank of the river hit Long's gun crews and their teams of horses by total surprise, throwing them into frenzied, unorganized confusion and havoc. Frightened animals balked and tried to flee. Many collapsed dead or wounded. Many of the gun crews also fell dead or wounded. Long himself fell mortally struck. He kept on uttering senseless exhortations about his splendid gunners until he breathed his last. It did not take long before retreat had to be sounded, and the assault on the center ended in utter disaster.

Strategic and dreaded Hlangwane Hill was attacked by troops under the command of Douglas Hamilton, 12th Earl of Dundonald. Overly apprehensive of the defensibility of their important position, the Boers fought more gallantly than expected. The onslaught advanced only to a certain point where it was checked and pinned down by the defenders. Hamilton requested reinforcements to achieve his objective, but he was denied.

The most dramatic, but also most tragic phase of the battle was to come on the opposite flank. Here a brigade was under command of Arthur FitzRoy Hart, famed for a command that he had at Aldershot. He espoused the theory that infantry, to be successful, should attack in closely knit phalanxes and steamroller their way through to victory, evidently regardless of vulnerability and possible heavy losses. He had planned to cross the Tugela River at a ford a short distance from a U-turn in the stream. His tactic would have worked, for the Boers were rather thinly spread out to cover their long front, and most likely would have been unable to stem such a forceful tide of infantry. But, fortunate for the Boers, Hart had not done his homework—reconnaissance and familiarity with the terrain. A black guide led them in error, as if into an ambush—into a loop of the river downstream of the the ford. As the tightly compacted formation advanced ignorantly into the U-turn, heading for a ford which was not there, they were abruptly raked in a murderous crossfire from the river level, intensified by some Boer rifles from the ridges beyond the river.

In the center Long had now expired, and without a leader disarray was the order of the day. The British troops had no choice but to fall back. About a dozen highly prized guns that were supposed to have blasted a wide gap through the Boer defense line, had to be abandoned within easy reach of their enemy.

Blissfully unaware of this monumental disaster, the Commander-in-Chief was devoting his attention to Hart's predicament.

An exacting taskmaster, Hart was bent on instant success. In spite of heavy losses sustained right from the opening shot, he kept on pouring in fresh troops and urging them to the imaginary ford. The guide by now had disappeared, or might even have been killed himself. Still the bloody cross raking continued to take its heavy, heavy toll. Buller exposed himself almost with reckless abandon. One of his surgeons was hit and killed by his side, but it did not alter his attitude. Usually quite concerned for his men, and recognizing the folly of Hart's determination, he ordered a retreat. Then, no wonder, Buller himself was wounded. About four hundred of Hart's men did not get out of the loop.

When the additional shock about the fate of Long and his indispensable field guns hit Buller, he immediately ordered the guns rescued. Their proximity to the Boer rifles rendered the task almost certain suicide. For the required bravery and the additional sacrifices the reward of only two pieces retrieved was indeed meager. The rest of Long's bold experiment fell into Boer hands.

The great army was in retreat. It had sustained the loss of about a thousand men as well as invaluable guns and equipment. Buller had been wounded, and Long had been killed. Among the casualties numbered the son of a famous British military figure, Frederick Sleigh Roberts, later to be quite prominent in the war.

As the casualties on the British side mounted in the course of the battle, some were evacuated to field hospitals. Ferrying back and forth as a stretcher bearer was a young, British trained lawyer from India, small of frame and with ears seemingly too big for his head. He was destined in later years to rise to world renown, a figure who would make even the British listen—Gandhi.

The Boers, in spite of all the punishment intended for them, because of being the defenders, rather than the attackers, and because of defending mostly from surprise and unexpected locations—level ground near the river—lost only about forty men!

Botha, aided by colossal blunders on the part of Buller's lieutenants, had scored a momentous victory. December 16 was not for Buller and his forces.

A brief armistice was agreed upon by the Boers enabling Buller to remove his dead and wounded from the battlefield.

For all intents and purposes Ladysmith was a lost cause as far as Buller was concerned. He got a message through to White advising him to destroy his records and to surrender. But White refused.

As Christmas 1899 approached an uneasy lull had fallen over Natal, a region named on December 25, 1497 in commemoration of the birth of Jesus Christ by the intrepid Portuguese navigator, Vasco da Gama—a beautiful landscape, a breath-taking discovery for the early pioneers as they stood triumphant on the Dragon Mountains after unbelievable toil with their covered, jawbone wagons through ravines and over rocks to the top. Incongruous with its name its history had been written in warfare, blood, and violence—Zulu spears dripping with blood of other tribes; wheels of pioneer wagons encamped along a tributary of the same Tugela River in 1838, spattered with the blood and caked with the brains of children whom the Zulu marauders, swinging them by their feet, had dashed against the iron rims; the water of a river scarlet with blood of Dingaan's soldiers as they waded in, vainly seeking to penetrate the pioneer *laager*, and now massive boulders that had quietly rested for millennia untold, dislodged and exploded into the air as bombshell after bombshell pockmarked the hills; the moaning of wounded men, some wrestling in the last moments of life, clawing the gravel with their nails; and then the silent horror of violent death itself in the valley of the swift flowing, playfully gurgling Tugela!

The torrent of bad news that broke over England about the reverses at Stormberg and Magersfontein Hill culminated in the disaster of the Tugela River. The long lists of dead, wounded, missing in action, or prisoners of war could not be disguised or camouflaged by clever propaganda. The continuing strangleholds on Mafeking, Kimberley, and Ladysmith deepened the gloom of what became known as Black Week. In Kimberley dogs were shot for meat. In Ladysmith the Boers allowed White a separate camp for women, children, and the sick. For a mighty empire at its zenith and for its people, arrogant and lording it over all, it was hard to take.

The Boers were elated. For them it was a case of God vindicating their cause. They had ended the first war against Great Britain in 1881 with a decisive battle. Now they had just won a series of important battles and they were hoping that this war would end in the same way. They were not professional soldiers, by any means. Three months away from their farms and their families was a long time and a great sacrifice. Nagging impatience became a demoralizing influence.

The honor of the British Empire, on which the sun literally never set, a mighty power, had been stung to the quick. The British armies, deemed and painted at home as so gloriously victorious elsewhere (although fighting mostly primitive and ill-equipped peoples), led by generals burdened, as it were, with a dazzling array of titles and medals, boasting far superior military training and credentials, had been outfoxed, outfought, and sent reeling by much smaller armies of humble farmers of two small republics. Not that they were free of great blunders, either.

England, although expected to vindicate her honor, could nevertheless have devised a face-saving excuse to negotiate a peace, as great nations usually find when needed. But the glitter of Johannesburg's gold and Cecil Rhode's dream of a Cape to Cairo domination of the British Empire presented such an irresistible prize.

In the war there were many trump cards that determined its course, individual battles, and their final outcomes: innovation, surprise, mobility, superior marksmanship, and emotion born out of love of freedom. The Boers had all of these, except the most important one, the ace of spades, overwhelming numbers—numbers, numbers, and numbers again and again.

It had become amply clear to the British warlords that their forces present in South Africa by December 1899, although outnumbering the Boer forces by far, would not be able to bring the conflict to a successful conclusion. In fact Roberts said he feared, as stated in a letter to Lansdown, Secretary of War, that a significant setback could be detrimental to the Empire. Such a setback he envisioned in Southern Africa in spite of the fact that the forces that they had in the field at that time were much larger than had been in the time of Marlborough or Wellington. This seems to have been nonsense. Roberts was a small, egotistical man who wanted to head the British forces fighting the Boers. Revenge for the death of his son at the Tugela as well as his desire to be numbered among England's great who had fought Napoleon, probably played a major role in his hyperbole to Landsdown.

He got his way. Preparations were already underway for a massive infusion of additional troops and equipment. Appeals had also gone out to various loyal colonies of the empire to send volunteers. Australia, New Zealand, Canada, and others sent close to forty thousand men and contributed about £3,000,000 to the war chest. The volunteers alone numbered almost two-thirds of the entire force that the Boers could muster.

With the influx of thousands of troops from British colonies it was no longer the English War, but it had escalated into the Empire War, against a mere handful of courageous Boers. The British colonies were to sacrifice thousands of their young men on the battlefields in a cause that was neither any of their business, nor of any benefit to them. Sometimes, as at Renosterkop on November 27, 1900, New Zealanders and Australians were recklessly being thrown in to bear the brunt of an onslaught, and offered for slaughter to satisfy the vanity of a British commander.

A fundamental decision had also been made as to the leadership of the British South African Expeditionary Force which meant that Lord Frederick Sleigh Roberts, whose son fell at the Tugela, was to become Commander-in-Chief. He had sailed from Southampton in the Dunnottar Castle shortly before Christmas 1899. He stopped at Gibraltar where he was joined by General Horatio Herbert Kitchener, renowned for his expedition in North Africa and his conquest of the Sudan from defenseless natives. He would be Roberts' Chief of Staff.

Because the eastern front was of such great importance, Buller was informed that Roberts would assume responsibility of overall command in order to permit him (Buller) to devote full attention to the war in Natal. The face-saving ploy, devised for Buller, was not lost on him. At various times he seemed to find deliberate excuses to ignore Roberts and his orders, and to go his own way.

While the British were reorganizing and reinforcing on a large scale, a lull descended on all fronts, except for minor skirmishes. The lull brought laxity. Women with children began to arrive in wagons at the southwestern front to be with their husbands. This not only undermined discipline, but also impeded the mobility of Cronje's army. For his failure to deal with the matter promptly, all later paid very dearly. This colossal mistake made by Cronje seemed to have been surpassed only by Joubert's failure to capitalize on and to press his early victories home in Natal, taking advantage of the Boers' initial momentum and enthusiasm.

Inaction, lack of decisive victories, and the ever present hope for peace, which proved illusive, had dampened the Boers' emotion for the war. They were like a charged up, victorious team that had cooled off during too long a half-time.

The shake-up of the British command, the steady influx of huge reinforcements from all parts of the globe, aided by the world's mightiest fleet, and the failure of friends abroad to come to their aid, inevitably raised the demoralizing question in many a mind of how long the gallant resistance could be sustained by the two small republics against vastly larger and better equipped armies.

As the world's mightiest empire was hurling itself irreversibly against the Boers, it became obvious that the days of large scale confrontations such as made the battles of the Modder River, Magersfontein Hill, and the Tugela famous, were numbered as far as the Boers were concerned.

On January 10, 1900 Roberts arrived in Cape Town. Additional troops were arriving as well.

South of Kimberley camps were spread out all along the railway line, a huge force, swarming like locusts.

Advice from Roberts to the contrary, cabled several times to Buller, to remain on the defensive, rather than to attack, he nevertheless went ahead with further plans to relieve Ladysmith. He had now amassed an army of about thirty thousand on the eastern front. On January 16 he set out again, this time with more than twenty thousand men to accomplish his purpose.

In his customary fashion he temporized for a number of days to bring up huge quantities of materiel. It was quite apparent by this time that he would attack in the region of the upper Tugela. This area was dominated by a prominent hill called Spioenkop (Spy Hill). Control of Spioenkop seems a *sine qua non* to safeguard the route which he had in mind to reach the invested town.

Buller evidently had had enough of defeat at the hands of the Boers. Be that as it may, he did not assume personal charge of the new effort, but entrusted it to General Sir Charles Warren. The War Office had plans to transfer Warren to the Western front to replace Methuen. This was against Buller's judgment, and the transfer did not go through. Should Warren fail, Buller would not bear the blame. On the other hand, should he succeed, it would be very easy as commander in Natal to claim the victory. This would not only aid to vindicate him, but would also help ease his humiliating demotion.

Buller's twenty plus thousand outnumbered the Boers better than three to one. Their line of defense had to be stretched precariously thin, especially since Buller's staging area was a good deal up the river. The only factor in the Boers' favor was that they had been adequately forewarned. Thus far they seemed to have been much better at reconnaissance than their enemy. But Buller's forces made several advances along the front and threw the discouraged Boers into debilitating confusion. Fortunate for them, however, the British command was not all honey and light either. Buller and Warren were soon at odds as to the precise point of establishing a bridgehead. Out of this came a compromise to dare the impossible—take Spioenkop first.

The night of the 23rd an assault force under Sir Edward Woodgate, who was not well, started up the hill. It was no easy climb, but it progressed without resistance. They finally reached the ridge at the top, as they thought, where they drove off a lone picket into the night. But the ridge turned out to be only one of several and was not the top of the hill at all. Besides, the hill stretched for about four miles. A detachment is dispatched to occupy the real summit. But here they encountered the Boers who had crept up the hill from the other side in the early morning hours. A fierce exchange erupted at very close quarters. The casualties sustained signaled an ominous foreboding of what was in store. The advanced British troops were hurled back and the Boers held on to the summit.

Then the mist lifted and Woodgate must have felt sick at his predicament. He was not on the summit as originally thought; he occupied only a small portion of the four mile long rugged hill. But worst of all, one leg of a V-shaped trench, which his men had dug with great difficulty during the night, was exposed on the right to virtually direct murderous Boer fire. As the mist lifted the battle intensified. Woodgate was shot in the head and died. A senior officer, Crofton, had to assume command on the hill. More British troops arrived from time to time, all concentrated in a small area on the hill.

British artillery, frequently of great help to the Boers in other battles, was conspicuously silent for fear of hitting their own men. Boer guns, on the other hand, coordinated most effectively and rained bombs incessantly on closely knit British positions, causing untold death and havoc. So accurate was the Boers' sharpshooting that about seventy of the troops in the exposed trench perished from head wounds inflicted from the right.

Then, at Buller's insistence, command was transferred from Crofton to Colonel A. W. Thorneycroft. The battle continued to drag on with unequaled fierceness. Some of the British soldiers surrendered, but Thorneycroft would not hear of a general capitulation and carried on.

The Boers suffered heavily. A contingent from Carolina of eighty-eight men lost fifty-five. As the fighting raged on throughout the day, casualties mounted on both sides. The

British trench in places was piled up three deep in dead and wounded. The sun became hot and there was little water to relieve the suffering of the wounded and dying and of the hard pressed soldiers.

Night brought a merciful end to the inhumane butchering. Both sides had had it. Unknown to the Boers, the British quietly withdrew. But unknown to the British, the Boers also withdrew. At the foot of the hill the Boers began to ready their wagons for a general retreat. Then the hoofs of a horse came thundering through the night. The rider was either General Louis Botha or Commandant Hendrik F. Prinsloo. (Prinsloo had distinguished himself with great valor and courage during the day. If it had not been for his resolute leadership at one particular juncture, the Boers might have lost the hill.) The rider addressed the men from the saddle and pleaded urgently with them to return and not to yield the hill and their cause. Then the hoofs of the horse clattered off into the night to the next stop for the gallant rider to infuse courage in the outnumbered Boers.

Some of the Boers gave heed and returned. About three o'clock on the early morning of January 25th a few Boers got to the top of the wind-swept hill. Darkness hid the ghastly sight of dead and wounded and blood-drenched earth. Only the muffled groaning of wounded and dying men left behind by those who had fled earlier the previous evening broke the eerie silence.

To their utter surprise the Boers discovered that the British had also abandoned the ridges.

Word soon spread among the Boers who had been ready to retreat and they began to drag themselves up the slopes once more. They had hardly slept a wink for two nights. Then the new day rose over the Indian Ocean and those who could get themselves to the top stood triumphant on Spioenkop, and rightly so, for they had fought gallantly and with one accord against incredible odds!

Then both sides set about the gruesome task of sorting out the dead and wounded, for in some places Boer and Brit were lying side by side. Incongruous with the ferocity of the previous day, the workers were helping each other in their grim assignments.

The Boers counted sixty-four dead on the hill, most from the Carolina commando under the able leadership of Hendrik F. Prinsloo. Among them numbered a Mrs. Berrett, who had fought with the Boers for several months. In the total battle for Spioenkop one hundred and six Boers died altogether. Another hundred and fifty were wounded. The British, who had probably close to four thousand soldiers concentrated in the small area, had over two thousand either dead or wounded, including about sixty officers.

The Boers probably had only about six hundred men on the mountain at one time. In proportion their casualties were high, and would most likely have been much higher, had the British artillery not been silent in fear of hitting their own men, and consequently caused little damage to the Boers. On the other hand, had it not been for the effective shelling of Boer artillery which threw up an impenetrable barrage, it seems doubtful that such a small Boer force could have held the overwhelming opposing British force in check for long.

In addition the undertaking was marked by a comedy of errors and oversights, and a mess of bungling. Buller kept on interfering with Warren; command on the hill was switched several times with great confusion when a general (John T. Coke) also arrived without even knowing who was in charge; communications were poor. In spite of the huge amount of supplies amassed by Buller, the soldiers on Spioenkop were in want; but worst of all thousands of troops stood idly by not far from the battle while their comrades were being shot down in heaps. No attempt to outflank the Boers was made. With their meager forces they would not have been able to check it. But the British command evidently thought that their path of an outflanking move was barred by Boers, while in fact there were few if any, in the way.

Buller indeed did lay the blame for Spioenkop on Warren in his report to Roberts. But he made it known that he now had a new way to reach Ladysmith.

Almost two months had elapsed since Buller had wanted to stick it to the Boers on December 16. The first week of February Buller's troops were on the move to open up the new way. With various feints he once again threw the Boer command into confusion. Then he made a concerted attack on a hill called Vaalkrantz. The Boers defending the hill were under Commandant Benjamin Viljoen with only four hundred men. Indeed, the Boers did not expect a major attack on Vaalkrantz, since it did not seem a very likely passage to Ladysmith.

Buller started out by hurling about twenty artillery pieces, including several heavy naval guns from the Terrible, against his target. Now the Boers knew what Buller's plans were. The guns plowed up and wrapped the hill in dust and lyddite, but the Boers had been entrenched there for some time. Their defenses were adequately prepared and protected them well, but eventually, they had to retreat.

Fortunately, Boer reinforcements arrived in the nick of time. Buller's advance was stopped and even repulsed. Boer artillery arrived to supplement the lonely Long Tom, a formidable long-range gun, which Viljoen had at his disposal. The British had landed once again in a position swept by crossfire and could not advance.

Botha, on leave in Pretoria, was persuaded to rush back and take overall charge.

During February 7th and 8th the battle continued. Success was hard to achieve. Finally, Buller consulted with Roberts indicating that victory would cost up to three thousand men. Roberts replied that the beleaguered town must be relieved, even at the sacrifice anticipated by Buller. But Buller, always conscious of the welfare and lives of his men, scuttled the Vaalkrantz plan in spite of Roberts' opinion. Again he began to ferry hundreds of wagon loads back across the river, earning himself the derisive nickname, "Ferryman of the Tugela."

*   *   *   *   *

On February 6, his plans carefully worked out with his staff, Roberts secretly left Cape Town by train for the southwestern front.

The relief of Kimberley would be of immeasurable psychological value. In spite of Methuen's avowed intention and fixed date to reach Kimberley as early as about the end of November 1899, the Boers had denied him the honor. While he was still pinned down by the Boers at Magersfontein Hill, General French set out with a cavalry force of about six thousand, accompanied by a convoy of wagons carrying supplies, and some forty artillery pieces. There was no way, short of a miracle, that the meager forces of the Boers could stop him. A few skirmishes, a major charge by the cavalry, and a few days later the siege of Kimberley was yielded.

Farther to the east was General Piet Cronje. His force numbered about five thousand men. In itself it was a respectable and dangerous army which the British could not treat lightly. But the army had a clubfoot—about four hundred wagons, many of them carrying women and children that had assembled during the relatively quiet month or two preceding, a herd of loose cattle, and some loose spare horses. In its appearance and movement it resembled a great trek rather than a great army on the warpath to defend home and hearth. Roberts' forces could move more swiftly and soon overtook Cronje. Vastly outnumbered and lumbering he was easily outflanked and in serious danger of encirclement.

But Roberts, exactly because of the vast army under him, which required logistics hard to maintain, had become more vulnerable each day. The area was inhospitable without much for the horses and oxen to eat off the land, and very limited water supply away from the rivers. His lines of communication and his convoy of supply were getting more and more stretched out and subject to attack.

De Wet, the ubiquitous fox of the veld, always a daring opportunist was keenly aware of Roberts' Achilles heel. With a thousand men he unexpectedly set upon the supply convoy at a ford. The Tommies hastily threw up ramparts with what they had. Sacks of oats, cases of biscuits, and containers of bully beef came off the wagons in a hurry to build a breastwork. From behind their comical, makeshift defense works the Tommies fought bravely, but de Wet kept on pressing his surprise assault relentlessly. His men got the teams of oxen pulling the wagons into a wild stampede. Drivers and team leaders, white or black, fled to take cover the best they could, and the teams, frightened by the barrage of gunfire, took off running uncontrolled over the veld with the wagons behind them as if in a driverless chuck wagon race at a western Canadian fair. If there was ever something hilarious and comical to laugh about during the war this was it. In a brilliant stroke de Wet had captured or destroyed about half of Roberts' convoy of provisions, wagons, oxen and all!

In contrast to swift moving de Wet, Cronje's lumbering "army" was overtaken by Roberts and he had no choice but to make a stand on the banks of the Modder River, about thirty miles upstream from where, some two months earlier, de la Rey had surprised Methuen early one morning on his intended march to Kimberley .

The hopelessness of the cause of the two republics against England's vast power, which had at last invaded their territory, and the apparent futility of their sacrifices, brave fighting, and victories, seemed to have sapped Cronje's spirit of the will to fight. A religious man, he sought the solitude of meditation and prayer. But in war one can not afford to pray too long.

Roberts became indisposed and was laid up in Jacobsdal. Kitchener assumed command in his stead. He was a soldier with little fear of God, little concern for men, and hardly any love for women. He was bent on taking the honors of vanquishing a great Boer general in short order all by himself. But not unlike Methuen in his advance to Kimberley, he greatly underestimated his task.

After a long march and without breakfast he threw his army of about fifteen thousand against Cronje's wagon *laager*. About seven o'clock in the morning of February 18 he unleashed his first attack, hoping to have Cronje capitulate within a few hours. Breakfast could evidently wait until then.

Cronje did not have much time to be despondent. An artillery barrage began to explode upon the *laager*. Some wagons were set ablaze, horses and cattle fell dead. Occasionally, a direct hit was scored on an ammunition wagon, exploding it into the air with a deafening roar and and with a spectacular display of fireworks. Within a few hours the intense bombardment had wiped out almost all of the visible *laager*. But still there was no sign of capitulation. The Boers held well entrenched positions along the river on the opposite side. They checked the advancing British troops, mowing them down and exacting a dear price for each step of progress. Kitchener threw in the Highland Brigade, but they met about the same fate as Wauchope at Magersfontein Hill. Wave after wave of new units were committed recklessly, but to no avail. Their assaults were stalemated by an impenetrable curtain of lead from Boer Mausers, greatly encouraged by the arrival on the scene of de Wet and reinforcements under Ferreira from Bloemfontein, the Orange Free State capital.

They attacked the British forces from the rear and put them in an uncomfortable position, to say the least.

The soldier's instinct was rekindled in Cronje. He held his men together and determined to fight. The suffering among his people was heart-rending, but hardship to them was part of life. The doctors, of whom there were precious few, had been left at Jacobsdal with the sick and wounded of earlier encounters. The women stepped in and attended the wounded. As farmers' wives, far removed from doctors most of their lives, they had learned to deal with accidents and wounds of various kinds many a time without professional help.

Towards evening Kitchener had suffered about fifteen hundred casualties, dead and wounded. If this cruel sacrifice did not bring him to his senses, nightfall of a horribly bloody day forced him to end the massacre of his own men. It was a bitter pill for him to swallow. He had never lost a battle before. The Boers were not primitive people fighting with sticks and swords. His intention to take the *laager* by about ten that morning was more than frustrated by Cronje's men.

Kitchener's conduct of the onslaught, his callousness toward his own men and his merciless shelling of the *laager* filled with women and children, forebode what could be anticipated, should he finally assume sole command of the British forces, as he eventually did. . . .

Rather than repeat the slaughtering, the next day Kitchener's subordinates themselves appealed to Roberts. He journeyed to the front by wagon.

Cronje requested an armistice to bury the dead and to treat the wounded. It was customary with the Boers to grant such courtesy after previous battles where the British forces were at a disadvantage. They had even regarded it as humanitarian the night before to allow the Tommies, almost dying with thirst, to fetch water from the river unmolested.

Roberts refused. Instead he demanded Cronje's surrender. Although hopelessly surrounded and by now outnumbered six to one, Cronje was far from spent. He rejected the demand outright.

Then Roberts ordered the shelling resumed.

The third day Roberts offered safe conduct of women and children to the British lines. For obvious reasons Cronje refused this, but he accepted an offer of medical aid. However, afraid that medical personnel would supply valuable intelligence to Roberts about his precarious situation, once they return, he stipulated that they remain. This Roberts refused, and all pleasantries ceased when Roberts also refused Cronje's suggestion of a neutral hospital.

Had the Boers shown the same callousness toward women and children and civilians in their sieges of Mafeking, Kimberley, and Ladysmith, as Roberts and Kitchener had shown the *laager*, and shelled them with utter disregard of innocent life, these sieges would soon have been over with unconditional capitulation.

Desperate as Cronje's position might have been, there was an ever present ray of hope in the war genius of Christiaan de Wet. He was always in the wings, and would always, for the duration of the war, be a continuous, painful thorn in the flesh of the enemy, not knowing when or where he might strike, or pull a surprise. They had located him and attempted to lure him into an ambush, but with the alertness of his potato speculator temperament, he seemed to have an instinctive sense of danger. Before the noose of superior numbers could close around him, he ordered his men to take advantage of the only opening still available. With a wild and daring charge they rushed out. He then joined other Boer forces about fifteen miles east of Cronje's position. He assembled an army of about four thousand men and attempted to relieve the invested *laager*. But the Boers, because of their smaller numbers, and consequently unwilling to sacrifice needlessly, were usually less adept to offensive than at defensive warfare. In addition Cronje did not get the message to stage a simultaneous breakout. So, de Wet's attack failed, and one of the last chances to rescue the *laager* was missed.

Then the rains came. The fighting was slowed down. The Boers defending Cronje's *laager* became waterlogged in their trenches, polluted with their own feces. The stench of the rotting carcasses of dead animals made the *laager* and its environment absolutely unbearable. Food grew scarcer. Their main staple was meat, but by now, due to the incessant bombardment, most of their cattle were reduced to food for vultures only.

Among de Wet's officers was a daredevil like himself, Captain Danie Theron. He was fluent in English and could disguise himself very easily to pass for a Britisher.

Cloudy skies foiled attempts to communicate with Cronje by heliograph. De Wet needed to know just what the situation was, and was eager to urge Cronje not to give up, but to make a break-out attempt. Theron volunteered for the dangerous mission to get through the British encirclement and to contact Cronje personally.

It was a rainy night when he set out on his dangerous mission. Should the skies clear, the moon would be shining after midnight, and by then he had to be beyond the British lines. For a long distance he crawled until he could discern the guards as they paced their beats to and fro. His knees were sore and bleeding, but he had to go on. He waited near the path of one, jumped him with his revolver, stuck it into his belly, and demanded in a whisper to be let through and not to make a sound, or else he would "be a corpse." With the cold steel of the revolver's barrel thrust in his belly, the Tommy obliged, and Theron got through yet to face other pickets. Astonished Boer pickets received him into the *laager* later that night. He remained with Cronje for a day, and the next night set out to make the return trip through the British lines again. He had left some of the scouts under him at a designated place where they were supposed to meet him the next night. Knowing how hazardous his undertaking was, they waited in anguish as the hours of the night slowly ticked away. Again he picked his way carefully through the British lines and completed his mission scot-free. He reached his scouts where he had appointed them. He reported to de Wet and sent a long telegram to President Kruger: "The situation in the *laager* cannot be described, wretched, horrible. . . About twenty-five are dead and fifty wounded. It is heart rending to see how people, rather slightly wounded, pine away and die due to lack of nursing care and food. . . . Lee Medford bullets whistled over our heads all day long. The English sharpshooters in the immediate vicinity of the *laager* made it unsafe for us all day long. . . . The *laager* is completely surrounded and is being raked by numerous cannons. . . ."

Cronje would indeed attempt a break-through, but when the attempt was made, a devastating artillery bombardment rendered it futile, and the inexorable death grip tightened to choke the *laager* in its ultimate quest for life.

February 27, anniversary of Amajuba Day, when the Boers scored their renowned victory over the British in 1881 to win the First English War, was at hand. In 1881 Roberts was supposed to have set out to South Africa with an army to avenge Majuba, but peace was made before he could get started. Therefore, it seems more likely that with a flair for the dramatic, he purposely dragged out the siege to post a decisive victory on that very day. It would be as great a morale booster for the British as it would be a severe blow and discouragement to the Boers.

Either due to Roberts' vanity for historical coincidence, or due to the Boers' stubborn perseverance, or due to both perhaps, the siege dragged on for nine days with untold misery and suffering, and very heavy British casualties.

If Roberts suffered from vanity, he, or rather the British army paid very, very dearly for it, for while the Boers were enduring hell, an insidious, silent, but deadly enemy had time to begin inflicting a scourge on the British army far worse than the Boers could ever have hoped to administer with their Mausers.

Were they by any chance able to hold out for another week, the situation might have taken a dramatic turn in their favor.

Ultimately, conditions in the *laager* had become so unbearable with lack of food and the stench of dead animals, and their position so untenable that on February 27 the white flag of surrender went up over the *laager*.

Bedraggled and stunned Cronje's men emerged from the smelly trenches, unkempt and caked with mud, their few belongings tied in dirty bundles, their guns now cold and silent, in their hands. Reluctantly, very reluctantly, four thousand men laid down their weapons to become prisoners of war.

Cronje himself dressed formally in a frock coat, still the formal dress for men at that time, came on his beautiful, white horse and surrendered personally to Roberts, who was resplendent in his own uniform.

The effectiveness of trench warfare, made popular by de la Rey, had proven itself once again. To the astonishment of all, the Boers had only about one hundred and fifty wounded men.

The women and children did not belong at the front. Cronje could not be pardoned for this, one of the greatest blunders of the war. Nevertheless, a woman who could take an ox wagon, in some cases for several hundred miles, to join her husband, or one who could handle a gun next to her husband on the firing line, was one to be reckoned with in serious terms. During the siege they showed courage and determination that would characterize the Boer women for the remainder of the war, and that would have a profound influence on its course and development. Ultimately, no one would come to know this better than Kitchener himself.

A few days after the formalities of surrender at Paardeberg were over, the prisoners of war found themselves bumping and swaying in open cattle cars on the railway through the Cape Colony to be shipped to prisoner of war camps, some to Ceylon, others to a few small islands in the Great Sound of Bermuda.

The British realized from early on that Boer prisoners of war could not be kept in South Africa. They would continually attempt escapes, or such camps would be in constant danger of being attacked by Boers from the outside to free the prisoners.

Roberts, evidently aware of history and obviously desirous to carve a place for himself next to the great in British military annals, had several times, in writing about his South African expedition, made reference to Wellington, who had defeated Napoleon. This was just part of Roberts' vanity. In reality there was little comparison, except that several of the opposing Boer generals, Cronje, Joubert, Olivier, were of French descent. It was therefore, in all likelihood, little less than coincidence that he had Cronje (with his wife) shipped to St. Helena where Napoleon had spent his last days.

The loss at Paardeberg of Cronje with four thousand was a staggering blow to the entire Boer population. In spite of an urgent, personal appeal by President Kruger, an exhortation by ailing General Joubert, and prayer vigils in churches for the beleaguered army, they could not be relieved. If the prayers were answered, the answer seemed well hidden indeed. Real defeat for the hitherto successful Boer warriors, still craving peace and liberty, was hard to swallow and to live with. Paardeberg coupled with an avalanche of huge armies breaking like waves upon them from all over the world, made morale sink to a dismally low ebb.

British troops now swarmed into the Orange Free State from the exposed southwestern front. With thirty thousand men and more than one hundred artillery pieces Roberts stood poised to march on Bloemfontein, the capital.

Mistakenly, he had thought that in European tradition, the fall of the capital would mean the end of the war. But not so for the Boers, as he later found out.

*   *   *   *   *

On Helderfontein the yellow peach season was just about over. A good supply was still drying in the sun for use in the winter. The little bit of maize that had been planted was in full ear. Within about six weeks early touches of frost could begin to kill the summer.

The invasion of their country by thousands and thousands of Tommies who would sooner or later show up at their doorstep, added an element of apprehension and a chilling fear which the women would rather not have to face.

Rumors of all kinds were making the rounds and growing more frightening and awesome as they were passed on by word of mouth.

Dawid de Villiers, a venerable patriarch with a flowing white beard, had a much needed stabilizing influence on the neighborhood. He visited his daughter, Lenie, and her seven children as often as possible. The children were very fond of him and he made up in some way for the absence of their father.

In spite of his brush with death at the hands of Basuto marauders during his earlier pioneer days in the area, he had developed a great rapport with his Basuto help. It was no secret to them that one of his sons, Johannes, was to study for the ministry to become a *maruti*, a missionary "to teach them about God." While many Basutos were returning to their homeland, Dawid was able to persuade some of his help to remain on the farm.

* * * * *

Since the painful setbacks dealt Buller and his forces, the eastern front had settled down to a stalemate. But in the meantime he had continued to build up his already large forces and to increase his already awesome array of equipment. For this the harbor of Durban was conveniently close.

By February 10 he began to make a move with a force of twenty-five thousand. The Boers along the Tugela front were now hopelessly outnumbered five to one! From his earlier encounters Buller was reasonably informed about the Boer defense line. The element of surprise would virtually be eliminated. His movement was deliberately slow—almost to the point of standing still. He did not attack until February 17. Relentless pressure was exerted on Hlangwane Hill, the vital key to the Tugela line of defense. Its defenders held on bravely against crushing odds, but on the 18th sustained bombardment and attack could no longer be endured. The Boers took to confused, headlong flight. Like Joubert, earlier in the war, Buller did not press his victory to its logical conclusion and he probably missed a golden opportunity to vanquish the Boer army completely. For several days he contented himself with his initial triumph, and busied himself with his favorite pastime, ferrying supplies in enormous quantities across the river.

President Kruger, an inveterate fighter himself, kept a close watch on all fronts. He dispatched a long, preachy message, laced with Biblical quotations, especially from the Psalms, to Botha's army, admonishing them to stand firm. The ailing Piet Joubert also made a hasty trip to the front.

Buller's temporizing had created an opportunity for the Boers to turn despondency into defiance. Consequently, when Buller eventually got ready to commence what would otherwise have been a mere mop-up operation, he ran into a stonewall of opposition, probably tougher than anything he had faced before.

The Boers had manned two back-up hills to Hlangwane, Wynne Hill and Inniskilling Hill.

The advance on Wynne Hill by a formidable brigade met with fierce resistance from a much smaller force of Botha's men, coupled with accurate rifle fire as well as shells from Boer positions on neighboring hills. Due to the size of Buller's army there was no lack of targets. But surviving British attackers clung to the edge of the hill under heavy fire.

Then Buller summoned Hart of Tugela loop disaster to advance against Inniskilling Hill. His brigade made it along the Tugela River at the foot of Wynne Hill. But the Tugela just was not Hart's cup of tea. At one point his troops were utterly exposed to Boer positions on the opposite side. As in the loop back in December, hundreds fell dead or wounded, even trampled in the mud and water as their rushing comrades gallantly tried to slosh their way along, away from Boer fire. With heavy losses some charged and scrambled to the top of the hill, only to be hurled back by a dense barrage from Boer rifles. Hart's loss now already far exceeded the four hundred in the loop.

The next day was February 24. The Boers on Wynne and Inniskilling Hill kept the attackers pinned down rather hopelessly on the slopes. Their continuous fire repelled reinforcements, so much so that provisions, and aid for the wounded could not get through either. Many wounded soldiers, who could have been saved died, surrounded by other, moaning and groaning fallen.

The following day Botha agreed to a twenty-four hour armistice to handle the dead and wounded. He could not afford it, but his men, weary with battle, and without replacements, needed a respite, and this was a way to get it. His opponent used the time to reinforce and to plan strategy. Botha, on the other hand, had no spare resources at his disposal.

Buller had already sacrificed about fifteen hundred men since the advance began, but he could afford it, if human lives were that cheap.

The ace of spades was already on the table for some time—numbers, numbers, numbers. Ultimately, there is no higher trump card.

Then the battle resumed. Ruthless pressure was brought to bear on the two hills by both artillery and troops at the same time. Bomb shells exploded with muffled roars like drumsticks beating on a huge bass drum, floating a steady background crescendo, reverberating over the hills, contrasted with the rhythmic, crisp staccato of machine gun bursts, crackling of thousands of rifles, and the frightening zing of deformed bullets ricocheting from rocks everywhere—a bizarre symphony of death.

To the drumbeat of cannons British troops scaled the slopes, oblivious to heavy casualties as they progressed. At the top hand-to-hand fighting ensued with the Boers in pitiful minority. Some boldly hung on defending their gun emplacements and breastworks to the bitter end when a bullet, or a thrust of a bayonet, flashing in the sun, ended it all.

With rushing waves of British troops now dashing against it, the Boer line of defense, stubborn for so long, buckled. Fatigued by continuous stress, it cracked and could not but break. Those who survived had no choice—flight!

The siege of Ladysmith, which became inevitable due to Joubert's failure to capitalize on the rout of the British army at the beginning of the war, was now ordered by the same man to be lifted.

Again Buller did not take advantage of his momentous victory, so hard and dearly won, by routing the fleeing Boer army. Although in gross confusion, the Boers got away. Instead, Buller spent his time planning a formal entry into Ladysmith with appropriate pomp and circumstance. It would make good reading in jubilant England, and would be excellent for the propaganda machine. He had stolen a march on Roberts.

The battles on the Tugela and in mountainous Natal, marked by colossal blunders and glaring incompetence, had finally exacted their costly tribute of men. Such for ages has been death in battle—*dulce et decorum pro patria mori.*

CHAPTER III

THE STEAMROLLER

Roberts realized all too well that it was of the essence to move as rapidly as possible upon the capital of the Orange Free State, Bloemfontein. His supplies, due to de Wet's exploits and also due to the length of time that Cronje was able to hold out, not to mention Robert's vanity to have the surrender fall on Majuba Day, were so low that he had to cut rations for both soldier and animal to a bare minimum.

In his path stood the fox of the veld, de Wet. He had only about six thousand men, reinforced by a thousand men drawn from the Transvaal police force. They were under de la Rey. Some Boer forces were also withdrawn from the eastern front to help stem the tide.

President Paul Kruger made a hasty visit to the front. He traveled in a cart drawn by four horses with a small police escort. He and President Steyn thought it wise to make a peace overture—withdrawal of all troops to the boundary lines and full independence for the two republics. It was rejected. Kruger narrowly escaped from the front just as fighting broke out.

Attempts to delay the overwhelming numbers could meet only with disappointment. Boer morale was sinking lower as Roberts marched victoriously across the high veld toward Bloemfontein with a force of about thirty-four thousand men. The flat terrain of the high veld did not lend itself well for defense.

The capital was yielded on March 13, 1900 without a shot being fired to spare it destruction. President Steyn barely escaped northward to Kroonstad, which would be his new capital. Shortly after the last car of his train had rattled out of the station, the line was blocked.

Upon occupying Bloemfontein, Roberts made an offer to the Free State burghers. If they would sign an oath of neutrality, they could return to their farms unmolested. Some of them were not too eager for the war anyway, and about eight thousand accepted his offer.

Although Jacob Storm had a wife and seven children to think of who had to shift for themselves, he did not accept the offer, and neither did his two brothers and other members of the family under arms, but remained with their units in hopes of salvaging the liberty of their little republic.

As the Boer numbers continued to dwindle, morale sank still lower and lower. At the rate Roberts' huge army rolled on, hardly unopposed, it seemed that the war might soon be over, had it not been destined that the battle of Paardeberg first had to have its last, tragic say, and allow time for the Boers to reassess their struggle and to boost their morale to fight on.

Roberts had planned to rest his troops for a short while, to replenish his store of provisions, and to obtain more horses before setting out northward in conquest of Pretoria, capital of the Transvaal. But the battle of Paardeberg had a long fuse with a charge that would give Roberts and his forces a jolt of devastating proportions. Even before he could reach Bloemfontein, his men began to fall ill on an alarmingly large scale. His departure from Bloemfontein was blocked as if by the phantom of Cronje's decimated *laager*, the remains of which was now being cleaned up by thousands of scavengers, yet it was waving a diabolical wand of death over the British army. The stubborn resistance of the *laager* at Paardeberg coupled with seemingly deliberate temporizing on Roberts' part to achieve historical coincidence, had allowed the animals, killed in the bombardment, to rot in the water and to contaminate the river from which the Tommies freely drank. All the way to Bloemfontein in their bellies and in their flasks they carried the deadly typhoid bacillus. It was soon to wreak vengeance and suffering unimaginable. As winter was approaching thousands of troops were down in make-shift hospitals, or in tents on the cold ground without mattresses. Doctors and nurses were hopelessly in short supply. Death was on the rampage at will. Ironically, thousands found their last resting place in Bloemfontein, the prized capital, which they had taken without a shot.

For seven weeks Roberts had to bide his time. By then

winter had set in on the high veld. Frost had turned the green pastures into a monotonous gray. Snow would soon cap the peaks of the Malutu Mountains to the east. Cold winds would sweep in and make the Tommies shiver in their thin khaki uniforms, add to the death rate, and exact a high toll among the imported horses and mules, not accustomed to the climate. In addition the green veld which supplemented fodder for the horses, mules, and oxen during the summer months was now dead and not of much value.

While Roberts was champing at the bit, impatiently waiting to regain the strength of his army, the Boer situation was radically affected by several major events. Cronje was a prisoner of war and in addition Piet Joubert of the Transvaal armies had died, a deeply disappointed and broken man. Younger, more energetic and more daring leaders replaced Cronje and Joubert and took charge. Louis Botha succeeded Joubert. De Wet, Hertzog, de la Rey, and others teamed up with him to infuse new morale into the armies that had to retreat. Slowly it dawned upon the Boers that in reality they had not been defeated at all.

Realizing that Roberts was unable to resume his march, de Wet sent many of his men on furlough. It was a much needed rest. Jacob Storm and his brothers also went home. At home there was plenty to be done. Towards the end of March they rejoined de Wet's commando. He had been home a few times now and his departure was easier on Lenie and the children. When he left this time, they had all right to expect that he might be home again within reasonable time, barring the worst. But war is unpredictable.

During the period of rest and regrouping the credit has to go to de Wet *par excellence* for lifting the ragged and downcast spirit of his countrymen in the Orange Free State. It took a few of his daring exploits to rekindle enthusiasm and to renew confidence. Whether this was good or bad in the long run, is easy to assess in peaceful retrospect many years later, but not while in the midst of a hot war.

De Wet and his brother, Pieter, headed a force of about two thousand men. Among them numbered Jacob Storm and his brothers. It was the end of March. As they moved around they made a fake advance in one direction, so characteristic of de Wet, to mislead British intelligence. Then they made for the water reservoir of Bloemfontein on the Modder River to the east at a place called Sannah's Post. It was secured by only a few hundred British soldiers. During the night Christiaan de Wet took up position under the banks of Koringspruit, a tributary. His brother had been instructed to attack the garrison at the water works and to drive them in his direction.

But de Wet was not the only one with surprises. The British had a force of about two thousand themselves in the vicinity of Sannah's Post, retreating westward from an unsuccessful encounter with General C. H. Olivier at Thaba 'Nchu. Unaware of Christiaan's presence, they arrived near where his men had taken position. He was now in rather serious trouble. He was unmistakably outnumbered for the moment. To make things worse, his brother lobbed several shells on the Tommies, who deemed it the better part of valor to ford the brook and get away. They had enough time to hitch their teams, and began fleeing in Christiaan's direction. He decided immediately that his best defense was a surprise offense. But he could hardly resist the temptation to capture the large convoy and the artillery pieces as well.

He had enough time while the British force got ready to depart to get to the ford personally under cover of the river banks. Then the first wagons began to bump across the ford, usually lined with stones to keep the wheels of vehicles from getting stuck in mud. The native drivers and team leaders, as they descended into the ford, were terror-struck upon seeing de Wet himself astride their path. They were instructed to proceed, but to stop on the other side of the ford, and under severe penalty, not to betray the Boers' presence. They did as ordered. De Wet remained positioned astride the path of the retreating convoy—an unmistakably imposing Boer general, the lower part of his stern face decked with a black trimmed beard, his otherwise dreamy dark eyes now alert to any hostile move, peering from under his slouch hat, his gun, cocked, in his hand, ready to fire when he had to. His men had their instructions to wait on his signal.

With ease and finesse, as if a professional shunter in a railroad yard, he quietly directed the drivers, one as terrified as the other, upon encountering him in their path, alternately to the right and to the left. They halted as ordered once through the ford. Several pieces of artillery also came along. The gunners were taken prisoner and the guns ordered to park with the wagons. Systematically the convoy was inextricably boxed in.

Two officers rode up to investigate the jam. They ran right into de Wet. He promptly covered them, told them that they were his prisoners, and ordered them to dismount. They did. But shortly one made heels and sounded the alarm. De Wet now opened fire. His men unleashed a devastating barrage. Consternation reigned. As the remaining British artillery boomed on them at very close range, but causing little damage, they cut down the gunners and the horses.

This was the kind of action in which de Wet excelled. The intended minor skirmish came off as a real battle with lucrative spoil indeed. About one third of the British force was lost, captured, dead, or wounded. Eighty wagons and seven pieces of artillery fell into the hands of the two de Wet brothers! This encounter became known among the Boers as the battle of Koringspruit, the tributary of the Modder River. The water works were wrested from the garrison and the supply of Bloemfontein cut off. Roberts had no choice but to tank water in by rail, a near impossible task, until he could recapture the water works for which he had more than enough troops.

Of infinitely greater importance than the booty to the Boers was a revival of a will to fight. Those still under arms were greatly buoyed up, and those who had gone home with the oath of neutrality, began to doubt the wisdom of their decision.

About fifty miles southeast of Bloemfontein lies the peaceful little village, Dewetsdorp. It was named for the father of the de Wet brothers. The military significance of the village was of little consequence, but to guard against any possible contingency, it was occupied by four hundred men under General Gatacre of the Kissieberg debacle. His sentimental attachment to the place rather disturbed de Wet. He could not tolerate this. Promptly he advanced upon the village and threw the garrison out.

Slowly the Boers became convinced that, all setbacks notwithstanding, their fighting strength was hardly diminished. De Wet persuaded many, who had signed the oath of neutrality, that they had done so under duress, and he pleaded with them to repudiate it. The urgent call of a respected, and sometimes feared leader, did not fall on deaf ears. Many began to drift back under arms.

De Wet coupled his inspiration and patriotism with stern discipline. As determined by a council of war, the intolerable nonsense of families in wagons with the men in the field was definitely out. The practice of women carrying arms and fighting with the men in the front lines, which happened on occasion, was no longer allowed. For de Wet orders were orders, and it was no more every man his own master. He carried a *sjambok*, a very highly respected type of whip, indeed. These whips were fashioned out of a strip of hippopotamus hide, about four feet long, whittled to about an inch in diameter at the handle and tapered to approximately one-half an inch in diameter at the other end. Here a piece of cured, tapered cattle hide was sewed on, which in turn was extended with a supple, deer or goat skin lash. A hole was drilled through the handle part, fitted with a thong, and slipped over the hand for carrying it conveniently. De Wet was known to have used his *sjambok* on occasion, a much needed instrument to achieve discipline. And a rap with a *sjambok* was not easily forgotten. With his appeal to the home-sitters bringing men back under arms, de Wet had gathered momentum, which he was to exploit without delay.

Some twenty-five miles southeast of Dewetsdorp is another town, Wepener. It was now occupied by a division consisting mainly of colonial mercenaries. Their kind was referred to contemptuously by the Boers as "traitors." De Wet despised them with a passion. It was the most natural move for him to attack and teach them a lesson. However, he had his work cut out for himself. They included Boers, and they could mete out some of de Wet's own medicine. They were positioned in trenches to the approach of the village. The beginning of the second week of

April 1900 he engaged them with a force numbering around six thousand. For four days he attacked relentlessly, sometimes in hand to hand combat, but could not overpower them. Inclement weather set in. The trenches were flooded and doomed the colonials to unbearable conditions like Cronje's men at Paardeberg. Flee they could not. It would be suicidal, and besides, their horses were almost all dead. So they held out, waiting for help from Roberts' forces in Bloemfontein.

De Wet was in a position more vulnerable than he had probably realized at first. To the east of Wepener was Basuto Land, inhospitable with its lofty, rugged mountains and hostile inhabitants. To the south was the Orange River, swollen by torrential rains, thundering through steep and narrow gorges. Behind him came strong reinforcements for beleaguered Wepener. To the north and east was the Caledon River also in flood. Roberts seemed in a position to deal with this foe once and for all. But this was easier contemplated than done. It did not take de Wet long to become fully alert to the impending danger. He sent small forces to engage and delay the approaching columns while he himself still pressed the siege and attack on the defenders of Wepener. When the reinforcements ultimately reached the battered trenches two weeks after the battle had started, the fox of the veld had eluded them to the north and the open plains, the Boers' best defense and friend.

De Wet had shored up the breastworks of morale; he had introduced discipline; he had called back many of the wavering; he had helped the Boers to catch their second breath, while Roberts was nursing his thousands of sick and burying his thousands of dead, the sorry aftermath of Paardeberg.

Delayed by the unforeseen events of losing large quantities of his provisions to de Wet and of sickness and death among his troops, Roberts was unable to resume his march northward for almost two months. But by then his overall strength had been built up to about two hundred thousand troops, outnumbering the Boers still under arms by better than six to one! Based on figures of troops under arms it seemed that the war would soon be over.

On May 3, 1900 Roberts left Bloemfontein to set in motion the carefully planned advance of about one hundred thousand troops in conquest of Pretoria. Armies were on the march from the eastern front in Natal, from the southwestern corner of the Transvaal, and from Bloemfontein in the south. Close to forty thousand troops swept the Orange Free State alone.

Afraid of being submerged by the tidal wave of armies dashing against them, and not favored by very suitable defense terrain, the Boers could offer only obstructing resistance.

The siege of Mafeking was now abandoned. It was May 17, 1900. Never was an insignificant little, dusty town so uproariously honored. News of its siege being lifted by the Boers set off wild celebrations in England. For two nights and a day there was no stopping the uncontrolled hoopla in London.

By May 24 Roberts had reached and crossed the Vaal River without any major difficulty. He was now in Paul Kruger's Transvaal and only forty miles from the city of gold, the main cause of the war.

Many of the *uitlanders*, foreigners, in Johannesburg had fled when war broke out. They had been clamoring for the franchise, which Kruger refused without a long requirement of residence, for fear of Boer rule in the Transvaal being dislodged. It was one of England's pretexts for precipitating the war. What it wanted to grab was gold, never mind the franchise of a few thousand British subjects so disadvantaged.

The Boers had taken over the mines and were operating them.

The hilly terrain to the approaches of Johannesburg offered the Boers the best opportunity yet to make a stand. Louis Botha was there, de la Rey was there, and so was Benjamin Viljoen, the indefatigable fighter of Vaalkrantz fame. There he had suffered a fractured skull and concussion, but he had sufficiently recovered to lead his Johannesburg commando into battle again.

For several days fierce fighting raged. Roberts was temporarily checked. But again it was numbers, numbers, numbers. The Boer defenses could not sustain their continuous onslaught, and in spite of heroic sacrifices, they had to sound the retreat or be encircled and captured.

Johannesburg itself was not defended, for that most certainly would have meant siege and destruction. Plans were conceived to blow up the mines, but were not carried out.

On May 31, 1900 Roberts entered the city, the streets of which were not paved with the coveted, glittering metal after all. In fact, most of it had a rather disreputable appearance.

Forty miles due north of Johannesburg, and about one thousand feet lower in altitude in a delightful, subtropical climate lies Pretoria, the prized capital and ultimate destination of Roberts' expedition. He surely thought that the fall of Pretoria would automatically force capitulation.

Paul Kruger grew up in a tradition that was unfavorably disposed to the British, to say the least. He was a boy of about ten years old when endless trains of wagons rumbled through the district of Colesberg in the northeastern Cape Colony, where he grew up. On a wave of gross dissatisfaction with British rule he was swept away into the interior. For almost three quarters of a century he had opposed and fought the British conquest of all of southern Africa. As President of the republic of Transvaal since 1883, he had forged a bulwark to safeguard the ideals of his people. But now his enemy was at the gates of his capital when age had sapped his once tough physique of its strength. His exact date of birth is not known, but he was most likely in his upper seventies, which for that era was quite advanced. He was a heavy man which does not dovetail well with old age.

*　　*　　*　　*　　*

War being what it is, and soldiers having been conditioned for their prime objective to kill, other offenses against property and human beings—looting, destruction, and violating women—come with a minimum of qualm of conscience, if any at all.

Naturally, the women were afraid of being molested by the soldiers. When the first of them came banging on Lenie's door in Helderfontein, she refused to open, let alone allow them entry. They lingered around the yard. Then from the house they heard the fluttering of chickens in a little coop and the squealing of piglets. As Lenie and the children's frightened eyes peered out from behind the drawn curtains, they could see the fixed bayonets ripping through whatever was in sight. The Tommies rummaged through the yard and storehouses. Jacob's farm wagon was appropriated. Some of the sheep and cattle also disappeared with their departure. The chickens in the coop were kept in readiness to prepare when Jacob would be home next time on furlough.

Personal belongings were no longer safe. Some of the women got their wagons away from the homesteads and hid them in remote places on the farms, in canyons, or ravines, or thickets where they remained out of sight. Some of their livestock they secured in the same way.

Poaching by unscrupulous Boers, who did not go to war, or who had taken the oath, and by white entrepreneurs from Basuto Land was not uncommon.

As the winter had now set in, it was possible to butcher hogs. (In the warmer summer months the meat would spoil soon without refrigeration.) Pork was a welcome variation from mutton, which was a staple during warmer seasons.

Before too long another rather large number of soldiers came and encamped on Helderfontein. They were under a certain Captain Mackenzie. He came to Lenie's house and when they saw him he was standing at the kitchen entrance, looking in over the half Dutch door. Lenie spoke to him through her eldest daughter, also named Lenie after her maternal grandmother, Magdalena Louw de Villiers. She was fluent in English. The captain, impressive in his uniform with shiny brass buttons and insignia, seemingly a perfect gentleman, was not invited in. He requested Lenie to sell him some bacon and eggs. But, small and helpless as she was, she refused. From where Mackenzie stood he could see a container of eggs and a slab of uncut bacon on a shelf. "But you have some," he countered. "Yes," she replied, "but I need it for my children." "We are butchering a few head of cattle this afternoon," he said, "and I will see that you get some meat." So Lenie let him have some of the eggs and a slab of bacon. Then he left with the admonition not to open the doors, should any of his men come to the house.

In the afternoon two natives arrived, bringing a hind quarter of beef hanging on a pole between them. Lenie accepted the "gift". She seemed to have gotten the better part of the bargain, had the butchered steers not most likely come from a Boer's herd, and even perhaps her own.

Several times soldiers from the camp came to the house, but the doors were kept bolted, and they were told to go away, that Captain Mackenzie had told them not to open the door. Upon hearing his name, they would give up and leave.

When camp was about to be broken, Mackenzie came to the house again. He told Lenie that they were abandoning a disabled trolley, a light horse wagon, and that she could have it, if she wanted it.

When the soldiers were safely out of sight, Lenie and the children ventured to the vacated camp site, delighted to get out after being cooped up in the house for so long. A vast amount of litter was strewn about, newspapers, tin cans, boxes, and broken gear. Some of the containers were left almost full of biscuits. It proved a rarity to the children which they relished as grand treat.

Among the disorderly mess stood a small forlorn, gray wagon. Little did they realize then what a god-send Mackenzie had left them. With Dawid's help it was repaired— farmers could do almost anything. They had to.

*   *   *   *   *

Wedged to the north and to the south between two parallel ranges of low hills with limited approaches, Pretoria was an ideal city to defend.

Along the Quaggapoort Hills de la Rey, with only a few thousand men, bravely made a stand against an overpowering force. For about a day they were able to hold Roberts at bay. Then they were outflanked by a newly arrived force, and had to yield.

As in the case of Johannesburg, defense of the city to the bitter end would not only mean destruction, but also possible annihilation of the force defending it. And they had precious few men to waste. Therefore, it had been decided much earlier by Kruger and his government to abandon their capital, just as

Steyn and his government had done in the case of Bloemfontein.

So Pretoria became an open city with the retreat of de la Rey and his men. Botha hastily completed the evacuation of the government.

In symbolic gesture of the participation of the entire British Empire in his expedition, Roberts had his own force made up of representatives from all over— Canada, Australia, New Zealand, Ceylon, South African colonials, etc.

The city was entered on June 5, 1900. The balmy, subtropical climate with poinsettias, palms, bougainvillea, and hibiscus, and only a few jakarandas offered a welcome relief from the gray, and sometimes blustery, winter of the high veld.

Roberts were as if sitting in Kruger's seat and waiting for the Boers to do obeisance. But, as in Bloemfontein, it was only a fond dream.

In long-standing European tradition, the capture of the castle, the fall of the citadel, or the surrender of the capital, usually meant that a war was over, except for the formalities of negotiating a peace treaty, because the defenders had exhausted themselves, or were vanquished in ultimate struggle. And for more complex societies and nations the fall of the capital is of major importance. The two republics were still largely agrarian in nature, and the yielding of the seat of government was of less importance. After their capitals had fallen both Steyn and Kruger continued their governments under protection of their armies in the in other places, even in the veld.

But hopes were high for cessation of hostilities when the Boer leaders did indeed meet outside Pretoria, of all places in a whiskey distillery, to consider the possibility of peace. The distillery was owned by a certain Sammy Marks, a wealthy Russian Jew, who had amassed a fortune in the Transvaal.

Some present criticized the Kruger government for its conduct of the war, and for its failure to provide adequately for the Boer armies.

As they met to consider the momentous matter of peace or war, there were many historical and inherent factors that would determine the outcome.

The pioneers, who had trekked out of the Cape Colony more

than sixty years ago to get away from British rule, and their descendants had never capitulated to it since then. In spite of short periods that Great Britain thought that the two republics were under her wing, they were, with little exception, always in agitation for independence. Tradition and history, mingled with bitter resentment, had molded attitudes against the British that could not be ignored or lightly be overcome in a few days of conference.

The Boers were firmly convinced that they had justice on their side, that they were entitled to liberty, and to fashion their own destiny. For this together with their forebears they had endured countless hardships and privations during three and a half centuries of taming a wilderness with sweat, blood, and tears. What they had gained at such a costly price was not easily yielded.

They knew that they had the sympathy of many nations and were fervently hoping for outside intervention sooner or later.

There was much, and even vocal sympathy for them in the very halls of the British government itself. They were encouraged by the dissent in Great Britain and by the possibility of a change of government, which would bring Lloyd George to power in London, which would most likely not have changed their fate by much, for British empire builders were determined to have the gold of the Transvaal, as they were to have the diamonds of the Orange Free State.

Closer to home were the Boers in the Cape Colony, most of whom not only sympathized and gave moral support, but whose rebels were willing to offer their lives on their behalf. It was a territory in ferment. If the indignation of the Cape Boers could erupt in a general rebellion, it could, overnight, radically alter the fortunes of their brethren across the Orange and Vaal Rivers. The effects of such an eventuality would, without doubt, have been devastating to the British. The Boers always cherished this hope to the very end.

Deeply seated in the Boers' heart and emotions was the animosity built up over a century of struggle against Great Britain in Southern Africa. Not that the Boers were that narrow minded. The presence of Britain in southern Africa was a reality of life with which they had to live. During the Great Trek already, Jacobus Archibald, a Wesleyan clergyman, and Daniel Lindley, and American clergyman, were officially called by the pioneers as ministers of the Gospel, although they were English speaking. They accepted the calls. Botha, for instance, was married to an Irish lady. Even a staunch warrior such as de la Rey had hired an English governess to help with the education of his children.

The Boers did not trust the British. They had established a reputation, not only in South Africa, but also in other parts of the world, as might-is-right grabbers of what appeared lucrative to finance and build an empire and estates at home. They had reached for, and grabbed the diamonds at Kimberley, and now they had precipitated a war for the gold of Johannesburg.

In the war itself the Boers could not but have disdain for the mediocre fighting ability of the average Khaki to whom he was loathe to submit as victor and conqueror. The losses that they had inflicted on the aggressors in previous encounters were staggering. They had taken between six and seven thousand prisoners of war, thousands were wounded and killed, and the quantities of loot were even more impressive.

More than once the Boers, although vastly outnumbered, had tasted the satisfaction of vanquishing their foes. Outstanding in their memories was Majuba of February 27, 1881. Their previous victories made it doubly hard for them, as celebrated and self-respecting fighters, to surrender. On the contrary, they fostered a hope for vindicating victories.

The double defeat of February 27, 1900, at Paardeberg and at the Tugela, whether purposely timed or not, might have been historically cute, but it stuck revoltingly in the Boers' craw. Paul Kruger voiced a common sentiment of indignation when he exclaimed: "They have taken our Majuba away!" The Boers' self-respect and pride were seared, and would in no way be soothed by an unconditional surrender.

And then there were the Boer women, the primary vehicle of Boer tradition. As long as they were ready to endure and resist, there would be little room for surrender. And they were in no mood to capitulate.

In reality the capitals, other towns, and villages held by the British were small enclaves compared to the wide expanses of the veld, mountains, and bush—the true home of the Boer. Towns and cities were places where he went on occasion to attend church, to shop, or to sell his produce. Often he did not even have to journey that far, for church was conducted in outlying, rural areas and peddlers brought to his home what he needed and bought what he had to sell. The fall of a capital or a town was not an irreparable disaster.

The seemingly simple question of peace or war was in reality a very complex one for the Boer, with a multitude of cross currents that expressed themselves in moods, feelings, and attitudes, rather then in words.

A powerful influence visibly at hand was the fact that, in spite of the Paardeberg trauma, where they lost more than four thousand warriors, and the fall of Bloemfontein, Johannesburg, Pretoria, and other towns, the Boer armies were not defeated at all. They still packed a wallop, the force of which they themselves did not realize. Neither could the British imagine it, or they would have strained more diligently to secure peace, which seemed to be within their grasp.

Unconditional surrender the Boers could not stomach.

While the meeting paused for a few fateful days to ponder and to ascertain just what terms Roberts had in mind for a peace treaty, the delicate balance of peace or war was irrevocably tipped by the very fighting power and spirit that still motivated the Boers.

Christiaan de Wet was not at the conference. He had been guarding President Steyn, who had set up government in Frankfort, a town in the north central part of the Orange Free State. On June 7, as his unpredictable nature was, de Wet struck like a bolt of lightning from the blue and probably exercised far greater influence on the proceedings in the Transvaal than if he had been present in person. He dashed out from Frankfort. He caught several British garrisons along the railway line north of Kroonstad by surprise. His main objective is Roodewal, a well-stocked depot. A brisk exchange of gunfire ensued. The colonel in charge is killed, and his men surrendered. One hundred and fifty were killed or wounded, and more than seven hundred were taken prisoner. Huge quantities of provisions and ammunition fell into his hands. A freight train, carrying bombs, is set to the torch, and the spectacular fireworks wrecked the railway line. The British had painstakingly repaired it after the Boers had destroyed much of it in their retreat northward by dropping dynamite charges at intervals on the tracks from the rear car of a train on Roberts' supply line, and communications with his forces in the south were badly disrupted.

Here was a gratifying taste of victory craved by all, and not least by the leaders attending the "peace meeting." In the electrifying charge, set off by de Wet's success, emotions began to run high. At one of the meetings a younger fire brand, Hendrik Beyers, launched a passionate accusation of cowardice, a charge by no means justified, but it was a goading dart nonetheless. Hopes for peace were tottering and collapsed. The struggle was to continue.

Roberts was vulnerable because of his hasty charge for Pretoria. The Boers were by no means taking things lying down. While headlines were proclaiming Roberts' triumphant entry into Johannesburg, the Freestaters inflicted a severe blow to their enemy at Biddulphsberg, near the town of Bethlehem. They captured the 13th Battalion Yeomanry. It was a stinging defeat because of the large number of wealthy aristocrats in the battalion, who had joined the South African Expedition at their own expense. Vast areas of the Orange Free State and Boer forces there were intact. Roberts could be like Napoleon in Moscow. He was not unaware of his predicament. So he dispatched Kitchener south to restore the supply line and communications.

Botha did not break off peace negotiations immediately, but used the opportunity to prepare. He got an army of about six thousand together and soon joined battle with the British east of Pretoria. As the first day came to a close, the Boers had once again proven their mettle. Their armies had indeed not been defeated. On one flank of Roberts' line, Hamilton was virtually surrounded. On the other flank French was encircled by de la Rey.

The British Commander-in-Chief was in a fix. He was up almost all night in Pretoria, to which he had retired, mapping strategy.

The next day fighting resumed. Roberts' forces were able to capture a vital position, Diamond Hill, and that would make a difference. Both sides were cautious.

The Boers, as usual, had to preserve manpower. The British seemed to have learned their lesson not to storm Boer positions protected with deadly aim. Thus far Roberts had lost only a few hundred men, while the Boers had suffered the loss of only about twenty. But the British always had one solution—more troops. Roberts ordered more men in from Pretoria for the third day of the battle. He had to rescue French, who seemed in dire straits.

Meanwhile, Botha had to reassess the chances of victory. The capture of Diamond Hill could expose his entire line of battle to ravaging bombardment. Should his men be routed during the day time, it would be disastrous. He was now outnumbered three to one.

A surprised Roberts found the next day that the Boers had slipped away quietly during the night to a more easterly position. Both sides claimed victory, although it seems obvious that the British had the edge.

This was, in reality, one of the last pitched battles of the war. Botha had been entrusted with sole decision making power. Officers in the Transvaal army were now by appointment and no longer by election. A new policy was implemented that would eliminate massive confrontations in which the Boers would have little chance of success.

On the eastern front Buller had at long last mastered the approaches to the Transvaal and the Orange Free State with his huge force. He crawled at a snail's pace and was now only as far as midway between Volksrust and Standerton along the Durban-Johannesburg line.

Roberts' supply lines were in constant danger. Kitchener was able to restore communications severed by de Wet, but the movement of troops and supplies were constantly being harassed by Boer forces along the way. No sooner had the task of restoration been completed when de Wet came from the west and cut the transportation line in several places.

Frustrated by his failure to have the Boers come to terms with the fall of their capitals, and irked at their continuous harassment, Roberts unfortunately fell back on a barbarous policy that had worked well for him in dealing with primitive people whose habitats he burnt down to force them into submission.

Christiaan de Wet had already caused him a great deal of embarrassment, not to mention heavy losses. Unsportsmanlike, to say the least, he singled out de Wet's farm and burned it to the ground. So began a policy of scorched earth, although limited in scope initially. As homes and barns went up in flames, terror spread through the countryside.

The Boer's farm was not only his source of supply, but also his castle, much more so than his capital and towns. A scorched earth policy stung the Boer's very heart. It set in motion a chain reaction of resentment that would bring the women into the picture, a force that could not be subdued with rifles or flames. It is worth the surmise that the war might have come to a speedier conclusion, had such barbaric measures not been employed.

Obviously filled with bitterness, de Wet attacked. He slammed into the railway line, severed it again in several places, and captured yet another convoy. When his brother, Pieter, surrendered voluntarily, it was hardly a surprise that he threatened to shoot him "like a dog."

The hard core of the Orange Free State burghers were very much at war in spite of the fact that Roberts had proclaimed it annexed as a British territory and had presented it to his queen on her birthday! He threatened to treat those under arms as rebels. They treated his proclamation and threat with contempt and disdain.

It was obvious that there had to be a showdown. This brought more war activity to the eastern part of the Orange Free State, close to Helderfontein, where the Storm family was still making ends meet as best they could.

Jacob Storm's commando under de Wet had moved into Brandwater Basin north of Ficksburg. Several other generals were here, too. Their troops numbered close to nine thousand. It was a dangerous geographical area to have so many men. Escape routes were limited in number. British forces, outnumbering them about two to one, were advancing. It seemed as if they might have de Wet at their mercy. But the Boers knew the territory well enough to be aware of its danger to them. At a meeting it was decided to abandon the Brandwater Basin since it was obvious that the enemy was bent on trapping them there. They would divide into four commandos. Three were to leave the area on successive days. The fourth, under Marthinus Prinsloo, would remain to defend the passes.

In the reshuffle, Jacob and his brothers were reassigned under Prinsloo. It was Jacob's home area.

The night of July 15, 1900 de Wet, commanding the largest force, began to move. He was entrusted with the task of guarding Steyn. With iron clad discipline he enforced an unbelievable silence as the army and convoy, stretching for several miles, moved out through the intended pass. The British campfires were clearly visible almost directly in front of them. De Wet kept pressing relentlessly. As the convoy rolled ever closer to the fires and the horses walked silently, their hooves muffled in the veld, the Boers could see the Khakis warming themselves at their fires in the cold winter night. Daylight revealed to the British what had happened, but it was too late to head off de Wet and his army.

With de Wet and Theron gone, effective leadership and discipline were lacking. Indecisiveness delayed the urgent departure scheduled for the next night. Five days later no one had left yet, and their fate was almost sealed by British troops that had by now occupied some of the passes to the seventy mile wide basin. But there was still a faint hope, should they act immediately and attempt getting through the pass called Golden Gate. But then, as if unaware of the urgency, a vote had to be taken to determine leadership—Prinsloo, or Paul Roux, a non-arms-carrying clergyman general. The Orange Free State had retained the old method of electing officers, rather than having them appointed, which now, more than ever, showed its weakness. On the first vote Prinsloo won, but then votes from burghers outside Golden Gate, who had arrived from the Natal front under General C. J. de Villiers, gave Roux the edge.

By now the passes had to be defended. For a day the battle raged on. Then Prinsloo requested an armistice, but it was refused. Thereupon he proposed a conditional surrender. When this was also refused, he accepted unconditional surrender. Then Roux came to the fore. He was supposed to be in charge, and stated that the surrender did not apply as far as he and General Jan Crowther were concerned. In the end, he felt himself honor-bound to accept Prinsloo's capitulation. But in the darkness that night many Boers, who could not accept surrender, made a last and desperate dash for freedom, which they should have done much earlier. So casual was the enemy's handling of the situation that about fifteen hundred got away with wagons, guns, and all.

Jacob Storm and his brothers did not get away. On the frosty morning of July 30, 1900, one day less than two weeks after they were supposed to have left the treacherous basin, they surrendered on a farm Verliesfontein. (*Verlies*, strangely enough, means "loss".) Grown men cried in anger and frustration, but there was little they could do. Jacob laid down his rifle. Over four thousand men were taken prisoner.

The entire tragedy for the Boers contained some strange elements. It was small wonder that Prinsloo was accused of treason. He retired to his farm with permission of his captors. He died a lonely and ignored man a few years later.

*   *   *   *   *

The prisoners of war were processed, and under miserable conditions shipped to a camp at Diyatalowa in Ceylon. The news of the disaster at Verliesfontein that had inundated the country, had also dashed many hopes of Lenie Storm and her children. Word that Jacob and other members of the family had been made prisoners of war and would be shipped far away across the ocean brought many tears and sobs. Apart from what they had read in books, learned in school, and heard from others, their world had been confined to a small part of the eastern Orange Free State.

They had never even seen the ocean, and for Jacob to have been exiled to an island, thousands of miles across it, was just as good as death itself, if not worse. It all added immensely to the burden of a mother of seven children. A very soft-hearted woman, small of frame, but a priceless mother, Lenie tried to assure the children as best she could, unable to restrain her own tears, that their father would some day return. She could not help to doubt it herself, but she had to put up a brave front. She was a deeply religious woman, and her trust in the Almighty's providence was an invaluable succor to her.

The families on and around Helderfontein visited frequently. There was hardly a household without one or two men on their way to Ceylon as prisoners of war. Dawid came to see Lenie even more now than before. Several of his sons were under Prinsloo when he capitulated. Her brothers-in-law, Stephanus and Willem Storm, and a nephew, Henry Storm, were also gone.

The men were gone, but they had enough to eat, and they had roofs over their heads. Clothing was getting scarce, and it became harder to meet the needs of children as they outgrew what they had. There was no income because they did not have produce to sell, and the animals that had not been appropriated, they wanted to keep for the farm.

*   *   *   *   *

An overriding issue prior to the outbreak of the war was the three hundred mile long railway between Pretoria and Delgoa Bay, because it meant independence for the two republics from surrounding British territories, harbors, and transportation, although they did still make a great deal of use of these facilities as well. In fact much of the arms build-up in anticipation of war came by the British railway system! With the failure of peace to eventuate after the fall of the two capitals, Roberts set his mind on choking this artery of lifeblood to the stubborn Boers.

If he could strike a fatal blow at Botha's forces in the process of capturing the two hundred and fifty mile stretch of the line which runs through the eastern Transvaal, it would most likely force capitulation. And there was always the likelihood of capturing Kruger himself in the process, who had now moved farther east to Machadodorp.

But Botha had changed his strategy. He had come to realize that the Boer armies could no longer fight massive, pitched battles. British forces were too overwhelming and the danger of a major loss was a constant threat. Quietly he had dispersed a large part of the Boer forces as commandos to their home districts. The move had yielded an unexpected dividend. Being better provided for now, and being nearer their homes and families, boosted morale immensely.

Roberts was precariously short of rolling stock for the railway system to supply his now sprawling array of armed forces, for the steam locomotive that pulls a train is impressive and fascinating, but it is demon to keep in dependable running order.

It took Roberts a good deal of effort and time to prepare for his eastward thrust. It began the second week of July 1900. The Boers had kept on hammering away at the rail traffic under British control. The threat was so serious that eventually almost half of the British forces in South Africa were guarding the transportation system instead of fighting.

Botha gave Roberts' forces stiff opposition as they ventured eastward along the railway line. In addition, his new policy was beginning to pay off. It was indeed to change the entire mode of warfare, and would eventually have the British generals wring their hands in despair.

The campaign to the east had not progressed too far from Pretoria when the Transvaal west of the city, a region which Roberts had regarded as safe, caught fire behind his back. It was no small wonder, for this was the home territory to which inveterate de la Rey had deployed with his forces. There were about seven thousand Boers in the area. The former State Attorney, Jan C. Smuts, had changed hats and now had a command under the tutelage of de la Rey. With marked success they struck at the British, complacently resting on their laurels, and created a situation not much unlike that caused by de Wet at various times in the Orange Free State.

To make things worse, plots were discovered in

Johannesburg as well as in Pretoria against the British. If the plot in Pretoria had been pulled off, it would have had dire consequences. A German immigrant, Hans Cordau, who had signed the oath, had hatched and was masterminding it. Houses were to be set on fire in the city. In the confusion some British officers were to be assassinated and Roberts captured and turned over to the Boers.

Cordau died calmly facing a firing squad.

In addition to the Boers' continuous onslaught against the railways, the Hollanders, whom the republics had employed on the railways, refused to serve the British.

The annexation of the Orange Free State was a laughing matter. The Transvaal was nowhere near capitulation. The life lines from the southern ports through the Orange Free State and from Cape Town along the western railway on the border of the now unsafe western Transvaal were torturously long. From Cape Town to Mafeking is about one thousand miles, and from Port Elizabeth and East London to Pretoria about seven hundred miles, three hundred of which ran through the heart of the Orange Free State. About one hundred and fifty miles of the Durban-Johannesburg line runs through the eastern Transvaal. Even in the Cape Colony the safety of the railways could not be taken for granted. As thousands of troops stood watch over supply lines and large numbers of repair crews were needed at all times to keep the trains running, Roberts no longer had at his disposal the huge numbers of troops to steamroller his way eastward as he did to Bloemfontein and Pretoria. By the end of July the eastward thrust had progressed only as far as Middelburg, sixty miles from Pretoria.

The bane of Roberts and his generals, more so than Botha and de la Rey, still remained de Wet. They were keenly aware of his electrifying presence, his discipline, but above all of the humiliation which he had visited upon them on various occasions. He had no sooner made good his escape from the Brandwater Basin, when several British columns set out in hot pursuit. Roberts assigned Broadwood, de Wet's victim at the Bloemfontein water works, to direct the chase. Revenge would be a goading incentive.

But de Wet, as before, figuring that a surprise offense is often the best defense, attacked one column, while Theron skirmished with the other under Broadwood. They were able to keep the two columns apart and made for the heavily patrolled Bloemfontein-Johannesburg railway. As daring as de Wet, Theron brought a passing train to a halt and ransacked it before crossing over.

With a much larger force than their own in pursuit, de Wet and Theron were fighting and fleeing for their lives. Their capture would be doubly rewarding to the British because they were still entrusted with the safeguarding of President Steyn, a highly esteemed and respected leader, able to ride like his burghers, willing to endure the privations of war with them, and no small source of inspiration. At times their would-be captors caught up with them and sharp exchanges ensued in which the British suffered more than their share of dead and wounded at the hands of a lot of daring and now well disciplined Boers.

After more than a hundred miles of chase, de Wet finally eluded his pursuers and took up positions south of the Vaal River in hills near the town of Reitzburg. Here they got a little respite.

Along the way many Boers, who had laid down their arms, changed their minds and continued to swell de Wet's ranks.

But rest was not for these two leaders. While biding their time for a while in the hills, Theron dashed southeast several times for about thirty miles and attacked the railway line.

If they were left alone here, it was simply because their pursuers were not up to the task assigned them, and needed more men and time to reorganize.

Roberts was bent on getting de Wet. When the undertaking was resumed, more than twenty thousand troops in the Orange Free State as well as across the Vaal River would directly, or indirectly be involved in an attempt to corner him. None other than Kitchener himself was in charge.

Theron was a scout *par excellence*, and it did not take long to determine that a huge force was throwing an impenetrable half moon around them from the south with the obvious intent of pinning them against the river. Should they manage to cross, beyond were even larger forces to receive them. Methuen,

Smith-Dorrien, Hamilton, and Baden-Powell were all in the area, trying to cope with de la Rey, who had turned part of the western Transvaal topsy-turvy. They were alerted to aid in the chase and capture the fox. If they were going to take de Wet, it would not be at a cheap price. De Wet's prospects seemed as bleak as the winter-killed veld.

With a plot in Johannesburg, with a plot in Pretoria against him personally, and with the western Transvaal up in arms, Roberts must have realized the more fully that the war had never simmered down to a mere mopping-up operation, as he had bragged.

The heterogeneous populations of Johannesburg and Pretoria made security and essential secrecy of military matters nearly impossible. To aggravate the problem numerous refugees, women, children, and old men, from the farms had flocked to the cities. Many of them were there because they feared outbreaks of violence by natives. It must be said, however, that many of the natives on the farms remained faithful to their employers and were invaluable to them as the war dragged out.

Roberts now evicted the refugees from the cities. Large numbers fled east to be under Botha's protection. Others were shipped towards the front on Roberts' orders and unloaded near where the Boer armies were. Botha began to encounter the same problem that Cronje once had. They were Cronje's downfall, and it seems to have been figured that their presence would sufficiently encumber Botha as to cause his demise as well.

Sporadically farms went up in flames. Women and children more and more became victims of the war. This was a strange phenomenon in a conflict in which the opposing soldiers usually treated each other with gentlemanly deference, nursing each other's wounded, allowing armistices to remove the wounded, to bury the dead, and even to exchange tobacco. The British on one occasion even listened to a Boer's prayer for peace, and on another accorded a fallen hero of the Boers a funeral with military honors.

Yet, in the final analysis, war was war. And this war was for wealth. The gold of the Witwatersrand mines, like the diamonds of Kimberley, so desperately needed to build up the land from which it came, now began to make its way to London. In fact, the major objective of the war had been accomplished.

De la Rey's operations in the western Transvaal made headlines again. He had surrounded a certain Colonel Hore, who was guarding large quantities of provisions, turned his artillery on him, and destroyed large numbers of cattle and horses in the process. A rescue column was driven off by de la Rey's men. Baden-Powell of Mafeking fame advanced to help, but in the end retreated without accomplishing much. Due to faulty judgment he just thought that Hore had already been relieved.

The western Transvaal was in such a precarious situation militarily for the British that Roberts began to fear for the safety of Pretoria itself. This was the more so since he had several undertakings launched simultaneously—the attack on the Pretoria-Delgoa Bay railway line to the east and his full-scale hunt for de Wet. So Baden-Powell and Hamilton were ordered closer to Pretoria, where they could be nearer the capital and also serve as back-ups for cornering de Wet.

In the process Hore was left to the mercy of de la Rey, who had now settled down and leisurely castigated the trapped colonel behind his edible ramparts of flour sacks and bully beef containers.

In the eastern Transvaal Kruger was awaiting developments from his personal railway car to which his government had now been reduced. He had left his wife, Sannie, in Pretoria in their modest verandahed home on South Church Street. It was expedient for public relations' sake to treat her with respect. This Roberts realized and did.

Kruger was already in his seventies, as stated before. All his life, which spanned almost the entire involvement of Great Britain in South Africa, he had scorned British rule. He grew up as a young boy on the frontier of the northeastern Cape Colony from where the Krugers were swept across the Orange River in the Great Trek of 1835-1838. The Transvaal eventually became his home. Schooled in rugged frontier and pioneer life, he had a tough and forceful personality, enhanced by a massive, strong physique. His large face was carved in heavy, somewhat unattractive features. He was largely self-taught, stern, and orthodox. A great deal of the Bible he knew by heart. It was not uncommon for him, when President, to deliver a Sunday sermon in his church. For this he was richly endowed with a booming voice. There was nothing small about his person.

In political philosophy he had an arch rival in Cecil Rhodes. Rhodes' Cape-to-Cairo-for-Britain ideals were in direct conflict with Kruger's more limited, Cape-to-Limpopo-for-the-Boer dream. Kruger had an advantage. His aspirations were rooted in the fact that the Boers in the Cape Colony, the Orange Free State, and the Transvaal outnumbered the British. But even more important, through the years they had become indigenous. Southern Africa was their home, while most of the British descendants still regarded England as home. In the long run, these facts would determine the outcome of a conflict many years after both these two leaders had gone to their last resting places.

*   *   *   *   *

De Wet knew what the inevitable outcome of encirclement by the large forces, approaching him from the south, would mean. He determined to leave the hills, attractive as they were for defense and hiding. But some of his Freestaters were reluctant. He usually got what he wanted. He had the wagons packed and gave orders to proceed. So the doubters had no choice but to go. An unwieldy, yet thrilling chase now ensued. Whoever could capture de Wet would earn laurels of history— and some of the best that England boasted at the time had a shot at it.

The British knew how skillfully de Wet could maneuver and that he could not easily be second guessed. Close to his hide-out was a ford which he would obviously choose to cross the Vaal River. But judging from the direction in which he was sending part of his convoy, it seemed that he would not do the obvious, but cross the river farther down stream and break out of the encirclement at the tip of the westerly pincer. So British forces rushed west to cut him off. De Wet's move was a feint. He swung around and rushed through the ford closest at hand into the Transvaal anyway. He had done the obvious after all, but not before he had thrown his pursuers uncomfortably off balance. They still thought that he would arch back westward and reenter the Orange Free State at the lower ford. So more troops were concentrated there, but with great disappointment.

Instead of obliging Kitchener on the Vaal River, he had planned to head into the western Transvaal where de la Rey held sway, where Commandant P. J. Liebenberg had caused the evacuation of Potchefstroom, a vital point in the link with the western railway line, and where General Sarel Oosthuizen had successfully locked horns with General Horace Smith-Dorrien. At various times de Wet made fake moves like a rabbit flashing its tail in one direction and scampering off in the opposite, and continued to elude the bulldog panting and sniffing on his trail. He soon reached the hilly region sixty miles west of Johannesburg, called Gatsrand. He was now close to the railway line. Movements at night and the hills that made it difficult for scouts to track him were his protection. In this area Smith-Dorrien was waiting for him. He kept his force in readiness to swoop down on the now tired Boer force, and overpower it. But de Wet was a relentless driver, giving his oxen and horses only enough time at intervals to feed and rest a minimum, and his men to sleep a little. Smith-Dorrien's large army was easily evaded and he crossed the railway.

But the chase continued in all earnest. Methuen, still trying to "put the fear of God" into the Boers, took up the relentless pursuit. He caught up with de Wet and attacked the weary tail end of his convoy. Methuen's troops were fresher than de Wet's. It seemed as if the inevitable end had come, but not just yet. De Wet kept moving in spite of heavy shelling. He abandoned part of his convoy and some of the prisoners of war that he had kept in custody. Then mercifully a cold August night swallowed him up.

The next day Methuen was able to catch up. Again only gallant rear guard defense saved de Wet and Steyn.

Exhaustion was written all over the faces of harassed Boers. Their oxen, pulling the vital supplies of food and ammunition, were tired to the point of collapse. Their hooves were sore from an impossibly long trek in a matter of only about a week—sometimes over rough and taxing terrain. They had become cranky, hard to handle, and unresponsive to the drivers who were very much in the same mood. The wagons could be de Wet's demise, and mean the capture of Steyn, but he would not let them go.

As Methuen's troops closed in, the Boers fought like tigers in a corner, and turned them back temporarily until they could catch up again for the next round of the running battle.

With Methuen now breathing down his neck, de Wet swung north and headed for the Magalies Mountains. Beyond begins the bush veld and the area is dominated by de la Rey. It would offer much better protection. The mountain range runs east-west, made up of consecutive hills mostly sloping gently to the north into valleys. To the south they formed forbidding escarpments which stared de Wet in the face. It gave the appearance of wide hatchway covers made of rock, pushed halfway up as if a massive giant in primeval centuries had wrestled in vain to escape from beneath the crust of the earth.

The pursuit of the Boers was not without peril, and few knew it better than Methuen himself. Twice, at Modder River and at Magersfontein, his army had walked unexpectedly into the fire-belching Mausers of the Boers with humiliating defeat.

Centuries ago water had carved a pass across the mountain range through which the Hex River disgorged its contents eventually to help fill the Limpopo River, the northern boundary of the Transvaal. This pass is called Olifantsnek. A flight farther westward, or Olifantsnek to his north, was de Wet's only hope. But time was running out fast. Kitchener had now advanced from the south to within striking distance. Hamilton was moving parallel with the mountain range to block the pass.

With Kitchener and Hamilton closing in, Methuen abandoned his direct pursuit and set out on a forced rush around de Wet to block his escape westward. Escape here would indeed be tantamount to a glorious victory.

It seems as if de Wet and his men were surely doomed under overwhelming odds. But all knew well that he would fight to the finish to protect Steyn, and rather die, than be caught alive. For such an eventuality the British generals were more than adequately prepared and equipped.

As Methuen and Hamilton strained to achieve their objectives to cut him off, de Wet infused man and beast with his indomitable spirit to win, which had already made him a legend in the war. With all they had left they pushed for the mountain in a desperate last-ditch effort.

De la Rey was still holding Hore pinned down, waiting patiently for him to surrender. The dead animals in and around the camp made it an unbearable stench hole. Downwind the Boers were fully aware of the wretched situation. Cautious of the high price of capture by frontal assault, the Boers seldom brought a siege to a successful conclusion.

With satisfaction Methuen arrived at his destination to seal off the westward escape route. Then Hamilton arrived at Olifantsnek to administer the coupe de grace. All was quiet. They found only tracks of de Wet and his men. They had crossed the Magalies Mountains where others had thought that only baboons could cross. Hamilton, Methuen, and Kitchener had failed! Although only a miraculous escape had saved him, victory once again belonged to the fox of the veld, who had added yet another fabulous chapter to his amazing legend.

Once north of the mountain range, de Wet swung in an easterly direction. As he passed a gap held by Baden-Powell, he facetiously signaled him to surrender. The mountains which had once seemed his sure undoing had now become a bulwark. The pursuit was abandoned.

Steyn, who had made the hazardous flight with de Wet, now set out with a small escort on a dangerous journey of more than two hundred miles to meet with Kruger in the eastern Transvaal.

The pursuit of de Wet having come to an end, Roberts devoted more time to his eastward push against Botha, who had now moved to the mountainous vicinity of Belfast, more than a hundred miles from Pretoria.

Most of the Transvaal Boers under arms were operating in their home districts in commandos and making life miserable for the invaders wherever they could. Consequently, Botha had only about five thousand men with which he guarded Paul Kruger.

Buller had been ordered to abandon his leisurely advance to Johannesburg and to proceed to the Pretoria-Delgoa Bay railway. He was now only between Volksrust and Standerton in the southeastern Transvaal. At his customary snail's pace he trudged over the veld in a massive convoy of over seven hundred wagons and nine thousand troops.

When Roberts finally confronted Botha towards the end of August, he outnumbered him better than four to one. Botha's line was very thinly stretched out over many miles, hoping to forestall outflanking and still being able to shift men to critical points of battle, as needed.

Steyn had arrived behind the Boer lines and was conferring with Kruger.

The Boer positions would not be much of a match for the British forces. *Mirabile dictu*, it was Buller who drove a wedge through Botha's defenses. It happened at a place called Bergendal. A small unit of Zarps (*Zuid-Afrikaansche Republiek Politie*), some of Johannesburg's finest policemen under Commandant Oosthuizen, bore the brunt of the hellish bombardment for which Buller was famous. The defenders killed scores of storming British troops, but in the end had to yield to overpowering numbers as was usually the case. Oosthuizen was captured, badly wounded.

As Roberts' troops struggled north and south through the rugged mountains they took Baberton and Lydenburg with great quantities of provisions and ammunition carefully imported by the Boers through Delgoa Bay.

The Transvaal had now almost completely been deprived of its remaining link with the outside world, and Roberts deemed it beaten. On September 10, 1900, eleven months after the war had broken out, he declared the Transvaal annexed.

Kruger and Steyn went further east by rail.

With Kruger's consent more than two thousand prisoners of war were released. Thus far, for lack of secure places to keep them, they had to let go between seven and eight thousand prisoners of war.

To make things worse, Botha was taken ill. The men in his army, driven hither and yon, were dejected to say the least, and hopelessly discouraged. Steyn sized up the situation and stepped into the vacuum created by Botha's illness. He visited the crestfallen Boers and encouraged them with all the vigor at his command, even joked at times to buoy up their shattered spirits. He himself had once been where those men were now when his capital fell and his republic was overrun.

Then on September 11, 1900, Paul Kruger left Nelspruit for Delgoa Bay, from where he would depart for Europe to ask for help. If ever a man must have felt like Job, it was Kruger in those dark days of his life. He had always been deeply and rigidly religious, a man with great faith in God and his righteousness. But the lessons of the Bible, which was the main book of his education, must have supplied some comfort in his time of affliction as well.

Schalk Burger, Chief Justice, became Acting President. It seemed as if a great dream which Kruger had tried all his life to translate into reality had finally come to a tragic nothing. Yet, it was not the end. He had helped to bring a people into nationhood, and a nation does not die in losing a battle, or a war.

Kruger's departure, labeled as a leave of absence, could not be disguised. It had a debilitating influence beyond measure on the Boers.

Steyn wanted to get back to his native Orange Free State to which de Wet had already returned. He left with several hundred men on a circuitous route. He went first to Pietersburg in the northern Transvaal where an important meeting was held, then to the western Transvaal from where he journeyed south, back into his own republic.

Spring arrives early in the region towards the Mozambique border. It would soon be hot and malaria infested. Botha saw no need to linger and expose his men.

The relentless drive of the British forces to the eastern Transvaal, the capture of the railway line, and the departure of Kruger had discouraged many of the Boers. Some did not want to continue with the fighting, but they were loathe to surrender to the British. So they went unarmed into the Portuguese colony and took themselves out of the war.

Botha and Viljoen trekked north with the intent of doubling

back to the high veld in due time. Viljoen was cut off by Buller's forces and had to go much farther north to avoid being trapped.

The eastern railway line, a vexing thorn since its inception in the flesh of Great Britain in southern Africa, had now been wrested from the Boers, and their last lifeline to the outside world severed. It was no small wonder that Roberts deemed the war over. He called for a full scale surrender. He threatened seizure, or even destruction of the property of those who continued to fight. In fact, he was so confident that his assigned task had been completed that he informed his government that most of the troops could be recalled.

Roberts, like the leaders of his nation for almost a century, misread the Boers completely in many respects. They were a thrifty people, of necessity imbued with an almost religious respect for property. For Roberts to have burned some of their farms and threatening more such barbarism, strengthened a conviction, built up over many decades in the Cape Colony, that the British were not desirable overlords. Threats by a general of armies which could not stand up to them man for man was fat on the fire for the self-respecting farmers with their inbred passion for freedom and self-determination.

Boer emissaries who had gone to European nations, Holland, France, Germany, and Russia, as well as to the United States of America, begging for help, got polite receptions and what was cheap and most convenient, but of little practical use— sympathy. Now Kruger's departure to Europe rekindled hope that he would be able to turn sympathy into deeds.

*   *   *   *   *

Convinced that the war was a success, and providing an opportune time, an election was called in England by the party in power. The victories in the two republics after humiliating defeats at the outset of the campaign would aid in carrying them to victory and power again to conclude the vast expansion of the empire and the addition of much coveted riches. But the liberal opposition party was as vocal and sardonically outspoken as the government was imperturbable. The bitterness of the election campaign was sweet to the Boers' ears. It kept alive the distant hope, coupled with Kruger's appeals for help, for a change of government in London and a favorable end to the war. [Sixty-five years later an interesting parallel developed in the Vietnam war. Vocal critics of American involvement on behalf of South Vietnam were paraded daily by the news media with approval before the public. Some even went to visit North Vietnam, lambasting their own country, and thus encouraging North Vietnam to drag on the war for years, causing thousands of casualties on both sides and squandering billions of dollars.]

With the conquest of the eastern Transvaal the Boers had lost a great deal of provisions and stored-up ammunition. Their production facilities in Johannesburg which supplied in some of their war necessities were long in the hands of their enemies. In addition they were now deprived of supplies from abroad. It was difficult to conceive how they could possibly continue the struggle.

Tradition has it that Kruger once had a conversation with an Englishman before the war broke out. The Englishman, aware of the Boers' vulnerability in continuing to receive war materiel from abroad, presumably posed the question where he would get supplies if his outside sources were cut off. Kruger is said to have replied: "You will give it to us." This was already happening on a rather large scale. Great quantities of ammunition and other supplies had been captured from the British right from the beginning of the war, along with thousands of prisoners of war. With the deployment of the Boer armies to their home districts in smaller, more mobile commandos, they were better able to pounce on British troops and convoys and take what they needed.

The Boers in their history of taming a wild interior had to learn a great many things of necessity. It was no small wonder that they became experts in wrecking trains. Guns with the triggers exposed were secured on the tracks. They were so rigged that trains passing over them would activate the triggers and discharge them into well-placed sacks of dynamite!! More than one locomotive flew into the air over a thundering dynamite blast, wrecking the locomotive and disabling the supply train

100

from which the Boers then freely helped themselves. This tied up a railway line for days while crews removed the wrecks and repaired the tracks. Locomotives and rolling stock were in short supply already, and these capers immensely taxed the British efforts to provide for their forces deep in the interior. And they had a lot of mouths to feed and to supply with other necessities—between two and three hundred thousand, not counting the many thousands of black people who were in their employ.

The foundation was laid for the only type of resistance which the Boers could now conduct with any measure of success in the face of a crushing predicament— guerrilla war.

As the bitterly fought election in England stirred emotions in the British Isles, fights broke out and riots erupted at political rallies. Lloyd George, leader of the Liberals, kept up his sometimes sarcastic scourging of the Conservatives, but sometimes at the peril of his life. As the contest drew to a close Salisbury's party administered the final blow to the embattled liberal opposition with the claim that the war was over and that they had added greatly to the expansion and riches of the Empire. To reinforce the impression that the war was indeed over, that all was well and about to be peaceful in South Africa, Roberts was appointed Commander-in-Chief at the War Office, as if his leadership in the war was no longer necessary. His impending departure from the war theater in South Africa would confirm the impression in the minds of the voters that the harangue of the Liberals was about a matter passe.

Nations seldom change horses in midstream. The Conservatives, unpopular with many, garnered the votes even of numerous opponents, and returned handsomely to power. In this Parliament Winston Churchill, once a prisoner of war of the Boers, took a seat for the first time.

The British election had knocked another prop out from under the Boers. About all they gained was the useless comfort that many in Great Britain itself condemned the scourge being visited upon them. But sympathy does not win wars.

Courtesy the Queen of Holland, Paul Kruger sailed from Delgoa Bay on October 19, 1900 in the Dutch cruiser,

Gelderland. Cheers of thousands greeted his arrival in Holland and other European countries. But few nations in world history, if any, have ever taken up arms to right a wrong done to some other people, and the plight of the Boers, an insignificant nation, was no exception. Kruger got no help for his people.

In the end, as always, the Boers, although seemingly down and out, had to rise from the debris, rely on themselves, and fashion their own destiny as they had done throughout their history.

During his pause at Pietersburg in the northern Transvaal Steyn met with Acting President Burger of the Transvaal, Botha, and other leaders. They mapped their strategy for an all-out guerrilla war that would not only stir up the countryside of the Transvaal and the Orange Free State, but also include invasion of both Natal and the Cape Colony.

Meanwhile de Wet, who had sneaked back into the Orange Free State after his epoch-making trek and escape through the Magalies Mountains, never let up. While still maneuvering to escape Kitchener's forces, he had let Theron separate from him. This lessened their vulnerability and also served as a diversionary tactic. Theron then turned to what he knew well—disrupt railway traffic between Klerksdorp and Johannesburg. It was while operating in this area that he died a hero's death in a blazing shootout at very close range.

Back in the Orange Free State de Wet turned the Cape rebel, Scheepers, who had claimed Orange Free State citizenship, loose against the Bloemfontein-Johannesburg railway. He managed to blow it up in a dozen places.

The relentless hunt for the capture of de Wet continued unabated. Sir Charles Knox was placed in immediate charge of the operation. But de Wet was not always to flee. He had a mission in the Transvaal, and when he had crossed the Vaal River he turned the tables and attacked a British column on the Klerksdorp-Johannesburg line. For almost a week he kept it up, but was forced to evacuate his position upon the arrival of Knox with reinforcements. He diverted Knox's attention by sending most of his men and convoy in a southerly direction while he himself penetrated into the western Transvaal again with a small, mobile commando. He was heading for Ventersdorp.

Although the Boers were seemingly without means of communication, they displayed a remarkable ability to get dispatches around. De Wet's mission was to rendezvous with Steyn in Ventersdorp during the last day of October to escort him back home.

Within a week he returned with Steyn, rejoining his convoy. But Knox was not to be denied. He was right on their heels. Early one morning his men surprised de Wet. A guard had fallen asleep and had failed to sound the alarm. Some of the Boers were cornered on a farm, but de Wet and Steyn got away. The beleaguered Boers fought as they knew how. While they were fiercely contesting their position, de Wet returned and launched a counter attack. He was on the verge of success to relieve his men when reinforcements rushed to the aid of the hard pressed British troops, and he had to yield more than a hundred men. The British also got back at him for the various times that he had captured their supplies by taking all his wagons with supplies, as well his guns. Had it not been that these could easily be replaced by daring Boer raids, it would have been a disastrous loss.

De Wet's men were exhausted. They had been on the go for many months now under trying conditions. For lack of substitutes, there was no such thing as a regular rotation. So he let most of them go on what might be called furlough. He himself, with Steyn at his side, hastened to the eastern Orange Free State. He was a hero greatly admired by now, with the result that in a short time he had whistled up a new commando. Only a few weeks later he stood outside Dewetsdorp again, the small village in the southeastern part, named after his father. Its recapture by de Wet after the fall of Bloemfontein was one of a series of events that had played such a vital role in rallying the despondent Boers. It was now garrisoned by some five hundred Gloucesters and Highland Light Infantry. For a change the Boers were in the majority. Fierce fighting ensued. Once again he relieved Dewetsdorp. In doing so he replaced supplies that he had lost to Knox only several weeks before. Those of the garrison that had survived the Boers' marksmanship were taken prisoner of war and marched south. De Wet was poised to invade the Cape Colony, an assignment entrusted to him by Steyn in accordance with the Pietersburg council on strategy.

CHAPTER IV

THE HOLOCAUST

In the beginning of October 1900 Buller left for England. The English War had virtually undone him as a military leader.

So confident was Roberts that some of the British troops were also heading home. Delayed due to an illness in his family (his daughter had contracted typhoid fever that had taken so many of his men in Bloemfontein), he was not to turn his command over to Kitchener until the end of November, 1900.

But Roberts had misjudged the status of the war just as badly as he and the British War Office had misjudged the Boers all along. The defeat of the Boers and taking their gold and freedom were supposed to have been over within several months, by Christmas 1899; and here it was more than a year later since the war had started. He seemed to pretend that the war was all over. Perhaps it was a posture which he had to strike of necessity, justifying his departure to London to assume a new position as Commander-in-Chief at the War Office.

However, the forceful, inevitable thrust of history which had propelled the Boers into war with Great Britain at the outset, could not as easily be blunted as overpowering their capitals with huge forces which they did not have the manpower to withstand. Miraculously, time and again the force of history revived the Boers, even after stunning and seemingly final defeat.

So again the Boers began to organize. They were fighting once more and recruiting with astonishing success among those who had deemed their cause as lost, and had gone home.

Names of new, younger men would soon make the headlines as they emerged to help take the lead. There was Christiaan F. Beyers, a former British subject, who had migrated from the Cape Colony. He made his home in Boksburg where he practised law. He had already made himself felt by upbraiding his elders at the distillery meeting after the occupation of Pretoria. He had a striking personality and was a popular sportsman who had distinguished himself as a forward in the Transvaal rugby team. In keeping with his profession, he was an eloquent speaker.

Then there was Benjamin Viljoen, who had already made a name for himself at Vaalkrantz in Natal where he and his men held off Buller's superior onslaught, and in the eastern Transvaal, rendering invaluable service to Botha in fending off Roberts, Buller, and French. Jan Kemp would shortly prove himself an impetuous daredevil like de Wet. [The author remembers him well. He retired to Pretoria and lived on Marais Street not far from where the author boarded while attending the University of Pretoria until 1945. Having been wounded in the war, General Kemp, as he was then known, walked with a distinguished limp for the rest of his life, and he drove his green Chevrolet coupe like he fought—like a daredevil.]

On November 27, 1900, only a few days prior to Roberts' departure, Ben Viljoen encountered General A. H. F. Paget at Renosterkop, barely forty miles east of Pretoria. It was near Bronkhortspruit which gave its name to a famous battle of the First English War twenty years earlier. Viljoen commanded a mere five hundred men. Paget had over two thousand.

Paget was going to handle Viljoen trump up, as the saying goes, and he had the means to do so. The British would report the battle as a success, but the facts speak for themselves. At sunrise Paget launched his men in a frontal attack. The Boers, like at Modder River and Magersfontein Hill, let them approach up to a mere seventy yards before they opened fire. The result was death and destruction all around. A unit of New Zealand suffered heavily. Five of six officers perished. Paget ordered a second charge accompanied by two artillery pieces. Again the Boers let them approach to within deadly range. The result is the same as had befallen Colonel C. J. Long on the fateful day of December 15, 1900 at the battle of the Tugela. The artillery had to be evacuated without time to get into action. By ten o'clock Paget directed his fourth attack sacrificing men without regard. The Australian West Riding Regiment now were subjected to the dire fate that the New Zealanders had suffered in the first attack. More attacks followed as the sun rose in a hot sky, but with no success to dislodge Viljoen. By evening a last vicious storm-to-overpower came. The only cannon and pom-pom gun that Viljoen's Boers had at their disposal were not in working order and out of commission from the start. Repairmen tinkered with them all day, and fortunately, when the final attack pressed them hard, the pom-pom gun was ready at last. It helped to repel the attack. Then the curtain of night swept in from the east over the sordid battle field and ended Paget's senseless exploits of the troops offered by two colonies for the cause of the Empire.

Roberts departed just in time to leave his glitter as a hero and as a great general, untarnished. His tumultuous reception in England, his installation as Knight of the Garter by the Queen, a bonus of one hundred thousand pounds voted him by Parliament, a new position as Commander-in-Chief at the War Office, all created a glorious mirage that obscured for some time the inherent and later obvious shortcomings of his South African campaign. A more sober assessment with the passage of time and the judgment of history would put it all in proper perspective. A brilliant author and scholar of the English War, Rayne Kruger, states that no general has ever been so overrated in England's history, or any country so gulled (*Good-bye Dolly Gray*, J. B. Lippincott Co., Philadelphia and New York, 1960, p. 354).

When Kitchener took over command, he was already perilously awash in a new war, widely spread, and infinitely more difficult to handle than what Buller and Roberts had ever faced. They waged the war with armies of overwhelming numbers and inexhaustible mountains of war materiel. Kitchener faced a nation—man, women and child—and vast expanses of country that would easily hide his enemies and swallow up his huge armies.

Several unfortunate developments added to Kitchener's already tough predicament. Milner, whom the Boers detested and held largely responsible with Rhodes for the war, was appointed Governor of the two republics. It was all but a conciliatory move, and by hind sight poor diplomacy. To add salt to the wound he was installed in Pretoria, Kruger's seat.

Kitchener's attitude towards the Boers did not help matters in the least. He regarded them as savages, and his slip was showing more than convincingly in dealing with them. If his opinion of the Boers were gained from the way they fought, he was correct, but if he had formed his opinion on other grounds, then he had a lot to learn, indeed.

Kitchener, like the British leaders before him was noticeably short on diplomacy in dealing with the Boers. He deemed it appropriate to use a so-called Peace Committee to negotiate with them. The committee consisted of Boer handsuppers who were collaborating with the British. They were to persuade their countrymen to do the same. This seared the honor of the Boers who were in a desperate struggle for their freedom and infuriated them. They had no time for collaborators.

They had suffered a great deal at the hands of traitors who were spying for the British and betraying the positions of Boer commandos. Those who were actively working for the British in the field under arms were called National Scouts. A National Scout was anathema to the Boers. Upon reaching the commandos some of the Peace Committee were tried as traitors. A few were actually executed. One such accused came before de la Rey and Jan C. Smuts. Smuts as State's Attorney set his seal of approval on the death sentence and the man died before a firing squad. Four more National Scouts leading a British patrol were purposely rounded up on order of de la Rey and Smuts. They were brought to trial. De la Rey presided. Three belong to the same family, two of whom are condemned to death along with the fourth. A young boy is spared because of his age.

Probably with symbolic gesture several Cape rebels fighting with the Boers were assigned the gruesome task of executing the sentences and were supplied with Martini-Henris, British rifles. One of the condemned was an elder in his church. As they marched off to where three piles of fresh dirt were telling the foreboding story, he led the other two in singing a hymn in Dutch, more or less the equivalent of the last stanza of the great Welsh hymn: "Guide me, O Thou great Jehovah."

"When I tread the verge of Jordan,
"Bid my anxious fears subside;
"Death of death, and hell's destruction,
"Land me safe on Canaan's side;

"Songs of praises, songs of praises
"I will ever give to Thee,
"I will ever give to Thee."

With great reluctance, and with heavy hearts, the young Cape rebels carried out their assignment. A hush had fallen over the commando. As their custom was, the commando gathered at dusk for vespers. Grown men sobbed openly. Such is the incongruity of war.

Although Kitchener soft-pedaled it, even through the Peace Committee, there was little disguising the fact that unconditional surrender would be demanded. The Boers would not be prepared for any humiliation such as this.

Then in a desperation to be a successful general in the war, he made a disastrous determination. Roberts had already resorted to a policy of limited "scorched earth". Kitchener gave orders to apply it systematically on a full scale. To make things worse, he claimed that he did so on advice of the surrendered Boers.

Homesteads built over many years—investments of labor stretching over lifetimes, and of money saved from scant earnings of produce and livestock—were set to the torch as Tommies fanned out over the countryside. Cattle and sheep were rounded up or killed.

Homeless women and children were ordered on wagons and carted off to concentration camps. These camps held no lure for the Boer women. The British army in South Africa was notorious for its lack of care, facilities, and medicine even for its own sick and disabled. As the war dragged on the number of British soldiers that died of disease far exceeded the casualties suffered on the battlefield. Small wonder that reports from the concentration camps already in existence told of poor administration, unsanitary conditions, disease, and death. In addition to fear for the camps, the Boer women harbored an historic aversion of being under protective British custody.

By far the majority of women, children, and old men on the farms had no choice but to obey the orders of the Tommies. With their homes in flames and reduced to ashes before them, they had nowhere to go.

Men, who by nature are more likely to plunder and burn in

war, could more readily understand and forgive such deeds of violence, perpetrated by an enemy. But women, by nature more gentle, could not comprehend and tolerate such barbarism, much less forgive and let go with impunity. They became the conscience for justice and a powerful voice for revenge, not to yield, but to fight on.

The trekking spirit that had sent former generations into the interior and to new frontiers was still alive in many. They decided to flee for as long as they could, rather than be interned.

*   *   *   *   *

Dawid de Villiers and his wife, old as they were, and their daughter, Lenie, had made up their minds not to be interned.

It was late spring, 1900-1901. These were days of intensive preparation—what to take and what to abandon to the British torch. Wagons were loaded. The small, gray wagon stood in front of Lenie Storm's thatched roof house. A canvas covered frame had been built over most of it, extending over the sides. It was packed to capacity, mostly with food and clothing. Its overall measurements were no more than fifteen feet long and seven feet wide. Its width, overly stretched for its length, gave it a clumsy appearance. It was not intended for oxen, but for two or four horses, or mules. In front was a driver's seat, of the kind not found in ox wagons. This was to be the new home for the Storm family of eight!

Dawid de Villiers had been able to hold on to his own heavy wagon with much larger capacity. On good roads it could haul a load of three to four tons. Among their prized possessions, which he took along, was a small harmonium. Little did they know how useful it would be.

Dawid was able to persuade a few of his native servants to accompany him. Among them was old Jantjie, a faithful, venerable man who had been in his employment for many years. Dawid would need help. He had a full team of twelve to fourteen oxen to pull his wagon. Lenie had to make four oxen do for her wagon. A small herd of cattle would be taken along, mostly cows for milk, and other cattle for slaughter.

110

On a set day sad farewells were said to their homesteads, for they realized well that they would soon go up in flames. The wagons began to roll. They abandoned the furniture that they could not take along. Some of it was handmade, but some were heirlooms that had made the long trek from the Cape Colony, many years before. At various crossroads other families joined, forming a small convoy which grew to about a dozen wagons. A number of mounted Boers formed a small escort. They were under a certain Commandant Jan van Schalkwyk. He had been shot through his hips earlier in the war, qualified as disabled, and excused from regular duty. He could have remained at home, and would likely have been unmolested, especially if he was willing to sign the oath. But that was not for him. He and his men continuously reconnoitered, reported, and directed the flight along unchartered routes through the veld and mountains. A very practical tactic, wherever possible, was to keep a Boer commando between them and the British.

Sannie (de Villiers) Fourie with harmonium
Pictured about 1965

Since the large Boer armies had been broken up and commandos were assigned to their home districts all over the two republics, protection from these commandos made it safer for the *kappiekommandos* (bonnet commandos) to roam around, stay away, and sometimes flee from British forces.

They were deadly afraid of being overwhelmed by the

British for several reasons: While most of the British officers were gentlemen, like MacKenzie, there were some cruel ones too, like the one who ordered his troops to fix bayonets and storm overpowered Boers in Natal with orders to take no prisoners. If they would fall into the hands of one of those, they had no idea of what fate the women would have to endure. Their young boys, twelve or older, would be taken as prisoners of war. But worst of all, if they were overpowered, it would mean the horror of concentration camps.

When not in danger or being pursued, they remained stationary, otherwise the clumsy wagons went thudding along, avoiding open roads as far as possible to prevent the tell-tale column of dust and the too far reaching sound caused by the hoofs of the oxen, but especially the massive, steel-rimmed, wagon wheels. They knew that a trained ear pressed to the ground, could detect a moving wagon miles away, especially if it was on a hard road. The grass of the veld not only muffled the sound, but had no dust.

As they went along, heartbreaking scenes of "scorched earth" were in evidence all over the countryside. Burning homesteads lit up the night skies like torches. The roofs of barns had tumbled in on the grain left there and smoked like pyres for months on end. (The author could still dig up charcoaled grain in the ruins fifty years later.) The stench of slaughtered cattle and bayoneted sheep mingled with the smoke and crawled leisurely over the rises into the valleys. It was a great year for vultures.

*   *   *   *   *

Kitchener had barely taken over his new command when de la Rey, famous strategist of Magersfontein Hill, began to stir in the western Transvaal. A British convoy of about one hundred and fifty wagons was lazily lumbering along from Pretoria to Rustenburg on a wagon road north of the Magalies Mountains. It was being escorted by soldiers from the West Yorkshires and Victoria Mounted Rifles. They had several pieces of artillery. De la Rey knew of the convoy and gathered a force of about a thousand to take it. He moved south of the mountains out of

113

sight and crossed at Hartbees Pass. In the bush on both sides of the road they set up an ambush. The British cavalry moved right into the trap, but the Boers did not stir, hoping that the wagons would all move in further so that a commando of Boers under Commandants Koos Boshoff and Ben Bouwer could close in on them from the rear. But the Boers were discovered and a battle ensued. The rear guard of the British dismounted and took position to cover their tracks, expecting an attack from the rear. But Boshoff and Bouwer were slightly to their front. As a consequence they were almost totally exposed to the Boers, who got the order to open fire. Some of the British got away, but four hundred surrendered and here, on December 3, 1900, the Boers had struck a damaging blow, destroying many wagons and capturing about seventy with provisions.

De la Rey was now on the go. General R. A. P. Clements was in the area encamping in the open next to the Magalies Mountain rising precipitously on his flank and affording what seemed some adequate protection from that side. De la Rey was planning to attack him. But General Broadwood was also in the area and it would be much easier for de la Rey if he could be occupied elsewhere.

The British were accustomed to make use of natives, not only to obtain information, but also to spread rumors. Copying this practice stood de la Rey in good stead. He got a report to Chief Koos Mamagalie in the area that the Boers were indeed intent on attacking Rustenburg further to the west. Armed with this information which he readily got from Mamagalie, Broadwood set off for Rustenburg. Meanwhile de la Rey had summoned General Beyers to the area. The plan which he had devised called for an attack on Clements from the open side by his own troops. This would distract him, and while this was going on, Beyers and Kemp were to scale the mountain from the north side and launch a surprise attack on the camp. This was easier said than done, for Clements had the top of the mountain fortified with stone walls and occupied by about three hundred Northumberland Fusiliers. In addition there was always the danger that Broadwood might swing around and attack them from the rear, or that reinforcements might come from around

Johannesburg and attack de la Rey from the rear. As a safety precaution, Beyers had left a number of men to keep an eye on Broadwood, should he return to aid Clements. De la Rey, a veteran in war, also had a lookout for a surprise from unexpected quarters.

The plan had called for simultaneous attacks at dawn on December 13. Beyers and Kemp advanced through the night, but were delayed and when they were supposed to be launching their attack on the fortifications on top of the mountain, they were only as far as the foot of the mountain. De la Rey's men attacked at the time as scheduled under leadership of Assistant Commandant Badenhorst. Reports are conflicting as to what exactly took place. The end result told of a wild exchange of fire with the pickets and onrushing help from the camp. Fifty to sixty men on either side fell including all but one of the British pickets. While this took place, Beyers and Kemp charged up from the other side of the mountain and took the fortifications one by one in relentless onslaughts.

Broadwood did not come to Clements' aid. Rumor has it that a Boer heliographer had taken it upon himself to signal him that Clements did not need help.

However, the British heliographer from the top of the mountain continually signaled Clements for reinforcements. But he evidently fully realized the predicament in which he had fallen, and could spare only about one hundred men. They crawled up in a narrow ravine, but it was too late. Captain Mudie and Lieutenant Campbell fell almost immediately upon reaching the top, as did others. From the top the Boers now poured lead unmercifully down the ravine upon the brave hundred that had been assigned the deadly task of aiding their beleaguered comrades on top of the mountain. A small stream that trickled down into the camp, according to one eyewitness, was not just red, it was thick with human blood. Some survivors surrendered, but some lower down managed to turn and flee.

Now Beyers and Kemp opened fire on the camp and stormed it. Clemens and many of his men fled. In an heroic effort they were able to get the artillery pieces, of which they had nine, out. These would have fallen to the Boers and perhaps the entire

British force, but it seemed that de la Rey could not mount a sufficiently forceful second attack after the disappointment of the dawn encounter. The Boers were uncoordinated, but they did take the camp and vast amounts of provisions and ammunition. Here in the battle of Nooitgedacht (translated - "you'd never have thought") they had about one hundred dead and wounded, while the British had suffered about two hundred and fifty. Three hundred and fifty of Clements' force were taken prisoner.

On December 16 the commandos in the area met in solemn assembly commemorating Dingaans Day. A chaplain, The Rev. A. P. Kriel, took the lead, and other speakers followed, de la Rey, Beyers, Smuts, and Kemp. The climax of the proceedings came when each one brought a stone and piled them up in token of assuming the pledge made on December 9, 1838 near Blood River.

*　　　*　　　*　　　*　　　*

The British commanders' obsession to capture or eliminate de Wet grew stronger as attempt upon attempt ended in humiliating failure. His leadership was invaluable for Boer morale, and his enemies knew it. Very often he had President Steyn and what remained of the Orange Free State government with him. To capture him would very likely also yield the defiant President. It would be a shattering blow.

Knox was still in charge of the assignment to deal with de Wet. Again large concentrations of troops were dispatched to the southeastern part of the Orange Free State where de Wet was readying to sally forth into the eastern part of the Cape Colony. He threw his pursuers off his track and then rushed east while they dashed after him in an entirely different direction. The Caledon River was roaring ahead of him in full flood, but he crossed it with his men. He proceeded southward to negotiate his last and most formidable barrier, the Orange River. It was impassable due to heavy rains. In addition the area was teeming with British troops. Keenly aware of the danger of too large a concentration of Boers under one command, he left behind two detachments under Commandant Gideon Scheepers, who had rejoined him earlier, and General H. P. Kritzinger to carry on guerrilla war in the area, and to cross the Orange River, should they find an opportunity.

But de Wet, whose electrifying leadership it was hoped would stir up general rebellion in the Cape, was badly stuck between the Orange and Caledon Rivers in soggy terrain, hampering his mobility. British troops were poured in by railway to close in for the kill, again. The imminent capture of the legendary general once again became world headlines. De Wet about-faced from the Orange River, renegotiated the Caledon, and then, very much unlike him, unknowingly ran smack into strong British forces at Thaba 'Nchu. His position was utterly precarious. Behind him strong forces under Knox were making rapid progress, sealing in his much smaller force. All his men could do was to retreat helter-skelter, but fortunately without much loss. The debacle had one salutary effect. They were shocked into full alert.

Probing the net around them, one of de Wet's commandants, Pieter Fourie, found a weak link in the British encirclement. Immediately, he exploited it and in desperation drove in a solid wedge. Word spread through the ranks of the hard pressed Boers. De Wet was hurrying up the rear to get through the break. A concerted effort widened the wedge and the entire force, wagons and all, broke clean through. Once again de Wet was gone!

Some British forces were now drawn off from elsewhere to close in on him. This enabled Kritzinger and Scheepers with slightly under a thousand men to negotiate the Orange River at Odendaalsdrif under cover of darkness into the Cape Colony. It was December 15. Their presence posed a formidable threat to the central railway so vital to supplying British troops in the two republics. Meanwhile Hertzog also succeeded to land in the Cape Midlands by fording the river further westward at Sandrif, greatly endangering the all important railway junctions of De Aar and Naauwpoort. These had long been regarded secure since the relief of Kimberley and the demise of Cronje's *laager*. But more significant was the fact that potential uprising and rebellion once again became much more than an empty threat in the Cape Colony.

Hertzog entered the Cape Colony. On December 17 he captured Philipstown. On December 22 Britstown, barely thirty miles west of De Aar, was taken by Commandant T. C. Nieuwoudt; then Vosburg and Carnarvon were taken. Within two weeks Hertzog had reached Calvinia, about three hundred miles to the west of de Aar, while some of the Boer invaders got as far down as Sutherland. Kritzinger and Scheepers took Venterstad in the Cape Midlands and then moved southward to stir up the districts of Middelburg, C. P., and Steynsburg. From Calvinia Hertzog reached as far as Lamberts Bay on the Atlantic Ocean. From here he turned around to join de Wet, should he burst into the Cape Colony.

*   *   *   *   *

The war had become an obsession in South Africa. With the Boers resorting to guerrilla warfare, military operations were blanketing not only the two republics, but also some parts of the eastern and northeastern Cape Colony. There were British troops all over. As one Boer woman once remarked in desperation about the course of the war, and the ubiquitous British soldier: "You kill one, and ten appear!" Worthwhile road junctions or river crossings, or bridges were guarded and almost every town was garrisoned by British troops.

A century of British rule in the Cape Colony had accomplished only limited success in creating loyalty among the Boer colonists. Sympathy with their kin in the north was wide-spread and grew as resentment of the British way of conducting the war increased. The outbreak of rebellion remained a continual concern of Great Britain.

*   *   *   *   *

In the mountains of the District of Ceres, where Jacob Storm and his brothers came from, lived the family of Daniel Johannes Jacobus Theron. They had moved there to the farm Skurweberg from the vicinity of Sutherland a little more than twenty years earlier. His wife was Maria Johanna Hugo. They had fourteen children, of whom only five boys and three girls survived. Like most of the Boers in the Cape Colony, the family was in sympathy with the cause of the Boers in the north, but they had no intention of starting trouble or rebelling. However, the fact that they had four sons that were old enough to take up arms, brought them under the watchful eye of the English authorities.

Probably of more importance was that Theron was a wealthy man. He had a number of farms in the Sutherland area which he had sold prior to his move to the District of Ceres. He had money in the bank.

The farm was a busy place. They had several colored farm hands living on it with their families. Many years earlier the wife of one of their Hottentot servants became very seriously ill, and when she despaired of her life, she called for Maria. On her deathbed she requested Maria to take her little boy, Hendrik, and to bring him up. He was their only child and, being very young, needed someone to take care of him. Maria and her husband felt compassion for the little boy and duty bound to the woman who had been a trusted servant to them. So with his father consenting, Hendrik was brought up in the Theron home, very contrary to social custom, with their own children. They had a son, named Daniel after his father, who was about the same age as little Hendrik. It was about 1880, the time of the First English War.

As rebellion threatened, the farmers in the District of Ceres were restricted to their farms and could leave only if permission was granted. All fire arms had to be surrendered. The Theron family complied with the gun ordinance, but much to their dissatisfaction. There were still leopards in the mountains that preyed on farm animals, as well as baboons that had to be kept from the orchards, vineyards, and crops. Guns were needed on the farm. They kept one small handgun of which they thought no one knew. Not so. Unexpectedly policemen arrived on the farm from Ceres and demanded the handgun. There was no denying, but before the gun was handed over, it was broken and the stock destroyed in the stove fire. Daniel, as head of the household, was arrested and marched off to jail, about a fourteen mile walk. He was sentenced to a heavy fine or imprisonment. Cash had to be withdrawn from the bank to get him out of jail. But this was not

119

the end of it. He was arrested again for the minor infraction of going across the border of his farm to round up some stray sheep. Again it was a heavy fine. The intent of all this was not clear. It might have been to intimidate his sons and keep them from joining the Boer armies, or it was also surmised, that corrupt officials pocketed the fines.

It was suspected that someone on the farm was keeping the authorities informed. Unfortunately, their thoughts went to Hendrik, who was still living on the farm, although no longer in the main house. In the midst of all this, Hendrik disappeared and was never heard from again.

The harassment of their father and the humiliation of being dragged off to prison had just the opposite effect of intimidation. Their sympathy for the Boers now became a desire for revenge and action.

Incidents like these set tongues wagging and cemented support for the two republics among the Cape Boers.

Daniel Johannes Jacobus Theron (Sr.)
District of Ceres, Cape Colony
Pictured about 1925

*   *   *   *   *

Many Boers were heartened by events in the western Transvaal and by the entry of their commandos into the Cape Colony. As often happened before, many who had signed the agreement of neutrality left their farms and drifted back under arms. In order not to concentrate too many under a single command, a separate command was created for Jan C. Smuts.

The Boers were gathering momentum and were keeping the pressure up where they could. In the eastern Transvaal Botha and Ben Viljoen launched various attacks and inflicted heavy losses of both men and materiel. They were ready to carry out their assignment of invading Natal again.

Smuts struck near Johannesburg and overpowered a garrison.

Ubiquitous de Wet had regrouped after his narrow escape near Thaba 'Nchu and was riding south with several thousand men once again to test the border of the Cape Colony, where Hertzog and others were causing their enemy great concern.

*   *   *   *   *

Kappiekommandos (bonnet commandos), as the women convoys were called, began to roam the country in increasing numbers. Van Schalkwyk was able to keep his *kappiekommando* safe for some time, but one day as the oxen were straining forward at the yokes up a steep incline, they saw one of their scouts, Boy van der Merwe, on a wild gallop towards them from the flank. He spurred his steed over the veld teaming with the animal to avoid anthills and aardvark holes hidden in the tall grass. (There were few animals left to crop it short.) He pulled the horse up short when he got to van Schalkwyk and remained in the saddle as if ready to ride again. He had spotted British cavalry coming in their direction with only a few miles separating them. The wagons were in the open and, lumbering as they were, there was little or no protection against much faster moving cavalry.

Van Schalkwyk quickly had a consultation with the few men that he had under his command. They checked the wind. Word had swiftly spread through the convoy. They all knew that something serious was afoot. The few men that served under him hastily mounted, dispersed, and fanned out a mile or more on either side of the wagons. The wagons were ordered to drive on as hard as they could. In near panic they rolled on, the oxen sometimes at a trot. The Commandant rode a short distance himself and dismounted. He secured his horse with the bridles under a stone and hobbled downwind from the horse some distance, his war disability very much in evidence. Out came a tinderbox and his jackknife. With the back of the blade firmly struck against a flint stone the pieces of rag in the copper cylinder began to glow and flame as he gently, but earnestly blew on it. He set the grass on fire. Then he stepped back, half plucked, half cut tall grass stalks with his knife and gathered them in a small sheaf. He lit one end of the sheaf and dragged it along the ground sideways to the wind which was fortunately blowing towards the approaching cavalry. As he stooped along, fire broke out behind him.

Smoke was now beginning to rise all along Jan's battle front where the other men had followed his example. The wind lifted the flames over the tops of the tall, red grass. The heat created fierce fanning currents and the fire fed on itself. Charred stubbles, burning fragments, ashes, and smoke swirled aloft and forward in conflagration "attacking" the enemy. A blackened earth emerged behind the red phalanx, roaring several miles wide. Old cattle dung had caught fire where it had been deposited when this was a grazing pasture. Glowing little piles, last remnants of a once prosperous ranch, feebly dispatched smoke after the raging holocaust.

The cavalry thought better than to brave the fire attack.

Late in the afternoon van Schalkwyk halted the convoy. They had been satisfied that there was no immediate threat in sight. It was near a stream. The children with their buckets were ready to fetch water. Van Schalkwyk, as his custom was, first had to check the water supply. "No," he said firmly, as they were about to dip their buckets in, "you can't get water here. It is bad." Then he rode upstream, a brigade of little children hopping and skipping along with clanking bucket handles to keep up with him. A few hundred yards up was a large pool which the stream had culled out through the years. As they approached it, they could hardly endure the stench. The surface of the pool was a thick, greenish, nauseating mass of putrid carcasses. A flock of sheep had been killed and dumped in the water. Flies of all descriptions– blue, green, and large black– were feasting on the carcasses and depositing their eggs. Nature had summoned its own army to restore the imbalance of man's inhumanity.

Further upstream the water was uncontaminated. It was a long way for many little legs and hungry stomachs to haul water, but it had to be done.

The cattle were driven upstream to water.

As the sun lowered in the west each wagon became the center of a homestead on wheels. Belongings were unloaded and rearranged to make sleeping accommodations. Heavy, wooden stamp-blocks were unloaded in which wheat or maize were crushed for food. The grain was soaked in water for a while, if time permitted, to soften the outer skins of the kernels. This helped to remove the skins more easily to reduce roughage.

For the younger children, so blissfully unaware of the sorrow of abandoning home and hearth, this was sometimes a great deal of fun, as long as they had enough to eat. They had many newly found friends and playmates.

The girls played house. Lenie had made rag dolls for her daughters. The faces were painted on. A certain part of the intestines of butchered animals was so cured and prepared that it became like transparent celluloid when dry. This was pulled over the painted faces of the rag dolls and tied together behind the heads. It prevented the paint from wearing off. Young, girl "mothers" could wash their dolls' faces without letting the paint run.

The boys were always little farmers. They collected certain bones (*dolosse*) from butchered cattle. They remotely resemble oxen and in due time a boy could collect quite a herd. The same bones from sheep or goats would be calves. A particularly large bone would be the bull of the herd. Other bones were used as herders. Many of them had little toy wagons hammered together by their fathers before the war. Cotton spools were sawed in half and nailed on for wheels.

Whenever there were skeletons of cattle or sheep near the camp, the boys, in a great game of gathering riches, would go collecting *dolosse* and other bones.

At about sunset Jan van Schalkwyk summoned those who could come to Dawid de Villiers' wagon. He had their small harmonium so positioned on the wagon that it could be played where it stood. Van Schalkwyk read from the Bible. He knew it well, and often tried to suit the reading to their circumstances. He chose Exodus, Chapter 15: ". . .The Lord is my strength and my song, and he is become my salvation: He is my God, and I will prepare him a habitation; my father's God, and I will exult him. . . . Pharaoh's chariots and host hath he cast into the sea; his chosen captains also are drowned in the Read sea. . . .

"And when they came to Marah, they could not drink of the waters of Marah, for they were bitter. . . ."

He offered prayer and then announced the closing hymn. Lenie's younger sister, Sannie De Villiers, played the accompaniment on the harmonium, its melancholy tones warbling on the evening breeze as it mingled with their voices.

And so they closed each day with vespers consisting of Scripture reading, prayer and a hymn.

The little wagon was barely a substitute home for Lenie and her seven children. When darkness set in, she spread a cured animal skin under the wagon and placed a few belongings next to it on the side of the prevailing wind to serve as a breaker. Here Nellie, her sister Anna, and Hennie slept. Lenie with the three smaller children crammed in to the covered part, or tent, as it was called. The eldest sister, Lenie, slept between the driver's seat and the covered part of the wagon, which they called the tent.

So they bedded down every night for many months, winter and summer, under all kinds of weather — lightning and rain, snow occasionally, frost, or just a starry heaven above. Nearby, secured to the shaft of the wagon, in case flight by night became necessary, their oxen were chewing the cud.

Shortly after sunrise the next morning van Schalkwyk and several of his men took a two-wheel ox cart, which was part of the convoy, and set out around the vicinity in search of food. They went to several abandoned farms in the hope of finding something that had been left behind. Most of the homes were leveled by flames. They found one that was still standing, but the family was gone—either to a concentration camp, or otherwise, they too, had taken to flight. They found little or nothing in the way of grain, but they ran across several head of stray cattle and some sheep. These they brought along to be butchered and the meat distributed among the families according to need. Then they moved on to get away from the polluted water.

The Boers were now belatedly attempting to accomplish what they should have done at the very beginning of the war while they had the initiative—strike rapidly, deep, and decisively into Natal, but especially into the Cape Colony, to produce a general rebellion there. If they could at any time have caused a general uprising, it would have been almost impossible for the British forces to cope with the situation. Even during the first half of 1900 the British were keenly aware of the danger inherent in a war spread over such a vast territory. They had their hands sufficiently full in the north, fighting the Boers over the endless space of undulating veld, at intervals broken up by hilly areas, and bordered to the east by rugged mountain ranges.

Thus, when the Boers' plans of invasion became apparent, it was not surprising that Kitchener went all out to thwart their success. Not far into the Cape Colony vast British forces were waiting and alerted, not only to check any meaningful penetration, but also, and especially to deal once and for all with de Wet, the most distracting and inspiring maverick of the war.

De Wet needed provisions and ammunition for his foray into the Cape. For this he promptly captured a train on the Central Railway and ransacked it. Then he crossed the Orange River the second week of February 1901 without much opposition. But once in the Cape Colony, the tables were turned on him. Kitchener came from Pretoria to take personal charge of another attempt to annihilate him. He was outnumbered about seven to one. With such a tremendous show of strength by the British, the Boers in the Cape were obviously reluctant to rebel. Consequently, Hertzog, Kritzinger, and de Wet were unable to swell their forces to any significant extent from local citizenry. Instead of launching an offensive, de Wet became the object once again of relentless pursuit by fresh forces while hundreds of his own men lost their mounts in an area with sparse grazing. As the hunt intensified, he began to shed his convoy of provisions to gain greater mobility. But he kept his pursuers at a distance and wore out even new columns sent after him.

The futility of his undertaking became evident even to him, a man that would seldom give up. He decided to return to the Orange Free State, but the mighty Orange River, which he had crossed with relative ease, had also turned against him. Flowing beyond its banks like a muddy, swirling serpent, it now blocked his way decisively. All he could find was one small boat. He had it ferried back and forth feverishly, but was able to land only several hundred men on the other side before his pursuers were upon him again. He had to abandon the attempt to cross and had to make haste not to be encircled. From both east and west two British forces were converging upon him and south of him escape was blocked by other armies.

With the railways from De Aar to Orange River Station in the west and from Naauwpoort to Colesberg in the east Kitchener was bringing up more troops to converge along the murky barrier of the Orange River to snuff out de Wet as well as Hertzog, who had now joined forces with him.

Majuba Day, February 27, when the British were vanquished during the First English War in 1880-81, as well as when Cronje's *laager* had capitulated a year earlier, was at hand. Another great victory for the British would again be of invaluable psychological advantage. On the other hand, for the Boers, de Wet had become the personification of a people frantically fending off a giant that had been clawing at its liberty for a century, and was now about to wipe it out.

The odds against him seemed like one to a hundred. For days he had been probing ford after ford without success. The river in full flood seemed unyielding. British forces under such able leadership as provided by Knox, Plumer, and Kitchener himself, were at hand. Against their number there was little chance of victory in a direct confrontation, even with the help of Hertzog. It was evident that they were endangering a large force of Boers by remaining together. So they separated.

Fully confident that the end for de Wet had finally arrived, British columns moved along the river from opposite directions for the grande finale. Almost simultaneously the two forces encountered him, or they thought they did. They opened fire! It all took place barely fifty miles north of Kissie Mountain where British forces under Gatacre, earlier in the war, had blasted their own men off a hard-won mountain top, fled, and had given up six hundred prisoners of war without even knowing it.

What the British forces here along the river evidently did not realize, as they were converging on the same prey, was that they had mistaken each other for de Wet's men. Fortunately, for them, they sheepishly discovered their folly before capturing each other!

And where was de Wet? His pursuers were overly confident and preoccupied converting wagons into small forts to block his escape. Food supplies were stacked on the outside edges of the wagons and the space inside manned by soldiers. They forgot the very obvious. The prints of thousands of hooves in the dirt, tell-tales of a force that had recently moved in an opposite direction, should have alerted one of the British forces. In typical fashion de Wet had sneaked through their lines the previous night under cover of darkness, ingeniously armored wagons notwithstanding.

The only consolation for the British forces was that it was not an escape, but only a temporary eluding of the inevitable net. He was still south of the river on which the entire plan of entrapment had now been staked. Both upstream and downstream of de Wet they had control of the railway bridges, but had not planned for the contingency, should he by any chance ford the river. Should he manage this, his movement northward would be totally unhampered.

Despite all the gross misfortune, de Wet, unbeknown to his enemies, and perhaps not even evident to himself, had an infallible ally in the over-all geography of South Africa. The terrain rises to an inland, veld plateau between five and six thousand feet above sea level with mountains towering far beyond that. Consequently, rains, torrential or not, dispatch their waters with increasing swiftness to the oceans far below. Floods build up rapidly and run off quickly, leaving debris at the outer edges clearly delineating the high water marks. This was de Wet's only hope.

Along the outer rim of the flood debris deposits were beginning to write history, unless new rains inland had occurred to swell the flood some more. At one ford a few Boers were already able to swim their horses across, but at great peril. For a man with an impetuous temperament de Wet at times showed remarkable coolness when needed. He did not hazard a crossing. He would bide his time some more. He must have known of his enemy's overconfidence and their customary time-consuming concern with bringing up the baggage. A dozen fords had denied him, but characteristic of him, he never gave up. A small British contingent confronted him, but he managed to throw it out of his way. In utmost jeopardy and hard pressed, he would probe further along the river. The encirclement against the river was rapidly and ominously coming to a climax. Some force of the pursuers had now advanced to within firing range, and there was no darkness to cover him. He found another ford. A test of the waters proved still dangerous, but this had to be it! The order went out. They swung at right angles to the massive body of water. The horses were not in the best of condition, to say the least, and the riders were saddle weary after weeks of continuous maneuvering about. They plunged and waded in, braving the strong, silent current. The massive crossing aided immensely in the swift waters.

The river, which had at first seemed to be the Boers' undoing, in the end proved to be their salvation. The British generals had put so much faith in it to capture or annihilate de Wet that they had neglected to arrange a welcoming party for him and his tired men when they emerged jubilant on the opposite side. Even if they had the nerve to plunge in after him, they must have known how vulnerable they would be in midstream. Should his men turn and start firing in such an event, hundreds of the pursuers would no doubt have been killed and wounded and swept away by the flood waters to untimely graves in the Atlantic Ocean almost six hundred miles to the west.

De Wet's ambitious invasion of the Cape Colony had failed, but so had the third, massive hunt to annihilate him and his commando. He had to yield his convoy. But as in the past, this was no irreparable loss or disaster. He would replace it at the expense of His Most Excellent Majesty Edward VII By the Grace of God . . . . (He had succeeded Queen Victoria who had died on January 22, 1901.)

Magdalena Johanna (Hugo) Theron
District of Ceres, Cape Colony
Pictured about 1925

130

The daring Boer general was now back in his native Orange Free State to wage guerrilla war as he knew how.

Most of the eastern Transvaal, as most of the rural expanses, were open territory for the Boer commandos to roam.

French had earlier been ordered to clear and secure the area. To do so he staged a grandiose march of his army from the east to the outskirts of Johannesburg. The Boers did not try to stop him. Instead, they parted like water on either side of a moving ship, harass him as he passed, and close ranks again in his wake. They inflicted many casualties and grabbed a great deal of his provisions as the convoy moved on. The bold show of strength had produced little or nothing of the desired effect.

Fearful that Botha would invade Natal, Kitchener had again entrusted operations in the eastern Transvaal to French. He set out with a force exceeding twenty thousand about simultaneous with the third great hunt for de Wet along the Orange River.

The massive sweep was not aimed at Botha alone, but also at the farms where women, children, and elderly men had until now lived a fairly peaceful existence in the midst of war. The army moved slowly towards Bethal, Standerton, and Ermelo, the fertile maize belt of the Transvaal. The wake of the deliberate advance was a repetition of a now familiar pattern—homes bursting into flames, barns likewise being leveled, tumbling in on grain stored away, livestock rounded up or killed. A sorry and desolate landscape in smoke and charred ruins waited for the first touches of winter. Those still on the farms were rounded up and interned.

Word of the horror, which nauseated even some of the hardened British soldiers, spread quickly. Like many of the Boer families in the District of Ficksburg, hundreds from this chastened region also hastily packed their wagons and fled in droves before the approaching devastation and certain internment. With them they took as much of their possessions and livestock as possible—a pitiful exodus of refugees streaming eastward in search of salvation.

Some hastily dug holes on their farms to bury possessions in hope of saving them. But this practice soon became known to the British invaders. Where they suspected that possessions had been buried and the places camouflaged, they went around the yards tamping the earth with their gun stocks, listening for hollow sounds to find them.

Kitchener and French were visiting the benefits of the British Empire upon the Boers.

Botha did not have enough men to confront an army of this magnitude, but he assigned as large a force as he could to ensure the protection of defenseless women and children. They fought a delaying battle to aid their escape to the southeastern Transvaal.

Botha was in the vicinity of the town Ermelo. The town was abandoned. A pincer move by the British forces under French was in the making against Botha. But he staged a surprising night attack on Smith-Dorien, who was in command of the northern arm of the move. He was badly mauled by Botha, who broke through westward.

Kitchener had now returned from the front where de Wet had still frantically been pacing up and down the Orange River during the third, great hunt leveled at him. In his mind de Wet was about to be captured, but he most likely saw a greatly expanded war should Hertzog, Kritzinger, and Scheepers meet with any degree of success in the Cape and should Botha penetrate into Natal.

So Kitchener made a peace overture to Botha. On the last day of February 1901 the two generals met in Middelburg on the Pretoria-Delgoa Bay railway line. Kitchener proposed a rather generous settlement of various issues. The main problem was still surrender of sovereignty. This would be a bitter pill for the Boers. Its taste was somewhat sweetened by a promise of early self government. But what Kitchener and Botha had discussed was subject to review by Chamberlain in England and Milner in Pretoria. They were not involved in the hardship of war and failed to appreciate the Boer sentiments. The end was a peace proposal, vaguer in some crucial aspects and harsher in others. For the immediate future peace negotiations got nowhere.

The war had grown way out of proportion in relation to what the leaders in England had anticipated. Death and disease had stalked the British armies in South Africa like famished predators. The need of troops in the expedition kept on increasing. Fresh, but less efficient soldiers replaced units that had been recalled. Tens of thousands of horses and mules had to be imported from various parts of the world to keep the required strength. It was a constant struggle to maintain the extensive railway system in the face of relentless onslaught by the Boers. Food for the troops and animals had to be imported at great cost. Losses to skillfully executed Boer raids were enormous. It all escalated the daily cost of the war to a point where it became a heavy burden on the British economy, not to mention the government which had to raise funds by taxes and through loans.

These facts were not lost on the Boers. They had made supreme sacrifices, but they knew that the victories of the British in their midst were mixed blessings at best. A little more endurance might bring a much better peace settlement.

French's thorough-going drive had turned much of the eastern Transvaal into a land of desolation. It had stopped Botha from carrying the war into Natal at a most critical time. Some of the Boers surrendered, but despite the vast scope of the operation and the trauma inflicted upon land and inhabitants, it had failed to cripple those who were resolute to fight on. And last, but not least, the ever rolling plains, hills, and mountains still belonged to them—an endless haven where the dead grass provided some hay for their hardened horses in the winter, and where life would revive refreshing, come spring, and rain in August and September.

*   *   *   *   *

Autumn had stealthily crept over the high veld. Cold winds occasionally swept in from the south. Snow would soon white-cap the Malutu Mountains' rocky, serrated peaks eleven thousand feet against the horizon, stretching beyond and beyond.

A blanket of frost would more often glitter on the grass in the morning sun as tiny crystals, like prickly pear thorns, would nibble at the youngsters' bare feet, cracked in places from exposure.

Military activity had increased in the District of Ficksburg and so did the problems of the various convoys of *Wilde Boere* (wild Boers), as these *kappiekommandos* were also called, to stay out of the hands of the Tommies. Flight by night was often resorted to now as the only way to remain free.

The wagons, although a crude and rugged means of conveyance, needed a certain amount of maintenance, and so did the yoking gear. The domestically cured straps of cattle hide (called *rieme*) that were used to lash the chains to the yokes, wore thin with usage. Sometimes they would snap at the most inopportune time, leaving a pair of oxen detached and useless while in full progress. (These cattle hide straps were used because any kind of more durable lashing material, made of metal, would soon wear out, as well as damage the hardware of the yokes, all of which were expensive, if obtainable at all.)

The axles needed periodic greasing. This meant jacking up the wheels one by one, removing the pin and large washer at the outside of the tapered axle, sliding the wheel out only partially to maintain an emergency support, should the jack by any chance slip, and then applying a heavy grease to the exposed part of the axle and to the metal sleeve inside the hub from the open end. If a wheel should go too long before given proper care, the grease would burn on to the axle from friction and heat. Then the wheel had to be removed completely to scrape the affected parts before greasing. Permanent damage was not uncommon. It did not take too long to exhaust the original supply of grease, and they had to use rendered animal fat for grease, if they could spare it. This did not last as long as real grease, which meant more frequent lubricating chores.

The brakes of the wagons consisted of heavy blocks of soft wood (poplar or willow), which were cranked tight against the rear wheels when going downhill. A hard wood would heat up the steel rims of the wheels, cause them to come loose, and wear them out too soon.

Lenie Storm, apart from not being mechanically inclined, had her hands full with her family. Their little wagon's condition left more than something to be desired.

Again they were encamped close to a stream of water for a day or two. Washing and ironing were done, grain was crushed to have a supply on hand, "coffee" was roasted from grain, or

134

dried peaches, or dried pumpkin, and ground up. Those who thought of it, checked their wagons and did the necessary maintenance.

The sun was tilting towards three o'clock in the afternoon, when Jan van Schalkwyk's shrill whistle pierced the air and broke up a lazy afternoon. They had seen a scout charge in, and they knew instinctively that it meant trouble. British soldiers were heading their way. They had to pack up and go. The camp became an anthill of activity. Little boys grabbed up their *dolosse* and little play wagons and dumped them in the proper spots on their wagons. House play of the girls stopped and the dolls were stored. In these emergencies each member of a family had a specific task. The women scurried around flatfooted not to trip on their long dresses, driving the oxen to the wagons, their voices high-pitched with excitement. The teams were separated to their respective places, sorted, and yoked. The loads were lashed to the wagons. Invaluable in danger like this were the men of the escort as well as a few natives who had faithfully remained with them. When all was done at a particular wagon, the driver would call on the team and the oxen on the left hand would duck under the chain. The flight into the late afternoon and into the night was in full progress. Sometimes a ride was unusually rough, especially in the dark, as the wheels climb over rocks not spotted by the drivers or leaders, and crash down on the other side, unmercifully twisting the chassis of the wagon, and throwing the riders on it around.

It began to sound as if a cricket had hidden in one of the front wheels of Lenie's wagon, but they were too busy keeping up with the convoy to pay any attention. The chirping grew louder and louder.

The scouts literally kept their ears to the ground listening for the sound of hooves. There was no mistake. They were being followed.

It was a tense flight as word was passed on not to let up. Down a hill someone from each wagon had to jump off and apply the brakes to the rear wheels to keep the heavy wagons from crashing into the rear most oxen from behind.

A dry bed of a little stream at the bottom of the hill was easily forded.

The noise in the front wheel of Lenie's wagon had stopped, but there was now another sound. Sparks began to fly. The wheels had not been greased for a long time. The axle could break. They stopped. The teams behind her wagon bunched up. Several oxen got entangled as the chains slackened and began to drag on the ground. They began to buck and drivers and leaders had their hands full to calm them down.

Van Schalkwyk came up quickly. "We cannot lose a minute," he said to Lenie. "You will have to abandon your wagon." The front wagons had now stopped. He ordered the two-wheeled ox cart back which was used in times of no threat to roam the countryside in search of food . What little they could Lenie and the children tied into bundles with blankets and sheets. As a bundle was finished she dispatched a child with it to the other wagons to seek rides. A few men had now arrived and were transferring some of their possessions to the cart. Hennie, Lenie's older son, helped to hitch his team of four to those already pulling the cart. Lenie climbed on top of the loaded cart and a man raised bewildered little Dawie into Lenie's arms. Little time was lost. The small wagon was abandoned and the others creaked further into the night. It was past midnight before they came to a halt. The next morning the scouts determined that, for whatever reason, they were no longer being pursued. The British had learned that too eager a chase could easily lead into a deadly ambush.

Evidently, the troops had turned away before they had come to the abandoned little wagon. The next day the scouts found it where it had been left. They got the wheel in working order, and brought it back. The Storms were never so happy during all the months of their flight. It was a poor excuse for a house, but to them, it was their only, precious, little home.

*   *   *   *   *

The possibility of peace was still in the balance when the Boer leaders met in the eastern Transvaal to consider Kitchener's proposals made to Botha and revised by Chamberlain and Milner. War activities went on as usual.

It was April 1901. Frost had come as the harbinger of winter. Garden flowers had bent their heads on now dead, black stalks, and a few tomatoes, frost-bitten and pinkish, hung useless on the vines. British soldiers were arriving on a number of farms in the vicinity of Dewetsdorp in the southeastern part of the Orange Free State. What they were doing was only a small part of a large scale holocaust. They were there to torch homesteads and round up the women and children and old men. They loaded them on open wagons with a few belongings. Black servants still with them were sometimes also taken along. As the wagons rolled away, tell-tale columns of smoke rose from among the trees where homesteads, built over many years with love and hard work, full of furniture and other possessions, were going up in flames. Some wept as they rode along, others just sat in bitterness and stunned silence.

Instead of the usual clear days of early fall, clouds drifted over them. A cold rain set in, frequently soaking them to the skin. It took a week to reach the town of Edenburg. From various directions wagon loads of now homeless women and children were coming in. They had the same report of scorched earth—devastated farms and butchered livestock. When enough of them had been gathered, they were loaded into open, railway cattle cars. The baggage was dumped helter skelter, and the journey was resumed by rail.

The rains did not let up. For a week the slow freight would wind its way to a concentration camp, picking up other inmates as it went along. Rows of grey-white bell tents, rigidly arranged in close proximity to each other, made up the camps, their new "homes" and final destination. For many it would also be their final resting place.

About six were assigned to a tent. The only place they could stand erect was in the middle, next to the pole.

More inmates were constantly being freight-loaded in during subsequent months. The camp would be bursting at the seams. It was moved to a larger area that could accommodate more tents.

Sanitary conditions in these camps were almost non-existent.

In one instance the hole from which household water was supplied was down a slope from an old cemetery. The water had to be strained and boiled before using.

Latrines were open trenches with corrugated iron sheets planted in the ground to the side of the camps. Rough, loose planks with holes formed long benches over the trenches, from which all descriptions of flies swarmed freely, ferrying pestilence and death back to the tents, and even the hospital. The layouts of these latrines were so bad that children were known to have fallen into the trenches.

Food rationed out was totally inadequate. The small portion of meat was usually of such poor quality that it could often not be eaten.

The camps, originally started by Roberts as so-called "Refugee Camps" had degenerated into horror camps, especially when Roberts' successor, Kitchener, a ruthless man, succeeded him. Wherever these camps were found, and there were fifty of them throughout the two republics, the reports were the same. Women and children became emaciated, with little or no resistance to infection and disease. Epidemics of whooping cough, measles, and gastric fever swept the inmates. Mothers were afraid to send their children to the camp hospitals, for it was almost invariably a last journey preceding the grave. As a consequence, every tent became a little infirmary, and often a morgue as well.

In the end there were 136,000 in the camps. The staggering numbers posed impossible problems of logistics. The British war machine in South Africa was not prepared to cope with it, and did not seem to care.

The bitter cold winters of the high veld made living in tents unbearable, and contributed greatly to the death rate in these camps.

There were only few, if any coffins. The dead were wrapped in blankets, secured with safety pins. Sometimes there were not enough graves, and more than one body was assigned to a single grave.

Only less than six months since its beginning of the camps, funerals in some places had to be held twice a day to bury all the dead. A young girl would contract measles that would end up in pneumonia. Her emaciated little body would quiver with frequent chills. As the end neared a parson, a Boer, would be summoned to pray with her. He had witnessed many of these heart-rending scenes. He would say softly, as if afraid that he would invite death into the tent, "what shall I pray for you, and what must I tell your daddy?" These children had been brought up in homes where religion and faith were the strength of their existence. And sometimes the weak response would be, "Pray that God's will be done, and tell my daddy that I died of hunger." Shortly afterwards she would expire and be assigned to an unmarked grave, most likely holding more than one body wrapped in a blanket.

Once a woman sat up in the morgue, feebly struggling to free herself from the khaki blanket and safety pins. A confused and horrified attendant rushed over. "What shall we do with you?" he demanded, as if she was to say, "Bury me, anyway."

Children almost lifeless on hospital beds had flies running all over their faces. Sometimes maggots were crawling out of their nostrils.

Little boys and girls, their knee joints bulging out in the middle of their spiky legs with only skin and bone, stood silently by the graves of their former playmates. Their hollow eyes and jutting cheekbones belied their hope of life. Next week it would be their turn.

In one camp it was reported that a woman had lost her mind. Bedraggled, she stood around, monotonously beating on an empty can with a stick. "What are you doing?" someone asked. She paused for a moment, looking up with a blank stare, and answered: "I am making coffins, coffins," as if everybody should know. Then she resumed her hammering, making coffins.

In Heilbron, Orange Free State, there was such a camp. In the cemetery, where hundreds of these victims had been buried ignominiously, there was erected a modest monument with their names on it. One could only stand by it in stunned silence and shed a tear or two on the sacred ground where these innocent victims had been offered for freedom's sake.

*　　　*　　　*　　　*　　　*

The Boers had been in the saddle almost continuously for more than a year and a half. They were good riders to begin with, and became more expert as the war lengthened. They began to apply a new technique, said to have been started by Commandant J. G. Celliers, refined, and applied by de la Rey—charge and shoot-from-the saddle. It had various advantages. The speed with which they attacked the enemy had an unnerving effect. It made them difficult targets. In addition, they were protected by their horses.

This type of attack was just where Jan Kemp would excel. His turn came at Vlakfontein in the western Transvaal, on May 30, 1901. De la Rey and Kemp had skirmished the day before with the British troops in the area, but it was indecisive. The next day they attacked a British force under General Dixon. Some reports had it that Kemp set the grass alight with a trail of gunpowder, others had it that Dixon did so when the attack got too hot. Regardless of who did it, Kemp charged through the smoke and fire with his riders, pumping lead into the enemy as they rushed them at high speed. They were met by artillery and gun fire so fierce that they had to dismount and take position. But Commandant Jaap van Deventer mounted again with some of his men and charged the two artillery pieces. By now the British were in flight. The Boers took the guns and managed to turn their own artillery on the British. Almost two hundred Tommies were dead and wounded. The rest fled.

The western Transvaal, under the watchful eye of one of the best Boer generals, de la Rey, and of several daring commandants, Kemp, Celliers, and Bouwer, was just not for the British. Time and again they were mauled unmercifully. They tried to corner Kemp, but to no avail.

Kitchener busied his troops with massive drives devastating the countryside, rounding up women and children for the concentration camps. A concerted effort was launched to trap the Transvaal government, which was roaming in the southeastern Transvaal, but this proved an elusive task, just as it had proved hopeless to take Steyn, President of the Orange Free State, who was usually guarded by de Wet.

Daring Boer attacks continued to exact heavy tolls from unsuspecting British columns.

The country became more saturated with British troops, warring against space and the Boers. In spite of a supreme effort to prevent movements, the Boer leaders were about to gather for an all-important meeting in the southeastern Transvaal. Steyn and de Wet came through the heavily garrisoned Orange Free State. De la Rey had picked his way from as far distant as the western Transvaal—more than a hundred miles—to attend. Hertzog, Smuts, Beyers, and others were on their way, too.

They did not suggest free passage through British lines. They were not suppliants in their own countries, and if they could make their journeys on their own, it would be a significant bargaining point with the enemy. They met in June, 1901, near Standerton. The meeting lasted unduly long, because they felt that they had to consult Kruger in Europe. This was done through the Dutch embassy in Pretoria. Kruger in his reply wisely seemed to have left the decision of peace or war in the hands of the assembled leaders themselves. The sentiment of the most influential men, including Steyn, Botha, de la Rey, Hertzog, Smuts, and others, was against unconditional surrender. The war was to continue.

Many of the Boer commandos were left under junior officers for the duration of the meetings. Obviously eager to show their own ability, and despite diminished numbers, they kept the pressure up on the British forces, even while the meeting considering peace was in progress.

CHAPTER V

WHIRLWINDS

The idea of launching a foray into Natal and the determination of stirring up trouble in the Cape Colony by invading it, was still an integral part of the Boer strategy. Botha was still to tackle Natal. He had been born there and knew the terrain well.

Initially de la Rey would be designated to lead an expedition into the Cape Colony, but in the end it was decided to entrust this task to Smuts. He was born on May 24, 1870 near Riebeek West, District of Malmesbury, a British subject, of course. He had studied at Stellenbosch and had originally planned to enter the ministry, studying both Greek and Latin. Unlike his colleague, Hertzog, who went to Amsterdam for further study, Smuts went to Cambridge. He changed his intended career from the ministry to law, and was admitted to the bar in Cape Town in 1895. He was an admirer of Rhodes, but after the Jameson raid of 1896, he turned against Rhodes. He emigrated to the Transvaal, was admitted to the bar in Johannesburg, and in 1898 became States Attorney under Kruger. Although switching to law he carried his Greek New Testament in his saddlebag and read it daily.

The young general was to set out into his former home colony with only about three hundred men. He had several outstanding commandants serving under him—Jaap van Deventer, Ben Bouwer, F. Kirsten, T. Dreyer, and others. To make his commando less vulnerable, and not to attract too much attention, he divided it into several smaller groups. He was to build up his strength by recruiting rebels in the Cape Colony where ferment against the British had intensified due to the inhumanity towards women and children, and due to the harsh treatment of family and friends in their midst, although they were British subjects.

The various groups were to rendezvous with Smuts somewhere south of the Vaal River in the Orange Free State. But secrecy was hard to maintain, and Smuts was soon being tracked and harassed in attempts to snuff out the fuse that might trigger an explosion in the Cape Colony.

*   *   *   *   *

As the war was grinding on and as the months became years, the food supply had dwindled to almost nothing. The farms were destroyed, and the livestock either killed, or hustled away. Former grain fields had turned into lush gardens of weeds. The few sacks of grain that the wagons of the *kappiekommandos* could carry in addition to people and belongings, were exhausted. Such every day things as coffee, tea, sugar, and eggs had not been seen for months. Milk was scarce. They had the foresight to take cows with them, but a cow could produce milk for only a limited time after she had a calf, and then she would dry up. Not many new calves were born, if any. Sometimes grain was roasted like coffee, or even dried fruit to make something resembling the bitter taste of coffee to which they were accustomed. For the Boers there was nothing like a cup of coffee, even before breakfast. They called it *boeretroos*—farmers' consolation.

In the summer they could pick a certain kind of wild plant, *marog,* often used by the black people, and cook it as a vegetable. But the green mush had a bitter taste that only hunger could stand.

Van Schalkwyk and his men were invaluable to the refugees of Helderfontein and its neighborhood. Stray cattle, sheep, and goats became scarcer to find, but somehow they were always able to find a few animals for meat.

Clothing had worn out. What they had they washed and ironed when stationary for a while. Shoes wore out, or were outgrown, and there were no fathers to make new ones. Blankets were hardly enough to fight off the cold of frosty winter nights.

Lenie made dresses for the girls from the outer cover of a feather mattress, and bonnets from the house curtains that she had brought along in hopes of using them again in their home some day. But now the house had been torched and was in ruins. She used a burlap bag to make Hennie a pair of trousers. It was too rough to wear, but that was all she had. So she lined them with bed sheets.

Once she found a discarded khaki shirt of a Tommie next to the road. She grabbed it before someone else could, but found it teeming with lice. (Lice had a prosperous time during the war.) But she was not to let it go. She carried it on a stick and dropped it some distance from the wagon not to get the children infested. There she doused it with boiling water and then boiled it again in water to kill all the nits. Out of this old shirt she made Hennie some clothes.

Lenie had a little flour left and decided to bake a few loaves of bread. They had no oven, of course. So they made one. Close to where they were encamping she and the children hollowed out an old anthill from one side. A small hole was made at the top to provide a chimney. In the scooped out anthill they started a fire with old cattle dung from the pasture around. When the fire had burned out, she waited until the embers had a thin layer of ashes and the smell of dung had been burned up. She slipped a bread pan with two loaves of bread side-by-side into the anthill oven and closed the openings with stone and clay.

The baking had scarcely begun, when a scout came galloping on and quickly spoke to van Schalkwyk. Once again the piercing sound of his whistle sounded an alarm. The Khakis were coming. They were in danger of being caught and had to move immediately. "But Uncle Jan," Lenie protested, "I have just put my bread in to bake." "Lenie," he said firmly, "We can not all be caught because of a few loaves of bread."

Getting the teams yoked, although a complicated process to get the right ox in the right place, had been perfected with plenty of practice. Within a short while the wagon train, as so often, was in flight once more.

They moved on until evening when scouting reports indicated that the Khakis were no longer coming their way. Then they encamped for the night, but still very ill at ease. The next morning two men rode back to the spot of their previous encampment. When they returned one pulled a pillowcase from his saddle bag and handed it to Lenie. There were her two loaves of bread, rather well baked and hard, but an unusual treat nonetheless.

*   *   *   *   *

Smuts had planned to cross the Orange River near the town of Zastron in the southeastern Orange Free State. However, on arriving in the vicinity scouting reports indicated that the river crossings were well secured by the British who had anticipated his plans. He withdrew back into the hills to bide his time. He sent out men to look for guides. The next day he was joined by a certain Louis Wessels with fifty men. He reported that any retreat was fast being blocked by pursuing forces. Their only hope now was fording the river in the face of strong opposition. Fortunately, a veteran who was with Wessels knew of a possible crossing, steep and dangerous, that he thought they could try.

Under cover of darkness they advanced towards the river. Through a narrow gorge, between steep cliffs it plunged rapidly westward—a formidable challenge to tackle even with bright sunlight.

Fortunately, either because the British did not know of this possible crossing, or had never thought that anyone in his right mind would try to cross the river at that point, it was unguarded. If it were not for the desperation of the moment, no one in his right mind would have attempted a crossing at that point. The riders had to trust the unusual sight of their horses by night as they started the dangerous descent. The animals stumbled and staggered down the cliff, and in the early morning hours, long before sunrise, they braved the cold, swirling stream. The weary animals could hardly stay on their feet, but they carried their riders through.

As the British scoured the hills of the southeastern Orange Free State the next morning of September 4, 1901, Smuts and his men were safely across the river in a daring move, ready to operate and to recruit rebels in the Cape Colony.

If crossing the Orange River was daring and dangerous, it did not compare to the commando's untold hardship to which it

146

was subjected as it meandered over a tortuous route of fighting and dodging, pushing their way westward through the colony.

One night, as it was still late winter in the southern hemisphere, they came near freezing to death in an ice storm that swept the Storm Mountain range. Scores of their exhausted horses did indeed perish in the cold. The men survived by huddling between the front legs of their mounts, under their saddles, shivering without sleep, of course, as the horrible night howled about them. But the next day they proceeded under the Boer general who carried his Greek New Testament with him from which he daily read.

The British, fully aware of, and very much afraid of the potential threat that Smuts's presence in the Colony posed, hunted him and his commando relentlessly. The regular roads were usually blocked by British troops and they had to make their way along unchartered routes.

Once Smuts went with two scouts, Adendorffs, who had grown up in the area where they found themselves, and who were familiar with the territory, to survey the mountains in order to determine where to lead his commando. Four of them, the Adendorffs, and Neethling, his chief of staff, set out along a ravine. They had not been gone long when those left behind heard shots ring out from the direction where they had gone. Soon afterwards Smuts' horse came running back riderless to the farm house from where they had started. Mortally wounded, the animal collapsed and died in the yard. The Adendorff brothers were instantly killed. Neethling was mortally wounded and died later. Fortunately, a few minutes after his horse had arrived and died, Smuts came walking back all by himself. Miraculously he had escaped the murderous volley unharmed.

No, the war was not over. Once again it was brimming over not only into the Cape Colony, but also in Natal where Botha had hastened and at last entered with a sizable commando from the southeastern Transvaal. Names of places, now only memories of the early phases of the war, suddenly were on the front pages of the newspapers once again. Botha's brother-in-law, Cheere Emmett, overwhelmed a British convoy, killing and wounding about forty, and taking over two hundred prisoners of war. The danger existed that Botha might press through Natal and attack the soft eastern flank of the Cape Colony, linking up with Smuts and others in the area. Kitchener had no choice but to dispatch more troops as reinforcements to Natal.

Kitchener thought he would frighten the Boers by issuing his famous proclamation of August 9, 1901. The property of the Boers would be confiscated to pay for the keep of their dependents in the concentration camps, and all officers of the Boers, who would not surrender by September 15, would be exiled from the country.

His paper bomb, as it was dubbed, met with scorn. Steyn then wrote a long letter to Kitchener in which he issued his own renowned proclamation that Kitchener's authority reaches only as far as the range of his guns.

The Boers were ready to back up their disdain with deeds. They had penetrated the Cape Colony and Natal, and they were launching fresh attacks on British forces over a wide area, inflicting more than a thousand casualties and wounded, and taking large quantities of provisions and arms as well as a large number of prisoners.

Smuts' foray into the Cape Colony had to face almost insurmountable obstacles. The British command knew that they had to stop him, or risk possible upheaval among Boers in the Colony. His hand picked commando of between two and three hundred had been harassed since its departure from the Transvaal. They had lost many of their horses. Their clothes were worn; not that they were new when they started out anyway. Their ammunition was exhausted and they did not have many opportunities to replenish from British troops, as the Boers in the Transvaal and Orange Free State did almost at will, for there were not that many British troops around. But opportunity would present itself sooner or later. Despite hardship, they pressed on as best they could, many of them now on foot, carrying their saddles on their backs, hoping that somewhere they would find a horse. By September 15 they found themselves about a hundred miles south of the Orange River in the vicinity of Tarkastad. They had been subjected to merciless downpours accompanied by bitter cold and wet nights. Horses were dying daily—usually during the night. It was a miracle that the men were able to survive.

As they set out one morning, only sixty men were mounted. To make things worse, they were confronted by a British commando of about three hundred encamped on the farm Rietfontein. They must have known about Smuts' whereabouts and were of course, intent on capturing him and ending his expedition into the Colony right there and then. So two patrols set out from the camp unknowingly moving directly into the path of Smuts and his commando now reduced to mainly saddle carrying infantry. The Boers, obscured by trees, saw the patrols first and let them come. Prematurely, shots were exchanged with one of the patrols. They all turned their horses and flattened them out for the protection of the camp, with the Boers who were still mounted in hot pursuit. The patrols formed a perfect screen of protection for them to get close to the camp without being fired upon. Then fierce fighting ensued. The Boers dismounted and took positions behind rocks. The camp commander decided to turn his field guns loose on the Boers. The crews, without time to get dressed, were half naked. They were at close range, poor souls. The Boers picked them off as they knew how and silenced the field guns, but rifle fire continued to crackle incessantly. In the meantime the Boers, whose horses had died and were carrying their saddles, came running to reinforce their comrades. Then some Boers bravely stormed the camp on foot, setting an example for many others to follow. It was the end of the fight. Smuts had only one man killed and five wounded. The British had seventy dead and wounded. Lord Vivien and Captain Sandeman were among them.

The British soldiers who had not fled were taken prisoners and "shaken out", as the saying went, that is stripped naked and let go, for the Boer commando, and the Boers in general, had no way of guarding prisoners and taking them along. These "shaken out" prisoners had to shift for themselves to reach other British camps for new uniforms and food. And walking barefoot for miles was slow going, if they knew where they were going.

Smuts' commando now had plenty of ammunition, horses, food, and clothing. What they could not use they destroyed.

Then they continued their invasion with two loads of rifles and ammunition, and three hundred horses and mules. The threadbare commando had suddenly undergone a miraculous metamorphosis.

Smuts' position was such that he could not recruit actively. He first had to establish himself firmly in the Colony. Nevertheless, some Cape Boers joined him as well as others already operating in the Colony.

It took unusual courage to take the step of joining invading commandos from the Orange Free State and the Transvaal. On the day that Smuts set foot on British soil, the Cape Colony, September 4, a commando, mostly rebels under Commandant J. C. Lötter, was mercilessly mauled west of the town of Cradock. Those who were not killed or wounded (sixty in all), were captured. Lötter, Lieutenant Wolfaardt, and three field cornets, Kruger, Schoeman, and Breedt, were condemned to face a firing squad, and were publicly executed at Middelburg in the Cape Colony.

Beset on all sides, Smuts nevertheless, pressed on towards more populated areas of the Colony. He was greatly aided by local Boers who provided him with valuable information about British troop movements, and also about lesser known passages through which he led his men out of surrounding nets, meandering without much gain.

Food remained a problem. In the Sour Mountains they helped themselves to a type of wild fruit, called Hottentots bread (*Encehelartos Altenseini*). At a certain time of its development it becomes poisonous, and this was the time. It did not take long before many of the men, including Smuts, were unconscious. Had the British attacked at that moment, his commando would not have had a ghost of a chance.

The British force at the foot of the mountains, fortunately for the Boers, were ignorant of their plight. During the night some of the sick men began to come to. The next morning, with van Deventer and Bouwer in charge, they moved further into the mountains, the deadly sick men strapped to their saddles, including Smuts with a rider on either side of him. Had the British turned their cannon loose on them at that moment, it would have been the end of the invasion. When they eventually began to bombard them, the commando was out of reach.

Van Deventer and Bouwer divided the men into two groups. Bouwer took Smuts and his group deeper into the mountains while van Deventer decoyed the British away from the general.

Several days later the two groups united near the town of Uitenhage. They were now only fifty miles from Port Elizabeth, a vital seaport for the British to supply their forces. Rumor got around that Smuts was about to attack. This brought large British forces into the area to forestall such an attack. To have attempted it in the face of such formidable opposition, would have been foolhardy, and Smuts knew better.

The rumors did not make life easier for Smuts and his commando. So he withdrew into the mountains with the British hot on his heels. It was a narrow ascent. But then, like a wounded animal, the Boers turned in their tracks, and awaited their unsuspecting pursuers. They were within twenty yards from the Boer positions when Bouwer jumped up with his gun ready and demanded surrender. Surrender was refused, and he opened fire, signaling his men to follow suit. The pandemonium on the edge of a steep ledge among the British troops was something to behold. Not even Hollywood could simulate the debacle. As Smuts described it himself: "Men and animals trampled each other to death, pursued by embittered Boers." Dead and wounded numbered in the hundreds, and many more horses were lost. They lost their footing on the slope and tumbled, some riders and all, down the steep mountain slope.

After visiting this devastating defeat upon their enemy, the commando moved northward to Somerset East and entered the Karroo, inhospitable due to it sparse rainfall. Here they divided again, in case of attack, to lessen the danger of complete annihilation, should they be the losers in another encounter. It also made it easier for them to live off the land in the Karroo which was extremely sparsely populated.

Smuts' ultimate destination was Calvinia in the western Cape Colony, four hundred miles away.

In the eastern Cape Scheepers and his commando kept up pressure on the British and penetrated as far south as Uniondale, about a hundred and fifty miles east of Port Elizabeth. There were many Cape Boers in Uniondale, for it was the spring communion weekend, usually celebrated in October. In a daring move Scheepers overpowered a British fort in full view of those encamped for communion weekend, lowered the Union Jack, and raised the flag of the Orange Free State. Such daring undertakings could only serve as inspiring propaganda for the Boer cause, and helped to recruit rebels.

*   *   *   *   *

There were few medicines and no doctors in the event of serious illness. The *kappiekommandos* had to resort to their own ingenuity to cure disorders. Through the years of frontier living the Boers had developed fairly reliable procedures for dealing with the sick. Many times their best efforts did not produce the desired cure, and death was not uncommon from the more serious ailments. Van Schalkwyk's *kappiekommando* was extremely fortunate. They seemed to have been hardened by constant exposure to the elements and fresh air. Nellie, who had to sleep under their little wagon, woke up more than once on a cold, winter morning not able to distinguish between her own jet-black hair, that got out from under the covers, and the frost on the grass beside her. It was all one blanket of frost.

Once Lenie's oldest daughter, also called Lenie, had developed an excruciating ear ache. Her mother had tried all she could—heat, cotton plugs in her ears, and hot drops of medicine from the little medicine chest, but to no avail. She went to bed in the open in the small space assigned to her in front of the wagon, still crying. In desperation she kept on soaking the cotton plugs in her tears and putting them back into her ears. She fell asleep and when she woke up she felt much better.

It was amazing that through the long months of flight, in spite of hunger, exposure to cold and rain, and hardship, difficult to believe, the *kappiekommando* did not have a single death due to disease.

Once after a long flight they had reached the farm Wonderkop shortly before sunset. All seemed safe. They were going to camp for the night. As darkness began to set in the flames of campfires began to dispel the darkness near each wagon. They prepared meals from what they had. All were huddling around the fires to keep warm. The meal of the Storm family consisted of crushed grain, and if they did not have time for crushing the grain, the whole kernels were boiled slowly over a low fire. In the process the kernels would swell to about twice their original size. At times a cup of this *kaboe* grain was the only ration a child had for an entire day. At night they would pull their little knees tightly together to still the pain of hunger and to fall asleep.

That evening at Wonderkop they had scarcely had their meals when above the crackling of fires they suddenly heard the hoofs of a horse rapidly approaching. They all knew instinctively that they were in trouble. It was one of their scouts. A brief consultation with van Schalkwyk followed. He blew his whistle as usual and gave orders to inspan the oxen and to be on the move. All that separated them from the Khakis was a hill.

In the dark they ran smack into a barbed wire fence. It was supported by massive sandstone blocks, about a foot square, serving as poles, spaced about fifty yards apart with wooden poles supporting the barbed wires in between. The lead wagon had to stop abruptly. As usual in cases like this the other teams, especially the first few, bunched up behind it. The chains slackened and the legs of some of the oxen got entangled. They began to kick and struggle, entangling themselves even more. The men of the escort came to their help. The fence was cut and dragged out of the way like a huge wire, concertina gate, as these gate closures, made of barbed wire and poles, were called. The teams were set straight and the wagons rolled through the opening.

Young Hennie Storm who was leading their small team of oxen had already had a hard day's trek behind him when they set out on their night flight. At times he could almost fall asleep while walking but for the pain of a few stubbed toes, with blood oozing out under the nails. The soles of his feet began to blister. He was in agony, but kept on going, trying to position his feet sideways not to expose the blisters to stubbles or gravel.

As the hours wore on into the night van Schalkwyk led them on, as he hoped farther and farther away from the enemy. At daybreak they arrived at a farm called Groenkloof. Here the convoy entered a ravine. It was a dangerous place to be, for they could easily be bottled up, if discovered, but it had the advantage that they could not readily be spotted. However, following the tracks, would have been an easy way to track them down. As stated before the British had learned from bitter experience to be cautious, for a harmless covered wagon could just by chance also be a death spewing little fort on wheels, manned by armed and sharp shooting Boers, or even women. Although a cumbersome vehicle, it was not lightly overtaken in the open, as the British soon found out.

The oxen and horses, as well as the people were exhausted, hungry, and irritable. They had reached the end of their endurance and had to rest.

The fires were lit again. The smoke, unfortunately, would be a dead giveaway. As soon as Lenie could get warm water, she took Hennie, washed his feet, and dressed them, using bandages ripped from old bed sheets. Then after a bite to eat, she put him to bed in the little wagon.

As the sun began to drench the hills around them, the women noticed that something unusual was afoot with the men. They began to climb the hill on their side and were spreading out in a sparse, long line on the ridge. A report had come that in spite of a tough night's flight the British troops were still quite near them on the other side of the hill. It was not clear whether they had followed them through the night guided by the sound of moving wagons which could not easily be muffled, or whether they had just happened to be in the area. Soon it was clear that they were not just there without a purpose, for they were quietly coming up the other side of the hill, evidently in an attempt to take the *kappiekommando* by surprise.

The *kappiekommando's* only salvation, whenever they found themselves in danger, was flight, putting as much distance between themselves and the British as possible, and not confrontation. In this van Schalkwyk had thus far been eminently successful. But now he was at his wits' end, and had no choice

154

but to try and defend the women and children and their possessions, and keep them from possibly being violated and carried off to a deadly concentration camp. The escorting posse could get on their horses and beat it, but they were honor bound not to do so, and abandon the helpless women and children. He looked at the sky for wind, but it was a still morning without a prevailing wind towards the enemy for another fire "attack."

If they were going to make a stand, and they had to, although they were hopelessly outnumbered, this was as good as any—certainly better than the open plains. They had a commanding position in their favor from the top of the hill, unless the British had field guns to lob shells on them.

Soon gunfire began to erupt on the side of the hill away from the wagons. A few Khakis were caught by surprise and bit the dust. One of van Schalkwyk's escorts, Boy van der Merwe, a young man over six feet tall with an outgoing personality, and liked by all, tried to improve his shelter and moved from behind the rock that was sheltering him. As soon as he came into the open a bullet struck him squarely in the forehead. The force threw him back several yards with this arms uncontrolled flung out and his gun flying through the air. He struggled for a few seconds with death. Then he was at peace for ever.

The bullets kept whirring up and down the hill. Some landed with dull thuds and sudden explosions of dry dust short of their targets, others slammed into rocks or stones and the disfigured fragments ricocheted away with frightening high pitched "pings" into nowhere over the hill. With a favored position, dogged determination, and good marksmanship van Schalkwyk and his few men seemed to be stemming the tide for the time being, and even seemed to cause a slight retreat.

But the defenders were not equipped for an encounter. They had a severely limited supply of ammunition. They did not have time to think that they had not had a wink of sleep the night before, although it had an effect on their fighting ability.

A stalemate seemed to develop, but in the end the small handful of Boers seemed to be doomed and the *kappiekommando* would share the same fate. Again it was numbers, numbers, numbers.

There was little chance of holding out until nightfall to flee again under cover of darkness. Then all hope seemed to disappear. They spotted what looked like reinforcements for the Khakis, wildly charging cavalry. When they came within range they began to open fire, but the bullets fell amazingly far short of van Schalkwyk's position. He and his men could hardly believe their eyes. It was like a miracle. It became obvious to them, observing the cavalry's horsemanship, that they were not British reinforcements, but indeed a Boer commando that had suddenly rushed up, seemingly from nowhere. It was an advantage for the *kappiekommandos* that the Boers, who were now deployed in their own areas, kept an eye out for them and provided protection.

The Tommies were now caught in the middle. What they thought would be an easy victory, had turned into a nightmare. They had no choice but to scramble for their mounts. A mad chase ensued with horses' hoofs thundering over the veld, interspersed now and then with echoes of rifle reports between the hills.

Van Schalkwyk and his small group of men could hardly believe their miraculous escape. When all was safe and quiet they came down the hill to the wagons. They took the two-wheel ox-cart as far up the hill as it could go to return the body of Boy van der Merwe.

Curious and awe-struck, Nellie and some of the other children ventured to the cart as it pulled up with its gruesome burden. Nellie well remembered for the rest of her life the gaping wound on the back of the dead young man's head where the bullet had made its shattering exit. His wrinkled old felt hat with a black sweat ring around the bottom of the ball, lay blood-spattered beside him. Even his worn and crumpled, home-made shoes somehow got blood-stained.

This was the first death in all the time that they had been on flight, in spite of sicknesses and hardship. The death of van der Merwe brought home to them the cruelty of war as it played itself out many thousands of times on other battlefields. He had been a close friend and always ready to lend a hand where needed. To the children he was a real big uncle.

A grave was immediately dug. There was no lumber for a coffin. Boy's body was wrapped in a blanket for burial.

As the mourners—and they all turned out—stood stark faced, many with tears in their eyes, van Schalkwyk read one of the passages from the Psalms, favored for funerals: "Lord, thou hast been our dwelling place in all generations . . . . Thou turnest man to destruction; and sayest, Return, ye children of men . . . . Thou carriest them way as with as flood; they are as a sheep: in the morning they are like grass which groweth up. In the morning it flourisheth, and groweth up; in the evening it is cut down, and withereth. . . ."

He spoke briefly of the deceased's exemplary life, a god-fearing and unselfish young man, who had now made the supreme sacrifice in their struggle for freedom. Then he offered a prayer. Even grown men wept as he took a handful of dirt and rained it gently through his slowly moving fingers on the blanket-coffin in the crude grave. He cleared his throat and with the composure of a man with a solid faith led the mourners in a parting hymn.

Wrapped in a blanket, like thousands of his compatriots, men, women, and children, Boy van der Merwe had become one with the veld on which he was born, out of which he was nourished, which he loved, and for which he had laid down his life. [There was a rumor that van der Merwe's body had been exhumed after the war and buried in the cemetery in Ficksburg, but the author sought in vain in the burial records of the town as well as in the Ficksburg cemetery itself for a grave bearing his name. His remains evidently still rest on the farm Groenkloof where he had been buried originally. A niece of Boy, Sarakie Steytler, provided the author with some valuable information. According to an extract from her grandfather's Bible, where their family's genealogy was kept, as was the custom, he was born August 11, 1885. His real name was Carel Frederick van der Merwe. He fell in battle November 30, 1901, and "was buried in Ficksburg." The record in the Bible does not state that he was reburied in Ficksburg. Perhaps the term Ficksburg includes the district. According to other family reports, although only sixteen years old, he was over six feet tall.]

As soon as their animals had rested and grazed a little, the convoy moved on, for the Khakis might return to bury their dead and to fetch their wounded.

The evening of that exhausting day found the refugees hiding in a distant place. As the custom was they gathered around Dawid de Villiers' wagon for evening devotions. There was reading from Scripture, a prayer, and then Sannie de Villiers, his daughter, pumped the bellows of the little harmonium with her feet, her fingers gliding over the key board, as its melancholy tones warbled off on the chill of evening, leading those gathered in a parting hymn.

One day they spotted a lot of white dots on a distant rise. They thought at first that they had spotted goats. It would mean meat! But then van Schalkwyk put his binoculars to his eyes and focused in. He smiled and gave them to someone else to see for himself. The dots were not goats. They were naked Tommies. The Boers had captured them, but for lack of a safe place to secure them, they had "shaken them out" as the expression was coined. Deprived of mounts, they had to find their way back to camp on foot, and that without shoes.

Now a long calm set in for the *kappiekommando*. They had moved away to an area where the British troops were less active. They encamped on the farm Skurwekop, near the town of Rosendal.

But their hiding place became known, or there was simply more military activity, and again they had to flee. They kept moving around and eventually encamped on the farm Leliefontein. Again many days went by without any sign of British troops. Their main problem remained obtaining enough food to keep body and soul together.

*   *   *   *   *

Finally, reports of the genocidal conditions in the concentration camps began to receive wide publicity in America and Europe, and even in England the truth began to stir bitter criticism of the government and Kitchener. So land-wide were the burning of farms and the rounding up of now homeless women and children and some elderly men that the number of camps had grown to fifty with 136,000 inmates. 26,000 were to die of malnutrition and epidemics which their emaciated bodies could not fight off.

From a military point of view the destruction of farms together with livestock and rounding up inmates into the camps were a disaster in almost all respects. Carrying out this policy was a task nearly equal in scope as trying to defeat the Boers commandos. The cost and logistics in trying to house, feed, and care for such a vast number of people, in addition to providing for the regular army, were staggering and increased the outlay of the war immensely. It is estimated that it contributed to making English War II the costliest war since the Napoleonic wars.

Rather than forcing the Boers into submission, this barbaric policy embittered them the more, and especially the women, who still kept on encouraging the men to fight on to the bitter end. It had seared a deep resentment and hatred into the hearts of those who had suffered through it that not even time could ever erase.

Even Lloyd George, although politically motivated, spoke of the concentration camps in terms of Herod's massacre of the infants, and saw it as building a wall of children's bodies between Boer and Englishmen in South Africa.

It stirred the conscience of Emily Hobhouse, a maiden lady of Quaker persuasion, and she in turn jarred the conscience of the British people to the point that a committee of women was deputized to South Africa to investigate the charges. They made an inspection tour that lasted four months. By that time the deaths in the camps had scaled to an unbelievable number. They found that in some camps the death rate of children had rocketed to seven hundred per thousand!

Reforms were proposed, camps were moved to better sites, and more doctors and nurses were sent from England. But all this took time, and in the meantime the death toll mounted.

Death had decreased the number of inmates considerably, and made it easier to care for the remainder. The weaker ones and those of lesser resistance had perished, and the survivors, by virtue of their stronger constitutions, were better equipped to cope with the unsanitary, disease ridden environment.

159

Due to the recommendations of the committee conditions were greatly improved.

Naturally, Emily Hobhouse was more than a thorn in the side of the man running this camp system, Kitchener. He called her "that bloody women," and had her forcibly deported when she tried to revisit South Africa. But in the hearts of the Boer women, men, and children she had won lasting respect, love, and gratitude. When she died her ashes were buried at the monument in Bloemfontein, erected by the Boers in memory of the thousands who had perished in the concentration camps.

The inadvisability of the whole undertaking now came home to Kitchener and the British government in a rather forceful manner. With the reforms the camps had become desirable places to live. Milner had even begun a program of education for the Boer children. Consequently, while the British government was spending thousands of pounds to support the Boer families whose homes they had burned to the ground and whose independent livelihood they had destroyed, the Boers were still carrying on a hot guerrilla war against its troops with unusual success.

In December 1901 Kitchener finally saw the folly of his scorched earth policy and of the concentration camps, and order went out to stop bringing new inmates to the concentration camps, unless they were in immediate danger of starvation. Word of this got around to the *kappiekommandos*. At first the report was received as a possible trick to catch them, but as time went on, it was gladly accepted as fact.

Where several homes, or buildings were in close proximity, they were in some instances left intact and used by the British to quarter their soldiers. This was the case on the farm Rooikrans. There were two family dwellings, a school building, and two stables. Van Schalkwyk took his *kappiekommando* there to settle down.

Lenie and her children together with two other families were assigned to one of the two houses.

Dawid hid his wagon and kept his oxen out of sight in a remote area, knowing full well that to have them in view would mean eventual loss. Because of his age he remained with the families on Rooikrans, but the other men, who had faithfully escorted them through many a difficult time, left and went on duty with the Boers. Their departure caused a void and a real problem for the women to find food and performing other chores to which they were not accustomed.

Food was always in short supply.

Wheat, maize, and sorghum, when it could be obtained, were the main staples, supplemented with wild herbs and fruit. Summer had now arrived, and as if by providence, there was some fruit in the orchards. Coffee was still roasted cereals mixed with dried fruit or dried vegetables, ground up in grinders, but they had to have their coffee, or Boer consolation (*boeretroos*) as it had been called long before. Tea was not available. They had no money to buy anything.

Communal meals were prepared and served in the house where the Storm family was quartered. It was custom among the Boers that when there were family gatherings, or parties, the adults eat first and then the children. But with the scarcity of food, when the children sat down to eat, only scraps were left over and they usually got up from the table hungrier than when they had started. But then they would hasten to the orchards in search of fruit to still the cramps of hunger. Then back home to do the rest with water, and wait hopefully for the next meal.

Painfully aware of the plight of her children, Lenie was in tears more than once. To solve the problem she finally decided to move into one of the stables where she could prepare meals for her children from her allotment of food. But the stables were not meant for people. Lenie followed an old custom of putting in dirt floors. She and the children dug up anthills and made mortar of the fine soil so well prepared by the ants in their own building process. With the mortar they put a smooth layer over the rough field stones with which the floors had been covered. They also plastered the stone walls which not only made them look better, but also helped to keep out the cold wind that blew in through the openings between the stones. Here in their newly prepared stable-house she cooked for her family, and they were better fed.

On the look out for food all the time, one day some women spotted three sheep on the farm. They had not had meat for

161

weeks, and here was a chance. A group of women and girls set out immediately to catch the sheep for slaughter. But the animals had not seen human beings for a long time and were absolutely wild. They could not get near them, no matter how hard they ran. They tried to surround them and stone them down, but the stones that they were able to hurl were too light, and most missed anyway, just making the sheep more frightened, wilder, scattering in different directions, and harder to come by. The wild chase went hither and thither with no success at all. The women and the girls were worn out, stopping now and then with their hands in utter frustration on their hips, the sweat pouring down their faces from under their long hair. But the sheep that had plenty to eat were strong and kept on running. The long dresses were torn in underbrush and were no outfits to run in, let alone catching wild sheep. They could not help wondering how men ever got hold of a sheep—a seemingly simple task which they had always taken for granted.

In one last attempt they gathered forces to map strategy. There was a cliff nearby, and they decided to drive the sheep to the cliff where they thought they could corner them. But the poor animals were so frightened and wild by now that, when they got to the cliff, instead of waiting to be caught, they jumped to their death.

The hunting party got around to the bottom of the cliff, slit the throats to drain some blood, otherwise it would affect the taste of the meat.

The long trek back home with the carcasses, bruised and bloody, slit throats, would have been comical, had it not been that they were in such dire need of food. The sheep were full grown, fat, and heavy. Two by two they took turns to carry, one grabbing the front legs and the other the rear. It meant that they had to walk sideways the whole distance back, and the one carrying the front end had to contend with the head that was continually in the way and threatening to knock her legs from under her.

*   *   *   *   *

162

The advance of Smuts and his commando into the western Cape was no secret, for they were continually being tracked by their enemy, especially the division under van Deventer with whom he was assumed to have been, since he was Bouwer's senior. In reality, he was with Bouwer. But the commandos got sufficient help from the Cape Boers on their farms so that they always knew what unusual and most unlikely routes to take. As a consequence the British troops trying to corner and end the expedition never succeeded—which was a marvel indeed.

What the British warlords were still fearing most was a large scale defection of Boer sympathizers in the Cape Colony, and worse a general rebellion. This was exactly what the various invasions into the Colony were designed to accomplish.

As said before, in the District of Ceres, on the farm Skurweberg, lived the family of Daniel Johannes Jakobus and Maria Johanna Hugo Theron. He had lived in Sutherland before where he owned several farms, but he sold them and bought Skurweberg. What was left over he put in the bank. He was regarded as a wealthy man. They had a large family, which was usual at the time. Three girls and five boys survived the vicissitudes of child illnesses like measles, whooping cough, and sometimes diphtheria. Infancy mortality was unusually high in those days of large families.

When Smuts' commandos approached the western Cape Colony, the opportunity for which two of the Theron sons on Skurweberg had been waiting was at hand, and they had plenty of reason to rebel against their government which had harassed the family unnecessarily and endlessly to the point of financial ruin. Daniel, named after his father, and called Danie, and his brother Jakobus, called Japie, took their elder sisters, Malie and Bettie, in their confidence, and divulged that they were ready to slip away one night to join the Boer commando under Smuts. The sisters concurred and kept the secret.

Early one morning as the family rose before sunrise for their customary dawn cup of coffee long before breakfast, and assembled for their usual brief, family devotions, Danie and Japie were missing. The flame of the candle on the table by the huge, Dutch, family Bible wavered in the slight draft and made the shadows of those assembled in the dining room dance on the walls. Malie, the elder sister, spoke up and told the rest of the family that Danie and Japie had left during the night to go to war under Smuts.

The words of the Psalm, which Daniel read—it was customary to read a Psalm for morning devotions—plunged unheard as if into emptiness. His usual prayer of gratitude for the rest of the night and supplication for sustenance and guidance during the day, would have gone the unheeded way of the Psalm as well, for all thoughts were on the gravity of the news that Malie had just broken to them. But then Daniel intertwined a short, terse deviation with the customary prayer as he commended his two sons, on their way to war, to God's care. Suddenly, they all realized that the prayer had meaning and that his prayer was the prayer of their hearts as well.

Their absence would most likely soon be known to the British authorities. They were not even supposed to leave the confines of the farm. Such an infraction alone, if caught, would land them in jail with possible, heavy fines. If they were captured far away from home, there would be no hiding that they were rebelling, and if they were captured under arms, there would be no defense. Other rebels had already faced firing squads.

The scuffing of feet and the creaking of wooden chairs where they had knelt ended the solemn family gathering.

Maria was left alone in the room. She had lost several of her children in infancy. She was a tough woman by nature. Her rather stoic attitude towards life, inherited from a German strain in her ancestry, was reinforced by the matter of fact way of life so necessary on a farm. Her mother was a Maritz who could saddle a horse in the middle of the night and gallop for more than two hours to tend to a daughter about to deliver a child. As sunlight began to stream over the mountains and into the valley where the house and the barn nestled, she cupped her hand behind the candle and blew it out. She could understand the decisions of her sons. She herself and Daniel have had enough of their government.

By now Danie and Japie had a night's journey on foot

behind them. It would have been foolish to travel any other way. They had planned to walk by night and sleep in hidden places during the day, avoiding discovery and capture.

The scant food supply which they had taken with them was soon exhausted. They purposely carried little with them not to betray the fact they were indeed on a journey, should they encounter anyone hostile.

The nights were warm. The dry season in the southern part of the Colony had now begun. Irrigated gardens and orchards were plentiful on the farms as they journeyed along. They spotted these from their hiding places during the day, and shortly after dark they would help themselves to watermelons, cantaloupes, carrots and fruit. A small supply was taken along for the next day. As they went along they became bolder and once in a while they would venture to a farmhouse at night. If they found a farmer sympathetic, and there was a good chance that he would be, they would enquire about the progress of Smuts. They always declined to enter the house for fear of being trapped or getting the owner into trouble for harboring rebels.

When they determined that a farmer was sympathetic, they would ask for food and enquire about other farmers further down their intended journey who would also be sympathetic where they could get food and further news.

Their journey went smoothly down the valley of the Olifant River towards van Rhynsdorp where they hoped to join Smuts and his commando (This river is not to be confused with the Olifant River in the Transvaal). It was the end of their first week of slipping away. Walking a long distance at night had worn them out much more than they had anticipated, and they were getting tired of their mostly vegetarian diet which they had "garnered" during the night from farms along the way.

The sun had set in a blistering red behind the Olifant Mountains, tapering towards the ocean. They approached a farm after dark where they had found out that a sympathetic Boer family lived. All was quiet and it seemed that all the help had retired to their quarters. There was the expected encounter with the watchdogs which were quieted down by the farmer as his figure silhouetted in the doorway against the light from inside. A

165

few moments of uneasiness, made heavy by darkness and suspicion, hung over them. Then Danie spoke up. He was the one who always took the lead. The aroma of food that still hung tantalizing in the air after supper made it less difficult to ask for food, which they hoped would be solid. Soon an atmosphere of confidence developed as they were treated generously. Enquiry was made about Smuts' progress.

The conversation ended with the farmer saying: "I can not invite you in, as you know, but down by the river is the threshing floor with a shelter. You can sleep there, if you want to." He whispered, for the darkness around them might have ears.

They had intended to walk further that night. Van Rhynsdorp was less than a week's walk away. But exhaustion and the good meal overcame them, and they decided against better judgment to accept the farmer's invitation to sleep in the shelter. There was plenty of chaff and straw of the wheat harvest and they made themselves beds of these far more comfortable than the hard ground of the preceding nights, and bedded down.

The day was dawning when they were awakened by the clanking of milk buckets and voices of the farm help. Disgusted with themselves that they had slept so long, they hunched down to the river to be out of sight under the bank shielded by a huge willow tree. They lit their pipes and were about to disappear further down the river away from the farm when they heard the hoofs of horses on the road to the farm. It took only one look to determine that British cavalry was approaching. They hurried downstream away from the advancing cavalry as fast as they could, but to their alarm more cavalry was already coming upstream only a few hundred yards from them. They were indeed trapped! Fortunately, if there was anything fortunate in this predicament, the huge willows, planted there by a farmer, probably more than a century before, obscured them from view for the moment. Under one of these trees, the two stunned brothers stopped for a moment to assess their fate. There was not much time, and it appeared even less to do. There was no sense in trying to swim the river and flee with horses in pursuit. They

166

could hear the hoofs of horses coming ever closer from both sides each moment.

The branches of the tree under which they stood, lush in their summer garb, hung over the water's edge and reached low enough to cover part of the level ground before a sharp roll at the water's edge from where the boughs tipped into the water. It would shield them from view from above as well as from the water, or other side of the river. Danie saw it as a shelter to hide. Without hesitation he scurried under the long, supple leaf-covered boughs. Had it been winter and the boughs bare, there would have been no place to hide.

He had thought that Japie would follow automatically. But Japie was unpredictable, unperturbed, and a daredevil at that. Once on the farm he had followed a leopard, that had been catching sheep, into the mountains and confronted it in a cave. When it charged, he shot and dropped it at his feet. At another time, as they were walking to a field, they surprised a full-grown yellow cobra in the grass that reared its head and got ready to strike. Danie, always the more cautious, jumped out of reach, but Japie stood just right where he was. It did not seem to occur to him that a strike by the cobra would most certainly mean death. He looked it right in the eye, and deliberate as quick he finished it off with a vicious, backhanded uppercut with a club that he was carrying.

A few seconds later, when Japie was not following, Danie moved the willow bough away to see where he was. He could not believe his eyes. He had sat down on the bank in the open and was still sucking his pipe. Instinctively he knew that Japie might act irrationally in an emergency. He could just see him jumping up on the upper bank of the river, knock an unsuspecting Tommy off his mount and attempt an escape. "My God, Japie," he whispered as urgently as the situation demanded without his voice projecting too far, "Come here!" The swearing—which they seldom did, if ever— had the desired effect. Japie came as if awakened out of a trance. There was not much room or time for the two under cover to maneuver for comfort, for soon the first of the cavalry had reached the trunk of the tree that was mercifully hiding them. Their hearts pounded when to their horror the Tommies stopped and dismounted. They waited for a few to jump down the bank and grab them with rifles or pistols drawn. But from the Tommies' casual, small talk they came to the conclusion that they had no such intention and that they had not noticed them. The only thing was to lie still and wait for them to move on. But they seemed to have no such intentions whatever. Both Danie and Japie understood English. They had learned it at school, although their home language was Dutch as it had begun to switch over to what became the Afrikaans language.

From the talk of two of the dismounted men, and the way they were being addressed by other soldiers, they gathered that they were officers in charge of the cavalry.

The horses were unsaddled and breakfast was being prepared. Breakfast was finished, but no sign of leaving. And were Danie and Japie's mouths watering when they got whiffs of breakfast? They were probably waiting for a report of a search of the farm. Danie became convinced that someone had seen them the previous evening and had reported it to the British for a reward. He could not help but wonder if by any chance Hendrik had found employment here. But he put the thought out of his mind as he had more important things to worry about.

The sun rose and heat waves began to dance in watery illusions on the horizon. It was great for swimming, and many of the Tommies availed themselves of the opportunity, cavorting in the water only a few yards from where a merciful willow was concealing two scared, young, rebel Boers.

Time seemed endless measured by limbs, tortured, unable to move the slightest, and by the ever mounting tension, which had produced a splitting headache for Danie. The Tommies were truly enjoying themselves. Some of them were now on the flat grassy part under the outer bank only a few yards from where the two brothers were hiding.

Lunch time came and the Tommies finally got out of the water. Two hungry mouths watered again, but, fortunately, no offer of lunch. Full stomachs and a hot day naturally invited a long siesta. Soon no voices were heard. Finch nests, artistically woven cradles, swayed gently over the water, well protected from cats, snakes, and other predators. The finches, the males in bright red or yellow, fluttered apprehensively overhead with disturbed chirping at all the activity in their otherwise peaceful surroundings. If anyone had spotted two men hiding under the boughs, the finches probably did.

As time went on, more and more disturbing thoughts ran through Danie's mind. He thought of Lötter and his officers who had been made a public spectacle at their execution for being rebels. And then there was Commandant Gideon Scheepers who had daringly raised the Orange Free State flag over the British fort at Uniondale. He was only twenty-four, but had made a name for himself in the Boer cause. On October 10, 1901, too ill to move, he was taken prisoner by the British, and nursed to health and then brought to trial. He was condemned to face a firing squad on charges of arson and murder. He had once burnt an Englishman's house to the ground in the Cape Province when he found that he was serving in the British army. He wondered what the verdict would have been, had Roberts and Kitchener stood on trial for burning down homes and causing the death of thousands in concentration camps.

About mid-afternoon one of the officers got up, stood at the edge of the bank, and voided again down the grassy level. About three o'clock activity began. Horses' hoofs could be heard and the clanking of stirrups. Then the muffled sound of hoofs echoed over the river several hundred yards away as they crossed a stone-lined ford. Danie and his brother thought they were safe and parted the willow bough ever so slightly to provide an opening in their shelter. Danie could see the the Tommies crossing the ford slowly and he counted about one hundred and fifty.

They waited for a long while to make sure that all was safe and then crawled out, hardly able to move, and dumbfounded at the miracle of their escape.

Almost overnight it became clear to Danie and Japie that military activity of the British would naturally increase the closer they came to where Smuts and his ever increasing commando were passing through, and that their journey would be made more difficult and hazardous.

Not long after their miraculous escape under the willow boughs, their nightly marches had brought them into the war zone. They had to pick their way carefully by night, sometimes through British lines, or else close to encampments.

Their beards had sprouted and they looked wild and unkempt.

When Smuts was not focusing on a particular military objective, he had his men scattered in small commandos over a larger geographical area where they could provide for themselves more easily. It also minimized the probability of a wipe-out by much larger forces, and it kept the British with their superior numbers off balance.

He now posed a real threat to the British. His initial, small commando of several hundred had eventually grown to over three thousand men, mostly rebels.

It was with one of these scattered commandos that Danie and Japie met two weeks after they had left their home in the District of Ceres. At first they were questioned carefully to ascertain that they were indeed rebels and not spies or traitors. They were provided with horses, saddles, guns, and ammunition, all of it looted from the British.

Danie got a fleet-footed mare which would be his faithful mount for the rest of the war. He named her Bella.

Among the many Cape rebels they met Manie Maritz, who was related to the Therons on their mother's side. He had come from Johannesburg as one of the Zarps. He was rather stocky, tough, and fearless. Smuts had advanced him to general in charge of Namakwaland, a vast area stretching south from the orange River where it flows into the Atlantic Ocean.

Van Rhynsdorp had fallen into the hands of the Boers. It served more or less as Smuts' headquarters in the area. However, when they moved farther northwestward, it was reoccupied by the British. Smuts decided to retake it. So he dispatched messengers to the mini commandos ordering them to pull together for action. One of the dispatch riders was Deneys Reitz, the young son of the Secretary of State of the Transvaal, who had been President of the Orange Free State before joining the Kruger government after his term of office.

The recapture of the town was easy. The British troops had pulled out obligingly and encamped about ten miles from Van Rhynsdorp at a place called Windhoek (not to be confused with Windhoek, the capital of South West Africa, now Namibia).

As they entered the town some of the Boers could not suppress the glee of a minor victory so generously yielded. A few of them rode their horses down the main street, kicking up the usual amount of dust as they leisurely trotted along. They dismounted in front of a store, fastened their horses to the hitching posts, and entered. They stopped before a display case with a sparkling assortment of rings. They ordered the owner, who was not a Boer, to open the case. Frantically he dashed around trying to gain time, pretending that he could not find the key, and obviously hoping that a miracle would save his merchandise, and perhaps his life.

Impatient with the stalling tactics, one of the men drew his revolver. The merchant was beside himself, thinking it was his last day. He pleaded for mercy. But the man with the revolver could care less about him. He wanted rings. He blasted the case open with a single shot and they helped themselves.

Under cover of darkness, on February 25, 1902, the commando moved out of the town towards Windhoek with the intention of launching an attack at dawn the next morning on the British now stationed there. The Boer attack was heavy and sustained. Being concentrated the Tommies were at a distinct disadvantage. They were suffering heavy losses as the bullets poured in on them incessantly from an outer ring. Fighting at very close quarters, the Boers rushed the farmhouse where the enemy had made its last stand, and engaged in hand to hand fighting. Tables and chairs were shoved across the rooms and overturned. China crashed in pieces to the floor adding to the great confusion as deadly gunfire erupted at frightfully and inescapably close range, and the results rather gruesome. From room to room the violence raged until a last "hands up!" shouted by a Boer brought surrender. The Tommies who remained stumbled out of the house. They had been badly mauled. Their casualties and wounded lay all over the place. About two hundred were taken prisoner.

The Boers too had suffered five dead and slightly more than a dozen wounded, some very seriously. Both Bouwer and van Deventer were wounded. Danie and Japie had their first, real taste of war. It was a bloody fight, but they had gone through it without a scratch.

As the Boers did not want to be burdened with keeping prisoners, they ordered them to remove their shoes and set them on their way on foot to their camp at Clan William, about fifty miles away. Smuts was merciful and let them keep their clothes.

When the fighting was over, the Boers found a man hiding in a large fireplace in the house. He was immediately recognized as a certain Colyn who had joined a Boer commando purporting to be a rebel. After a few days he was not seen around. Since discipline was rather lax, it was generally assumed that he had gone to visit friends, or perhaps attached himself to another commando. However, he turned out to have been a spy. He had betrayed a Boer outpost under Bouwer, which was then overran by the British. It was an anguishing, narrow escape, and Bouwer himself barely escaped death as British cavalry set upon him with sabers.

Smuts, who had retired to a farm, Aties, was informed about the capture of Colyn. He was brought before Smuts, who heard the evidence. The spy admitted to his treachery and gave as an excuse that he needed money for his family. Smuts sentenced him to death before a firing squad. The Boer chaplain, the Reverend A. P. Kriel, took him aside and prayed with him. Then he was lead away to where a few grave diggers were getting a grave ready. He requested again to see the chaplain, but it was refused. Then he requested to see Smuts again, but it was refused. Realizing that the end had come, he raised his hands, standing blindfolded, and slowly intoned the Lord's Prayer. With the Amen a burst of three shots rang out and executed the sentence. It was just the beginning, but the inhumanity of war had already made a lasting impression on the two Therons from Ceres.

With his breakthrough to the northwestern Cape Colony Smuts had achieved a major objective. With the growth of his army to over three thousand five hundred, mostly rebels, he became more and more of a real threat to the populous areas in the southern part. He had already begun to organize on a large scale: Maritz in charge of Namakwaland, van Deventer in charge of the area east of the main railway line, and general Wynand Malan in charge of a vast area west of the line. They hit hard when the opportunity availed itself. British convoys suffered heavily. Early in February both Malan and van Deventer took large quantities of materiel. Malan broke through westward to the Cape Midlands which the British once more had regarded as cleared.

CHAPTER VI

EMBERS

Since the beginning of the war it was not surprising to find teenagers in the Boer armies. Deneys Reitz, son of the Transvaal Secretary of State, fought throughout the entire war from beginning to end. Gideon Scheepers had a young adjutant, Karl Lehmkuel, sixteen years of age, serving with distinction. Among the rebels in Namakwaland was another young man, Abraham van Schalkwyk. His father was with the British, but he chose to fight with the Boers. In an encounter with the British cavalry he shot down four of them. The others fled. He dashed off to get the horses of those that he had shot, but was mistaken by one of the Boers for the enemy. The brave young man perished under bullets of his own men. Hendrik Storm, cousin of Lenie's children, was a teenager when he joined the Boer army. He was taken prisoner of war and spent years in Ceylon along with Lenie's husband and his brothers. Among them we must also note Boy van der Merwe who was killed in a skirmish on Groenkloof, as already mentioned earlier.

The boys with the *kappiekommandos* rendered invaluable service handling the oxen and performing other chores with which they were more familiar than the women. But it was especially as little scouts that they excelled. It was no wonder that the British in their drives were eager to round up these youngsters.

Hennie Storm, Lenie's son, had now reached the age where he too would become subject to being taken prisoner. He could serve as a Boer messenger or as an informer. The fullness of summer was culminating. It was February 1902. The war had already been dragging on and on for more than two years and four months. A calm had spread over the rolling hills with waving tall grass in the pastures. The branches of the trees swayed in the breeze weighed down under a heavy load of leaves. The birds were chattering endlessly as they frolicked among the branches, blissfully unaware of the suffering that war visits on a country. The children were playing outside and no one noticed until a patrol of British soldiers was in full view of the houses. When Lenie saw them she felt instinctively that they were out to get Hennie. She would hide him, but they might search the stable where they were living or the homes and find him. Sometimes the Tommies went into homes and pierced the mattresses with their bayonets or sabers to make sure nothing was hidden in them. She ran over to a neighbor, Betta Loots, who had some spare clothes and borrowed a girl's outfit. She dressed Hennie in it as fast as she could and covered his short boys haircut with her own bonnet secured tightly with a knot and a bow under his chin. She took a container of peaches and sat her children around it outside on the grass, Hennie among them. When the Tommies arrived, they were busily peeling away. They must have been informed that there was a boy among the families on the farm.

The soldiers walked around investigating. Finally, the officer in charge walked straight up to where Hennie was squatting down. A giveaway silence fell over the children. A few scuffed their feet a little as the officer's eyes visited from child to child. Then he bent over and grabbed the bonnet on Hennie's head and gave it a few hard tugs, but the knot and bow held. He turned to Lenie, and either in compassion, or in uncanny humor said to her, "All girls heah," and walked away.

Magdalena Johanna (de Villiers) Storm with great-granddaughters, Sophia and Neeltje Strydom, Pictured 1947.

Near the rows of tents in a concentration camp in the western Transvaal was a high heap of wood where the women had to fetch their own firewood for cooking. It consisted mostly of thin sticks that could not sustain a good fire. But here and there a thick piece was mixed in. A woman came along with her boy about ten years old to fetch wood. She spotted a thick branch way on top of the pile and started after it, falling down a few times and scratching her legs up in the process. When she got down with the piece of wood, one of the hands employed by the camp was waiting for her. He grabbed the wood and tried to take it from her, but she would not let go. Her boy had now joined her in the tug of war. The man got tired of the business and decided to teach the woman and her son a lesson. He went after the boy. The lad reared back when he saw what was coming. He was skinny from malnutrition. His knobby knees bulged out under a pair of worn and patch shorts. He wore a pair of English boots with steel reinforcements at the toes. These had worn sharp as blades. The woman stood dumbfounded, knowing that the man could kill the child. He stormed the boy in a slightly prone position to strike him with his head, like a ram, a technique commonly used by some Africans. He lowered his head for the impact. But the boy had retreated some and as a last resort let fly with the right foot as if kicking a ball. The sharpened iron reinforcement of the shoe hit the assailant squarely under his nose. He staggered and fell. His nose was completely stripped off. He was removed from the camp and never heard from again.

*   *   *   *

Jacob Storm with his two brothers as prisoners of war in Ceylon
L. to r. Stefanus, Jacob, and Willem

While Smuts was still struggling in the eastern Cape to break through the British defenses, great pressure was exerted on the Boers in the eastern Transvaal where the government of the republic roamed from place to place.

The British now tried a new tactic. Through information gained from local natives and with the help of National Scouts

178

they were able to ascertain where the Boers were camping at night. By attacking then at dawn, a fair amount of success was achieved, until the Boers learned soon not to overnight in the same place two nights in succession.

But large forces such as the British had in the field could be quite vulnerable, especially when they got complacent with success. It was the end of October. In the District of Bethal, Grobler and Opperman, two of Botha's commandants, were harassing a British force under General G. E. Benson. Botha had joined them and they attacked at Bakenlaagte employing the method, now famous with the Boers, of firing while storming in on horseback. They concentrated on the four artillery pieces which Benson had. Only three of the thirty-two men crew survived, three-quarters of the Scottish Horse of eighty fell. Benson himself perished with eleven of his officers. In all two hundred and fifty were dead or wounded.

De Wet had been very quiet, but on Christmas Eve 1901, he followed Washington's example at the Delaware. At a place called Tweefontein he let his men loose on a British force. They charged their camp, yelling and shouting as they came. In very short order it was all over. Almost one hundred and fifty British soldiers and officers fell dead or wounded. Five hundred were taken prisoner.

The British were finally coming to real grips with the main problem standing in their way to a successful conclusion of the war—endless space. Train loads of barbed wire, poles, and prefabricated blockhouses were pouring in. The blockhouses consisted of two large concentric corrugated-iron cylinders, a smaller one fitting into the larger one. When installed upright, the space between the two parts was filled with dirt. These blockhouses were spaced about one thousand yards apart, manned around the clock by about seven soldiers, connected with telephones and barbed wire fences. Thousands of cans were hung on these fences and filled with loose stones that rattled when anyone would try to cross. In the end five thousand miles of blockhouses and fences crisscrossed the plains of the Transvaal and particularly the Orange Free State in an attempt to hem the Boers in.

Blockhouse lines like these had already been protecting the railways for a long time and effectively cut sabotage by the Boers. The ever expanding system did indeed begin to hamper the Boers' war operations. In addition night raids by the British, aided by National Scouts and natives, who betrayed where they were staying overnight, continued to make life miserable for the Boers.

Kitchener had made many mistakes. He was now about to make another grievous one. For most of the war black people were employed by both the Boers and the British as animal keepers, drivers, trench diggers, and other jobs. When either the Boers or the British were attacking or being attacked, many of these black employees suffered also, and many of them, perhaps thousands, unsung in the annals of the war, perished along with their employers. But Kitchener needed all the help he could get. The war was dragging on at an awfully high cost. There were many black people, and they were much cheaper to employ as soldiers than Tommies who had to be shipped from England or from some distant colony, like Australia, New Zealand, Canada, and India. So he decided to arm black people to fight the Boers. It had been regarded as a white man's war, but he changed it all. It was in reality taking advantage of the natives. They were not trained in the way the war was being conducted and when caught, they paid with their lives, for they were regarded by the Boers as inhabitants of the two republics, who had become traitors. The charge by some ignorant Tommies in later times that the Boers shot black people indiscriminately "like dogs", is utter nonsense. They were just parroting what they had heard, and never saw any such inhumane treatment. While the Boers did have wars with the natives when they settled the Orange Free State and the Transvaal, once the wars were over, and especially at the time of English War II, blacks were treated with respect and civility. A charge that Smuts was inhumane towards natives is nonsense. Once when one of his generals did indeed kill a number of Colored people suspected of aiding the British, he was duly taken to task by Smuts himself.

January and February 1902 were hard months for Botha. He had to be on the move almost continually to remain free. He lost

General Ben Viljoen who was captured with a few men in January. He also lost General J. D. Opperman, and later his Irish brother-in-law, General Cheere Emmet.

Chamberlain, the British Colonial Secretary, found it hard to believe that the vast forces of His Majesty could not once and for all deal with Botha and de Wet. So Kitchener singled them out the more.

During February and early March three well planned drives were concentrated against de Wet. For the first drive Kitchener had mustered about twenty thousand troops and seven armored trains, in an area around Heilbron, dotted with hundreds of blockhouses, and obstructed by endless barbed wire fences. De Wet divided his men. Some broke through to the north, while he himself smashed through to the south. But two hundred and fifty of his men were taken prisoner. Unfortunately for de Wet, this was not the worst of his losses. A second drive netted the British almost six hundred prisoners of war. Again de Wet made world news, but remained free and managed to safeguard Steyn too. The third drive amounted to nothing, and was a failure.

At Botha's request de la Rey, who had been very quiet for months, readied himself to strike. He was assisted by Kemp, Celliers, and Liebenberg with their commandos to launch an attack on a British force. In customary fashion they stormed and fired from horseback. Celliers, the specialist in this tactic, delivered the crowning blow and put the enemy to flight. They were overtaken. In the process de la Rey and his commandos took thousands of rounds of ammunition, a number of pieces of artillery, and several hundred horses. The British had suffered almost two hundred dead and wounded. So ended the battle of Ysterspruit.

Now Methuen, de la Rey's counterpart early in the war at Modder River and Magersfontein Hill, rushed up to deal with de la Rey.

*   *   *   *   *

After the Windhoek victory Smuts moved his men northward in the direction of O'Okiep to take the copper mines.

181

He captured Springbok and Concordia near O'Okiep. There were several forts which had to be taken to be in full command of these towns. The Boers had a good number of Irishmen fighting with them as volunteers. They had expertise with dynamite, which they obtained in the area as it was used for the mining operations. So they made hand grenades with the dynamite. The forts were stormed and some of these grenades tossed on the roofs. The results were so debilitating to the occupants that they brought about the desired effects of surrender, almost immediately.

O'Okiep was more heavily garrisoned and better fortified. Several blockhouses commanded the approaches to the town. So Smuts set about attacking these. The assaults were launched at night. The first one was taken with ease. A wall collapsed under an exploding dynamite bomb and the defenders surrendered readily. The second blockhouse was more formidable to capture. It had with a more solid structure. A dozen or so dynamite bombs had little effect. Danie was one of those detailed for the attack. The loopholes in the blockhouse spewed fire at them as they took shelter behind rocks. He had to cover his eyes at times to shield them from the gravel sent flying by the bullets as they hit in front of him. When dawn came the blockhouse was still holding out. As it was an extremely dangerous and vulnerable position for the attackers during the daylight hours, a retreat was made to safer ground. The blockhouse was kept under surveillance throughout the day to prevent supplies from being brought in.

The next night Smuts put Manie Maritz in charge of the assault. He had been wounded extremely seriously earlier in the Cape campaign. One side of his chest was ripped open by a bullet. If it had not been for his superior physique and his indomitable will power, he would quite likely not have survived.

The attack began after dark. The Boers were met by a hailstorm of bullets, but with little damage. Maritz and a few men had gotten close to the blockhouse under cover of a ledge. Daring as he was, he got up on the shoulders of one of his men to find out how far he was from the target. Probably because the defenders were not expecting an attack from that side, they were not fired upon, or Maritz would have been dead. He jumped down, took three dynamite grenades and lashed them together. Then he climbed on the shoulders of one of his men again, supported by several others, lit the fuses and hurled the deadly mass with sizzling fuses on the roof. A thundering explosion lit up the sky all around. Then the Boers stormed from different directions. They found several of the defenders dead and the rest wounded.

The other fortifications were even more difficult and dangerous to attack. So Smuts decided not to press for their capture. Instead he determined to lay siege to O'Okiep in an attempt to force the British to ship troops from Capetown to Port Nolloth to relieve the town. In that event, it was surmised, he would quickly have rushed south. With a weakened British force around Capetown, his commandos would cause considerable trouble, and even gain more rebels to join.

The Boers were encamped in small contingents in the hills around O'Okiep. One commando was some twenty miles west of the town blocking the railroad from Port Nolloth. Some were quartered in houses in Concordia.

The British got messages to Port Nolloth by heliograph where a relief force of British troops was gathering.

As the days went by uneventfully, boredom set in and some strange things were done to pass the time. Japie got the idea to play a trick on a certain Boer who was a rather big mouth and somewhat annoying. He got him to smoke a pipe with a little gunpowder under the tobacco. With the second puff the powder caught and burned a path through the man's shock of unruly hair. It was a dangerous and bizarre kind of joke. Japie was sentenced to saddle and gear carrying. The next day he had to carry the whole load on his back and walk to and fro a distance of several hundred yards. It was within sight, but far enough away so as not to make it too embarrassing and to prevent heckling by others. After a while he disappeared down a bank, which was thought normal. He remained away for a while and then returned to resume his pacing. The only difference was that he had found a man nearby. He had hired him to do the walking while he sat in the shade of a tree out of sight. Since it was far enough away, no one was any wiser.

Danie had the same name as the famous scout and officer, Danie Theron, who had made a name for himself serving with de Wet in the Orange Free State and the Transvaal. It was probably partly due to his name that Smuts assigned him to a scouting patrol which kept him busy even when there was no fighting. It was a dangerous assignment, because being a spy in addition to being a rebel, if captured by the British, would have meant no mercy. He evidently did such a good job that he was invited to join Smuts and his officers for a picture. He is the first one standing on the far left in the picture which has been preserved.

One morning about ten o'clock he and someone in his group sat watching one of the blockhouses while smoking their pipes and talking about the exciting possibility of venturing south. Some of them even talked about the possibility of capturing Cape Town. Then suddenly fire flashed from the blockhouse more than half a mile away. Long before the report of a shot began to echo through the hills, a bullet whizzed by between Danie and his comrade right in front of his face and by the ear of the other man as they sat at right angles to each other. They clearly felt the air pressure as the projectile almost hit both of them in the head. Instinctively they tumbled out of sight.

The group had barely recovered from their fright, when a young man came crouching, rifle in hand, ready to fire yelling: "There goes a Khaki, there goes a Khaki!" And sure enough a man was running at top speed from the blockhouse at a right angle from where they were. The orders were explicit to keep the occupants of the blockhouse pinned down. The young fellow who had spotted the runner first, could not get over his excitement, could not steady his rifle, and did not get a single shot off. Then one of the group stretched himself on the ground, steadied his gun with its strap tightly wrapped around his left arm, and his elbow firmly planted in the ground. He tried to aim, but the man was sprinting so fast in the direction of another blockhouse that he could not get a good shot off. Then he tried moving his aim in on him from in front as he did when hunting deer in flight. He tried a couple of times before squeezing the trigger, when he thought it was about right. Exclamations of astonishment mingled with the echoes in the hills. The daring soldier, carried a few more yards by his speed, plunged forward, flat on his face. They focused in with their binoculars, but he did not move. Evidently, his comrades in the blockhouse though it so useless to fetch him, although they could have done so without danger under a white flag. The next morning he was gone.

The lull continued interrupted only by isolated instances of sniping at each other's positions.

Smuts' men were well off compared to the Boers in the Orange Free State and Transvaal. They had ample supply of food and ammunition, and had enough horses and mules to meet their needs, most if not all looted from the British. In the north the number of fighting men was now reduced from about sixty to seventy thousand at the onset of the war to only about twenty thousand. Some had been taken prisoner, some were killed, some had given up the war effort, and others had decided to work for the British as National Scouts. Winter was coming again on the high veld, taxing the ability of those under arms to the limit. The British were fastening their hold on the Boer republics. About a quarter of a million troops were against the handful of Boers. In all, about four hundred and fifty thousand British troops had seen duty in South Africa as they came and went to be replaced by fresh troops. For the Boers there was no rest and hardly such a thing as replacements. The hopelessness of their odds was readily apparent except to those who had fought so valiantly and knew that it was their last stand.

*   *   *   *   *

After the defeat inflicted on the British at Ysterspruit, Methuen stood poised to smash de la Rey and to recapture the artillery pieces taken by his old foe. On March 7, 1902 the two generals stood once again opposite each other ready to test their strength. This time Methuen had some of his men dug in, following de la Rey's example at Modder River and Magersfontein Hill. But the Boer war tactic had changed radically. First de la Rey let some of his cavalry dismount and take position to keep Methuen's infantry down in their trench. He had Kemp and Celliers with him, for whom no battle was ever too daring. While Methuen's men in their trench were being pinned down by some of de la Rey's men, he ordered the cavalry to storm, shooting from the saddle. Methuen's cavalry, numbering over a thousand, was put to flight. The Boers again concentrated on the artillery, felling the gunners with precision. The infantry could not get away and had to fight, but ultimately, with seventy dead and over a hundred wounded, six hundred of them capitulated. Methuen tried in vain to stem the tide of flight, and is severely wounded himself. His horse was shot. As it collapsed, it crushed one of his legs, and he fell captive to de le Rey. Then de la Rey had him transported in a British ambulance to a hospital. Instead of Methuen recapturing his cannons taken earlier from him, the Boers got six more.

With two decisive victories to his credit in a short time, the western Transvaal once again became a danger point for the British. Kitchener had to dispatch troops to that region and so pressure on Botha was eased.

*   *   *   *   *

At this time the Netherlands had a well known theologian, Abraham Kuyper, as Minister-politician. In January 1902 he had approached the British government with a proposal to mediate between Great Britain and the two republics, but his offer was rejected.

However, two months later Kitchener sent the correspondence to Acting President Burger. He regarded it as a tacit suggestion on the part of Kitchener for peace negotiations. He went to see Steyn and de Wet in the Orange Free State. As a result a meeting of the two governments was arranged in Klerksdorp in the western Transvaal. It took place on April 9, 1902. A letter is drafted to set forth Boer peace proposals. They were adamant on retaining their independence. Kitchener held a conference with Boer representatives in Pretoria, and at their insistence cabled their proposals to London.

*   *   *   *   *

The stalemate around O'Okiep kept on unchanged. The Boers were not good at siege. They just did not have enough men and were loathe to flatten a town with artillery, even if they had enough supplies to do so. One afternoon emissaries came by cart from the south under a white flag of truce to see Smuts. He was quartered in Concordia. They came from Kitchener asking Smuts to come to a peace conference. He would be furnished transportation and given safe conduct to the Transvaal. Both sides in and around O'Okiep would refrain from military operations while the conference lasted.

A patrol escorted Smuts westward towards Port Nolloth. Part of the journey would be by train. The escort bid Smuts a cheerful farewell as he boarded the train for a ship to steam south towards Capetown and Simonstown, a British naval base. Smuts was heavy at heart, for he knew what deep disappointment might await his men so full of high expectations. For the Cape rebels with him it had been all victory.

As Smuts journeyed northward into the Cape Midlands, through the Orange Free State, and the Transvaal, security was extremely tight for fear of attacks on the train by Boer commandos. Travel was done stealthily by night with an armored train escort.

The war had been fought with great bitterness for two and a half years and more. It had plowed deep scars into the countryside and hearts of the Boers that the passage of generations would not erase. Peace would not come easily. The Boers would be as determined in their negotiations for peace as they were in waging war, and fighting for their freedom.

On the Boers' side there was the ultimate crushing realization that they could not expect any help from abroad. There was plenty of sympathy, but it was a poor substitute for steel and flesh that win wars. They had also come to accept the truth that, in spite of loyal support of Cape Boers and active participation of Boer rebels, there would be no general uprising. The crushing mill of war had pulverized the country. Many of the Boers were in prisoner of war camps far across the seas—

some in the Atlantic in Bermuda, some in the Indian Ocean in Ceylon. Those still in the field in the eastern Transvaal and in the Orange Free State were in dire straits and their numbers still dwindling under heavy hammering of large British forces. In the western and northern Transvaal and in the Cape Colony they were much better off.

The women and children had suffered far beyond imagination. Twenty-six thousand women, children, and old men had perished in the British concentration camps. Some had feared that the entire Boer nation stood in danger of being wiped out. With the investigation of the committee that came from England and at the clamoring of Emily Hobhouse, radical improvements were made, but the Boers in the army could not visit their families, and many of them did not even know whether they were alive, or not. The grass waved tall over the veld with the flocks of sheep and herds of cattle that roamed there mostly slain. The towns and cities, the gold and diamond mines, the transportation system, the roads, important bridges and fords were all in the hands of the British. The main asset that the Boers had in abundance was an iron will to win and to be master of their own destiny, but it weighed very light in the scales of negotiation at the bargaining table.

On the British side of the conference table there was a weariness and disenchantment with the war. The vaunted British lion had turned out to be a wet cat against ordinary farmers. The prestige of the British armies had suffered immeasurably. They would never win a major war on their own again.

England's reputation as a champion of civilization was awash all over the world in reports of cruel malnutrition, disease, and death that had stalked the concentration camps, uncontrolled.

There was now indeed only a thimble full of Boers left. (The British estimated about twelve thousand under arms. There seemed to have been about twice that many. The low estimate was for propaganda purposes abroad where they maintained the Boers had only marauding bands roaming the country.) Yet, attempting to conquer this thimble full, the British were staggering under a war cost of about £1,500,000 per week! This was a large amount in those days.

188

The Boers were not beaten. Some lesser generals were captured lately with a few men, but the real leaders, Burger, Steyn, Botha, de Wet, de la Rey, Hertzog, Smuts, and others were still leading their commandos, eluding the most sustained drives ever conceived and inflicting heavy losses on their enemy. While the British were spending millions per month, the Boers had a war chest of only about £500,000 at the outset of the conflict.

A large portion of the Boer ammunition, food, horses, and other equipment they had taken almost at will from their enemy and turned against him. The blockhouses, drives, and night raids have had some success against the Boers, but there were still the vast expanses of the western Transvaal where de la Rey had recently won two important encounters, including the capture of one of their senior generals, Methuen. The northern Transvaal where Beyers held sway, and the even more vast territory of the Cape Colony to which the Boers from the eastern Transvaal and the Orange Free State could retreat away from the blockhouses and barbed wire obstructions to continue the seemingly endless war, were still options open to them.

Even the protected zone around Johannesburg and Pretoria, long deemed safe, had recently been penetrated by the Boers under Piet Viljoen. An attempt to carry out a night raid on him and his men ended in humiliating disaster for the British.

Kitchener's own mental state at this time was frayed by exhaustion and pressure. He had been in full charge now for almost a year and a half without rest despite long hours. When he learned of Methuen's disaster, he collapsed and stayed in bed for a day and a half. In addition, his relationship with Milner was a constant source of friction.

Out of the meetings at Klerksdorp came direct discussions and negotiations with Milner and Kitchener. Milner wanted to include the National Scouts and those who collaborated with the British to have a voice in the negotiations, but this would, without a doubt, have wrecked the peace effort immediately. National Scouts and collaborators, or "traitors", as the Boers had labeled them, or even handsuppers, were anathema to them and were never reconciled to Afrikanerdom, or ever fully accepted by their people again. For decades after the war whispers still circulated as to who were National Scouts or collaborators, "traitors." Rightly, or wrongly, the loss of the war would frequently be blamed on them, and, although not decisive, their aid did indeed contribute significantly to the British war effort, especially as informers and scouts. They were marked people for the rest of their lives.

Kitchener, humbled more than once by the Boers whom he had held in contempt at the outset of the war, and for that reason more sage, saw the folly of Milner's position. The upshot was that only those who had fought so gallantly, had suffered so much, and had made so many irreparable sacrifices would represent their people in negotiating a settlement.

Despite their precarious circumstances, the Boers were in no mood to negotiate on terms that would demand surrender. Steyn and de Wet stood out in this respect. But some, e. g. Burger and Botha, deemed surrender inevitable. The British, on the other hand, were equally adamant about surrender. The issue continually threatened to explode the delicate negotiations. But at each turn skillful diplomacy on both sides kept the ever closing doors of negotiation to reopen.

Those at Klerksdorp could not make final decisions about ending the war. So they dispersed to their respective commandos to have duly appointed representatives come to the table of peace negotiations. Sixty delegates—thirty from each republic— were so appointed and arrived at Vereniging in the Transvaal on the muddy Vaal River. (Vereniging means "reunion.") Here they met for the first time on May 15, 1902 together with members of their respective governments. It was for this meeting that Smuts had left the Cape.

The days that followed would be anguished and imbued with deep emotions. It was not only the culmination of a bitter, and excruciatingly painful war, but also of a century of frustrating opposition to continuous British meddling in South African affairs.

It was a solemn meeting as each member is sworn in and takes an oath faithfully to serve nation, country, and government in carrying out their duties, and keeping discussions in camera, "so truly help us Almighty God."

General Beyers, competent and well liked, was elected chairman of the proceedings. Minutes were duly kept. One of those entrusted with this task was a highly respected Boer chaplain, the Reverend John Daniel Kestell. Unselfishly he had endured the hardships of war with the Boers while ministering to them, sleeping, sitting up in his saddle, under the starry heavens, in the cold of winter as well as the stormy weather of the summer, and never expecting special favors because of his position.

De Wet not only knew how to fight a battle and how to elude a dragnet of overpowering forces, but he also knew how to win a majority at a meeting. Untiring as he was, he had visited his commandos, and even before the delegates had arrived, had extracted pledges from the commandos, representing the Orange Free State, that they would not surrender independence.

It was soon evident that the delegates from the Orange Free State were disposed to continue the war. A rift was evident, but Botha pled for unanimity. Reitz, Secretary of State of the Transvaal, proposed that Witwatersrand (Johannesburg—the gold mines, the real cause of the war), and Swaziland, a black enclave in the southeastern corner of the Transvaal, be ceded to Great Britain and that the rest of the republics be left independent.

It was a talking point and a commission took it to Pretoria to discuss it with Kitchener and Milner. It consisted of Botha, de Wet, de la Rey, Hertzog, and Smuts. With united front the Boer commissioners stood up to their British counterparts. When Milner snapped that he wanted only one language in the republics, Hertzog snapped back, yes, he wanted only one language too, Dutch! When Milner captioned the document on which they were laboring "Act of Surrender", Smuts wrote over it "Act of Peace".

It seems that it was an obvious axiom for the British that the more primitive the politically dominated people of a territory, the easier it could be controlled. If the natives in the two republics were in political control, they would be more manageable than if the independently minded Boers held political sway. It was, therefore, not surprising that in the course of the war England had frequently been beating the hypocritical propaganda drums of a war for the political rights of the natives. It created the noble overtones of a war for a cause, rather than for riches. But the truth of the matter is that the sincerity of such assertions was rather badly exposed by the almost total absence at that time, and decades later, of political participation of blacks in England's colonies bordering on, or near the two republics, where whites and blacks were mixed, and where blacks outnumbered whites by a large majority. Prime examples of the lack of black participation in government were the Cape Colony and Natal (where they had been involved in a fierce war with the Zulus not too long before English War II), as well as Northern and Southern Rhodesia. The whole question would be thrashed out and embodied in a clause of the final instrument of peace. From the 19th to the 27th of May they worked to hammer out a peace settlement.

De Wet's politicking with the delegates prior to the convention had created a pressure block among the Boers as well as against the British negotiators. It paid off in forging a better peace settlement.

Consultations with London finally produced the document which the commission took back to Vereniging.

It did not please many a delegate. Steyn had been suffering from a severe eye ailment and was absent from much of the proceedings. When the terms of the peace settlement was shown to him, he denounced it and rejected it completely. He also resigned as President. So de Wet succeeded him and became the last president of the Orange Free State. They had until May 31 to decide and to render a verdict, yes or no. Again agonizing discussions ensued as evidenced by the participation of General Pieter R. Viljoen: "I have prayed that God may grant that I would not trample on the precious blood that was shed—the blood of my own son . . . ." He made a motion indicating that they are forced to give up independence.

De Wet proposed that a document be drawn up reflecting the feelings of the delegates. It carried. Hertzog and Smuts were entrusted with the task.

The document when finished is blunt and direct about the brutal way the war had been conducted, about the destruction of private property, depriving people of a means of livelihood, about the concentration camps infamous with disease and death. They made a special plea for the Cape rebels.

The pledge made by the Orange Free State delegates to their commandos not to accept surrender was a stumbling block, but also a threatening bargaining point. Hertzog, a Dutch trained jurist and a member of the Orange Free State Supreme Court, had ruled earlier on this matter. Delegates, he maintained, were not just mouthpieces, but had an obligation to express their own, best judgments. He was greatly respected as a jurist, and his opinion as rendered was accepted by the delegates.

Earlier in the discussions Botha had already posed the sobering question: "What is the bitter end?" Would it be when they are all in their graves? Even de la Rey, one of the most successful generals, had concluded and expressed his view to the meeting that the bitter end had come.

The Boers were a fiercely proud and greatly self-respecting people, so much so that they were driven by a tenacity in their long struggle that had by now almost caused their utter annihilation. So, to no surprise, on the morning of May 31, the day of the deadline for a decision, the delegates were still torn by division and uncertainty as to how they would vote. Final conclusion remained elusive. Consultations continued. Botha and de la Rey had talked with de Wet that morning, urging him to accept the proposals. His support would swing many of the delegates. Then de Wet, with what must have been a most painful metamorphosis for such an indefatigable warrior, pronounced for acceptance of the document under consideration.

As they met that late autumn day, the inner pain of defeat was clearly etched in the stark faces of many. Their indomitable spirit to fight, to sacrifice, and to win, that had carried them through the years of privation, could no longer belie the reality that the bitter end was irrevocably upon them.

Three delegates from the Transvaal and three from the Orange Free State voted not to concur. Most notable among them was General Jan Kemp.

A preamble set the document of ten articles forth as an agreement between Great Britain, the Orange Free State and the Transvaal republics.

1. The Boers were to lay down their arms and acknowledge the King of England as their sovereign.
2. All prisoners and internees were to be returned by Great Britain, [the republics] making the same acknowledgment.
3. Burghers laying down their arms were not to lose their liberty and property.
4. There would be no legal prosecution of burghers, war crimes excepted.
5. Dutch was to be taught in schools, should parents so desire. It would also be admitted in courts of law.
6. Rifles were permitted for personal protection.
7. Civil administration would follow military administration and would be followed by self-government "as soon as circumstances permit it."
8. The question of franchise of Natives would not be decided before self-government was granted.
9. There would be no war tax.
10. District commissions were to be set up to aid in resettlement and provide necessities. Banks of the republics would be honored as well as promissory notes, for which purpose a free gift of £3, 000,000 would be provided by the United Kingdom. Liberal loans would be made available.

The only consolation for the Boers was that it was not unconditional surrender. It was surrender with dignity. Had the British been smart enough to have taken this course a year earlier, it would have saved many lives, not to mention needless destruction.

A mere hour before midnight on May 31, 1902, as if holding

out for a last minute miracle, the document was signed in Pretoria in Melrose House on Jacob Mare Street. Signatories were: For the Transvaal: Burger, Botha, de la Rey, Reitz, and J. C. Krogh; for the Orange Free State: De Wet, Hertzog, C. H. Olivier, and W. J. C. Brebner; for the British government: Kitchener and Milner.

It was humiliating for the Boers to give up the struggle. Nevertheless, considering the overwhelming power of a mighty Empire which they had just the same taught a dear lesson, and based on the terms that their leaders could extract, they stood victorious in defeat with their heads held high, an honor that they more than well deserved. It was far from an unconditional surrender!

The Boers had to sign that they would abide by the terms of the treaty. Many disposed of their remaining ammunition by shooting it away and broke their guns before surrendering them to presiding British officers. One man bent the barrel of his gun into a bow and humorously remarked: "Now the Englishmen can shoot in an arch and hit someone behind a rock."

At last, after more than two and a half years of a bitter war, peace had caused the echoes of artillery and the crackle of rifles to echo away into the past. Only scars remained of the wounds of flesh that could heal. The grass had grown over graves of small children and many fallen heroes. Burnt out farms were awaiting the return of the weary, devastated people of the two ruined republics. But the wounds of the heart would never heal.

The war had left little or nothing to the credit of the mighty British Empire, except that it had finally—over the dead bodies of thousands of its own soldiers, black people in their employ, Boers and their women and children—won control of the world's richest gold fields.

The British had lost a tremendous amount of prestige the world over as a so-called civilized people. The ability of the British to wage a simple war against untrained farmers, and the fighting ability of their Tommies as soldiers, regaled in splendid uniforms, on a man to man basis against the Boers, were barely above zero. This would have a devastating effect a little more than a decade later when World War I broke out. And had it not been for the assistance of the United States of America, England would have gone down in defeat, and sacrificed France in the process. The same, except to a much larger extent, was the case in World War II.

Total Boer casualties during the war were about 6,200, of whom about 4,000 died in battle, less than 1,000 succumbed to illness while on commando, about 150 died in accidents, and slightly more than 1,100 died as prisoners of war (Figures according to Dr. Fransjohan Pretorius, Professor of History, University of Pretoria).

Jacobus de la Ray, one of the most successful Boer generals, became Minister of Defense in the Botha cabinet. When rebellion broke out in 1914, he was on his way to the headquarters of the defense force near Pretoria, riding in the back of an automobile. Suddenly, shots rang out and de la Ray was assassinated. No one was ever apprehended or brought to trial.

Roberts, while visiting in France during World War I, succumbed to pneumonia on November 14, 1914. He was given an honorable place of burial in St. Paul's Cathedral. Kitchener, on a trip to Russia, drowned at sea in 1916 when a cruiser on which he was a passenger struck a mine. He also is honored in Saint Paul's Cathedral in London with a full size image reposed in death.

It is interesting to surmise: Had the Boers won the war, and had they applied the same criteria which the Allies had meted out to some of their enemies after World War II, would they also have been tried as war criminals, and hanged as well? Most likely not, but they would certainly not have been accorded ecclesiastical honors in a house of worship which is intended for the proclamation of love and the Kingdom of God.

A moving scene was witnessed in Jerusalem in 1999, almost a millennium after one of the crusades. A white-haired, German gentleman had made a special trip to Jerusalem. He was a descendant of a man who as a crusader had killed many a Muslim and many a Jew in Jerusalem in what was then a noble ideal to establish Christianity in its original cradle. There was a heavy burden on this gentleman's conscience. Walking the streets of that city he apologized personally to as many Jews and Muslims as he could find for his ancestor's cruelty. . . .

CHAPTER VII

THE PHOENIX

The courageous Boers had gone through hell, death, and damnation. They stood staring at ashes, thousands of graves of dead ones, without a means of livelihood, and there seemed to be no hope. A mood of despondency that all had been lost, in spite of supreme sacrifices, thousands of women and innocent children who would never return, loss of their worldly possessions that gave them security, loss of home and hearth, stretching out over two and a half years like a pain bench, filled them with bitterness and resentment day after day. It was like a horrible dream that was haunting them at awakening every morning for many months.

The refugees at Rooikrans received the terms of peace with extremely mixed feelings. There was no scarcity of tears. They could not but be tortured like others who had suffered and fought gallantly for their freedom until they finally grew callous, used to their fate, and accepted it as part of reality, whether they wanted to or not.

Fortunately, there was a solace to which they always repaired. Taking refuge in this solace was inherited from many generations before which had suffered during prolonged religious persecutions of the Dutch and the French Huguenots. It was their faith, deeply rooted in the Bible, hymns, and prayer. The Bible was their rule of faith and life, as it had been for their ancestors in tribulation, through ages and many generations before them. It contained for them the solution to human problems and the answer to human questions of the incongruities of life. Their hymns reaffirmed what they believed and lived. Prayers made their religion a strong reality. Tangible things around them had gone up in smoke and crumbled into ruins and ashes, but they had a spiritual stamina and security within themselves that could not be destroyed by fire and without which survival as a people would never have been possible. They accepted the fate of their nation, the loss of material things, and their privilege of self determination as part of divine will.

Now that all was over, they even sought to forgive their enemies and to forget. It was so dictated by their faith. But the refrain kept on coming back time and again: "We will forgive, but never forget," which really meant that they could not forgive, for forgiveness to truly take hold, demands restitution, some of which could never be made even if so desired, and of which there was none.

When a certain woman's son returned after surrendering and giving up his arms, when the peace treaty had been signed, she refused to receive him back. Lenie Storm heard about it and, the saint that she was, went to see her to bring about a reconciliation. "We have lost the war," she said, but remember, 'The pen is mightier than the sword.'" In time it proved that she had the right philosophy.

It was June, 1902 when Dawid de Villiers at last returned to his farm, Helderfontein. A cold, late autumn breeze played with the thin, white hair and white beard of this venerable patriarch. He was lucky to be alive, for had he been rounded up with many other old men to a concentration camp, he would most likely not have made it, like thousands of his contemporaries. His house had been put to the torch and destroyed, but fortunately a few small structures that he had built for storage before the war were still standing.

Always gentle, and although advanced in age, he was still tough. Under circumstances he had to be. Almost immediately he began reconstruction. He lived and slept in one of the small storage structures. The help that had fled to Basutoland early in the war for fear of being in harm's way, began to return and helped. And then there was faithful old Jantjie who had stood by him loyally throughout the long months of almost continuous flight.

When a few rooms were ready, he returned to Rooikrans to get his wife, Magdalena, and their daughter, Sannie.

Lenie's small wagon also carried her and her children back. Their home had been torched like others and was in ruins. Dawid set them up in the small storage structures, made of field stones and mortar. They were not suited for living quarters. There were no windows, or doors left in them. They were gone and the cold wind of the winter had free play. But it was a lot better than the small wagon.

Again Lenie and the children put in dirt floors. Anthills turned into mortar made good dirt floors. Again they plastered the stone walls with soil mortar. It made their "home" look a little better than the bare field stones. Some of the window openings they covered at night with small pieces of corrugated iron. The doors were covered at night as well as they could with larger pieces of corrugated iron. The windows for which they did not have covers were made smaller with stone and soil mortar and then plugged up at night with burlap bags.

The cattle and wagons, which they were able to save, while fleeing were invaluable. They could again begin to till the soil, and the wagons served as additional places to sleep and provided a means of transportation, although endlessly slower than horse carts would have been.

The rehabilitation program was slow to start. Finally, Lenie and her children got an old cow to provide milk. She had a white groin and they named her "Witlies", meaning white groin. What else could they have called her?

Reports came that the prisoners of war were being repatriated, but they had no idea when. Every day Lenie was hoping that perhaps Jacob would suddenly appear. But the captors of the prisoners of war were in no hurry.

They had been fortunate beyond comparison to others who had landed in the concentration camps. The *kappiekommando* was often hungry and ill-clad as it fled through the veld, but in spite of these privations, and utter poverty to which it had been reduced, there was only one death, Boy van der Merwe, who had fallen in the skirmish at Groenkloof.

Sometimes they had as many as twenty wagons together.

Clothing was utterly scarce and food was never enough. But

the Storm family was happy in their rough, new home, if it could be called a home. It was endlessly warmer and more spacious than their little old wagon with its canvas cover.

There were no tables and there were no chairs, no beds, and no mattresses, except what they had salvaged in the little wagon. The rest had all gone up in smoke. They slept on the floor, glad to have a roof over their heads. Sometimes they woke up during the night with hundreds of little red ants crawling over them.

Dawie was now about three years old, and a joy to all of them, a friendly little fellow with a warm disposition to his doting mother and sisters. Of some cloth Lenie had made him a shirt with a small pocket. He would force his little hand into the pocket and with sparkling eyes brag, "When Daddy comes home, he will buy me candy and fill my pocket!" All that he ever knew about candy was what he had been told, and he thought it was the greatest thing that could ever happen to a little boy.

One morning he woke up listless and sick. He had a fever as could be determined by touch. There was no thermometer. As the day wore on he grew worse. He was kept in bed and the help of his grandmother was sought. As his situation deteriorated during the days that followed, they tried all the remedies known to them, but to no avail. There was no doctor readily accessible. The nearest one, if available, would be Ficksburg, and the only way to reach him would be by ox wagon. But they were hoping for a turn in his condition as they nursed him and kept close to him. That was all that many of the farm folks could do in those days.

About a week after he had taken ill, he looked at his sister, Katerina, and with a weak, little voice, his lips dry with fever, he asked her to make him some milk porridge (a delicacy made with flour and milk, served with sugar). But they had not seen sugar for many, many months. While Katerina took the little milk left to make the porridge, his grandmother hastened to her home. She rummaged through the bottom of a chest where she had hid a little cloth in which she had tied a small quantity of sugar and hidden it from the early days when they had fled their homes. She brought it back and sprinkled a little over the small

202

dish of milk porridge. Dawie sat up and ate only part of it, but all were delighted that he seemed to relish the taste of sugar, and assumed that he was improving. Then he leaned back on his pillow with a faint smile of satisfaction.

Half an hour later his grandfather, Dawid, was hastily summoned. There was anguish on the faces of all. He pushed the curtain aside over the opening to the bedroom aside—there were no doors—and ducked in. When he came out a little later, a bewildered group of Dawie's sisters and his brother, Hennie, awaited him. They need not ask him. The old man's eyes, dim with tears that he could not restrain, and his lower lip quivering under his white beard, tacitly confirmed the worst of their fears.

There were no pictures. So Lenie placed one of Dawie's little hands, now white in death, on a piece of paper and drew an outline of it to show Jacob some day when he would return how much his little boy had grown when he died.

It was a severe blow to the Storm and de Villiers families. But considering that they had lost only one small child, they were so much better off than many, many other families whose children had been wiped out by the thousands in the concentration camps.

*   *   *   *   *

The Boer commandos around O'Okiep kept their positions and awaited the return of Smuts, ready to resume battle.

But a crushing blow awaited them, almost worse than defeat in a battle, for after defeat there was always the hope of regrouping, and fighting another day. They learned to their dismay that peace had been concluded with virtual surrender, and that the war was over. Many of the rebels had known only victory and any thought of capitulating filled them with immeasurable disgust and disappointment. Grumbling swept through the ranks. They simply could not believe it. The only consolation for Danie and the other rebels, who were subjects of the British Crown, was that they would not be prosecuted. They would be disenfranchised for five years. All had to surrender their arms, which they too did with utmost reluctance, although they were all taken from British soldiers that they had captured and disarmed.

Some were so embittered and determined not to become British subjects that they refused to sign the agreement. By virtue of the peace treaty the Transvaal and the Orange Free State had passed to British jurisdiction. Consequently, it was no haven for those who had refused to sign the agreement of surrender. Young Reitz, who was on Smuts' staff, and General Manie Maritz emigrated to Madagascar, under French jurisdiction. Maritz later went to Southwest Africa, then a German colony. Reitz's father, who was in Kruger's cabinet, had made it clear that he had signed the peace document in his capacity as Secretary of State, and not for himself. He was given two weeks to wind up his affairs, after which he sailed for the United States of America. His son later returned at the urging of Smuts and his wife. Eventually, he became a member of a Smuts cabinet.

The Cape rebels, deprived of their horses, saddles and bridles, were put into a camp where they were quartered seven to a bell tent. Their horses, they were told, were taken to better pasture. Indeed they were, for they never saw them again. Many were stranded hundreds of miles away from home without transportation.

After some time in the camp, they were informed that there were horses several miles away in an enclosure. Those who had money could purchase one of those horses. It was a motley collection of animals in poor condition and of poor quality. Danie bought one that did not look too bad, but the animal proved to be infected with scab. He braided a rope with a tough kind of water grass which he looped through the animal's mouth around the lower jaw to serve as a bridle. He put a blanket on its back to serve as a saddle. Japie did the same and they set out for home.

Those who had served under Smuts, especially the rebels, were deeply disappointed in him. They never saw him again. They felt that they had been left in the lurch, and that he could have struck a much better bargain for them, especially as far as their horses were concerned. Brilliant and sophisticated, unfortunately, Smuts was not a people person as would show time and again during his long political career. Antagonistic feelings against him ran very deep among the rebels. He had become to many of them what de Wet's brother, Pieter, had become to him when he had surrendered to the British. It was a tragedy that his loyal soldiers, who had risked everything and who had served him loyally, characterize him with the harsh accusation, "Jan Smuts, you have betrayed us!" From that day on many would oppose him for the rest of their lives. They would never vote for him or his South African Party, later called The United Party. The opposition grew through the years until he was ultimately toppled from power in 1924 and again, for the last time in 1948, his virtual demise from political life.

Danie and Japie's journey home was not much easier than their adventuresome and daring march to war. The letdown was crushing. To make things worse Danie contracted scab from his horse, although he had tried to protect himself with the blanket. At times the itching was absolutely unbearable, especially when it warmed up during the day and he perspired.

Of course, they were welcomed at home with open arms and many tears of gratitude that they were alive. Their father was an innocent man, and had been a wealthy gentleman before the war. He had unfairly been humiliated by imprisonment. He had been marched to Ceres on foot to be imprisoned several times. After what they had endured at the hands of their government, the family did not hold anything against them for joining the rebels, and had no regrets other than that they were unsuccessful in overthrowing the power to be.

It was soon realized that their act of rebellion in taking up arms against the Crown had brought near financial ruin to their family. Their father's livestock was confiscated and so were their own possessions. Even their clothes were taken away. All that Danie had left was an old nanny goat which was probably astray on the day of the roundup. Their father was reduced to poverty, and would die in poverty.

Danie had to begin from scratch. There was plenty of sympathy among the Afrikaners and a neighborliness to aid those ruined by the war. Danie borrowed money from a cousin with which he entered into a partnership with his eldest brother, Pieter. They began speculating in livestock. They would buy up sheep, have them clipped, if it was time, and sell the wool. Then they would fatten them up and sell them to butchers.

The business went well. Danie paid off the debt to his cousin. He had enough to invest in a new cart and a pair of fine horses. Their business prospered. At times they were carrying sizable sums of cash on their persons. Constantly aware that this might subject them to robbery, they took due precaution, especially when overnighting in hotels or boarding houses. They slept with the money right on their bodies. As a further precaution they would bring the cross-bar of their cart and lean it against the door. An unauthorized entry would bring it down with a clatter and awaken them. One night the door did indeed open, but their plan worked. They were instantly awake and the noise sent the would be robbers scurrying down the hall and out of sight.

But robbery was not always with violence, as they would find out by bitter experience. They had accumulated a large flock of sheep. They knew of a butcher who handled size. They sold the sheep to him. The papers were drawn up dutifully for the transaction. He asked for a week's grace to make payment, and it was unfortunately granted. When settlement was not made the next week, it came to light that the butcher had filed for bankruptcy! Danie and Pieter had to settle with other creditors for 2/6 to the £1, or one-eighth of their original claim. They had lost in one week a great deal of their capital that they had built up so carefully.

*   *   *   *   *

There was no school on Helderfontein or near it. Dawid and Lenie consulted about the children's education. Dawid went to Ficksburg where he had a house. There was a school in session in the town. To his surprise his house was intact, but it was occupied by a couple who had lost their own home. He asked them to vacate it since he needed it for his daughter and her children. A time was agreed upon.

Early one morning while it was still dark Dawid had his team of oxen yoked and the Storms took leave of their rough quarters for Ficksburg. They started early so that Dawid could make the return trip the same day.

On the way they had to cross a stream, called Sandspruit. The ford was still guarded by British troops who were living in nearby tents. A *pickaninny* was leisurely leading the team down to the crossing. The soldiers had a few dogs. When they saw the wagon approaching they viciously charged the boy leading the team. He let go to escape from being attacked. The lead oxen took fright and swung around sharply, pulling each successive pair of oxen with them. Dawid and old Jantjie, the driver, rushed as fast as they could to stop the panic and to avoid a serious accident, but in vain. In a few seconds the entire team was at right angles to the wagon. The front wheel, on the side to which the team had veered, jammed solidly under the frame, raising it precariously into the air, and with the sudden force now applied by the team, narrowing the angle with the wagon, it was about to topple. The load shifted. If anyone would be pinned under the wagon, there would be no hope of survival. In panic some began to jump off. But the strain on the shaft, as it was thrown against the massive wagon, was too much. Fortunately, it snapped, freeing the bewildered team from the wagon. In a wild flight they stampeded through the pasture amid distress calls from those on the wagon, or already on the ground. Thanks to the broken shaft, the wagon remained upright.

When the rage of the dogs had calmed down, the team was several hundred yards away pulling the broken part of the shaft behind them. They were brought back and unyoked. They could go no farther without a shaft.

Dawid and Jantjie took off on foot to a nearby farm for help. The soldiers at the ford paid no attention, and Dawid was loathe to seek help from them anyway.

The owner of the farm, a Boer, gave Dawid a tree to chop down for a shaft. They did not think of bringing a pair of oxen to drag it back. To save time they decided to carry it. It was too much for Dawid and also for old Jantjie. They were not young men anymore. Out of breath and their hearts pounding, they

207

made frequent stops to rest. Exhausted they got back to the wagon. Dawid had some tools in the customary tool box under the railings. So they could drill holes and install the new shaft.

The day was already well spent when the wagon clattered across the ford. Jantjie was ready with his long ox whip. Should the dogs charge again, he would send them helter-skelter back to where they came from.

It was mid afternoon when they entered the main street of Ficksburg. In front of Ross' General Store with people on the veranda a box of the younger girls' dolls and dolls' dresses fell off the rear of the wagon and spilled all over the street. Flustered Nellie and her younger sisters scurried around to retrieve the precious possessions. They were so embarrassed with all the people watching them.

When they arrived at the house, it had not been vacated. The occupants even refused to let Lenie in when she went to the door. The woman angrily claimed that the house did not belong to Lenie's father, but to her father. It was not until Dawid himself appeared on the scene that she backed off. Being a compassionate man, Dawid worked out a solution. He would allow the couple to share the house with Lenie and her children. The house was not too large to begin with. Before the war Dawid used to drive into town usually on weekends by horse cart with his wife so they could do their shopping, attend the morning and evening church services, and return home on Monday mornings.

Sharing of the house was a trying experience for Lenie and her six children. They were overcrowded, but she was a woman with a kind heart and well aware of the hardship that they all had to endure. Finally, after several weeks of bunching two families in the house, the other family found quarters elsewhere and moved out.

The house was in bad disrepair. It had been used by the Tommies during the war. The plaster had been knocked off on the inside in places. So for the third time in less than a year Lenie and her children were plastering walls.

The family was eligible for food rations. Twice a week Lenie and Hennie stood in line for almost half a day to receive their meager allotment.

Living in a larger house was a great relief to the family compared to the confines of the little wagon, the stable on Rooikrans, and the storerooms on Helderfontein. Yet, life was hard with food barely enough and clothing old and worn to the point of embarrassment in public.

But Lenie was resourceful and enterprising. With a large family to clothe she knew how to sew. It was expected of all females to be able to sew. She began to take in sewing to earn money. She also had an oven built in the yard to bake bread and biscuits which she sold to the British soldiers who were still garrisoned in the town. She bought hats for her eldest daughters, Lenie and Katerina, so that they could attend church with her. (Females just did not go to church without hats.) Eventually, she was able to clothe all the children better.

Nellie and her sister, Anna, who were very close to each other, darned socks for the British soldiers to earn money of their own. They were barely ten years old, but they had to swallow a great deal of pride. To work for British soldiers was hardly thinkable.

Many interesting stories were told after the war. On February 6, 1977 the author interviewed a survivor of the war, Pieter Hermanus de Jaeger, who was then ninety-four years old, living in a retirement home, Avondsvrede, in Vrede, OFS. (Avondsvrede means peace at eventide.) For a man of his age he still had a lot of spunk and a good sense of humor. He told of a certain, daring Field Cornet, Coenrad Strydom, who served under de Wet. During one of the several hunts to capture him, he and his commando were surrounded, and seemed to be doomed. During this hunt, he related that a British officer had told a Boer woman that de Wet had been captured. This would be double disaster, for de Wet was guarding President Steyn. "Not captured," she said, "but surrounded." Then she took a match box and put it on a table. "There is de Wet," she said. So much faith had the Boers developed in this fox of the veld that she grabbed the match box away. "Where is the box now?" she asked. "It is gone," he said. "Well," she said, "and so will de Wet be." It was a prophecy come true. De Wet found a week spot, and immediately gave the order to charge and break out at this soft point in the net around them. To hurry everybody along Strydom laid his *sambok* into men and horse alike. In the rush and by mistake, he also whipped the highly regarded President Steyn. And escape they did indeed.

After the war this Coenrad Strydom lived in or near Standerton in the Transvaal. There was not much love lost between the Boers and their conquerors who occupied the two republics. Several times, when Strydom would encounter a Khaki, or even several of them, he would charge them with his horse and just knock them over. His plea in court: "I could not help it. I had trained my horse during the war to charge a khaki whenever he smelled one, and I could not restrain him." De Jager did not say how effective the plea was, nor what the verdict was.

Then there was dear great-aunt Sannie de Villiers Fourie, who played the little organ for the vesper services held by the *kappiekommando* as they fled to escape the concentration camps. The author also interviewed her in 1977. "The poor Tommies," she said, "we felt so sorry for them. They could not help it."

*   *   *   *   *

With a burst of gold the sun rose from behind the Dragon Mountains in the east. As the shadows decreased before the rising sun, hundreds of weary feet were crunching over the winding, dusty roads leading from Ladybrand to distant places in the Orange Free State. A cattle train loaded with Boer prisoners of war returning from Ceylon had puffed up from the coast a few days earlier. They would be discharged at the railway terminal somewhere near Ficksburg. It is not clear how they came to Ladybrand, for it is uncertain whether it had been connected by rail at that time. Perhaps they were taken there by ox wagon, and from there they would be on their own to reach home, or what they used to call home. For Jacob Storm this was finally the end of his exile. With him on the road were his brothers Hendrik and Stephanus, a nephew, Henry J. Storm, and his brother-in-law, Johannes de Villiers. According to a letter by Henry J. Storm they had sailed from Ceylon on December 23, 1902, almost

210

seven months after peace had been concluded. It was now February 23, 1903.

As soon as possible they took to the road on foot for the town of Ficksburg about thirty miles to the northeast of Ladybrand. The few possessions they had were carried behind their backs in bundles attached to sticks and flung over their shoulders. While in exile Jacob, who was quite handy, had carved out of some unusual wood of Ceylon a few things to bring to Lenie and the children. For Lenie he had made a brooch in which she later mounted a small picture of Jacob.

It was mellow midsummer and the grass waved tall over the veld. Next to the road they noticed the sun-bleached bones of once proud Afrikaner oxen strewn around by vultures and other predators. The long, artistically curved horns were now dislodged from the skulls and half hidden in the grass some distance away. Ugly, perforated stumps stuck out from the skull where the horns once were. Two black holes where the eyes were gave a spooky stare at the passersby. Where the animal had fallen several years earlier its decomposed remains had fertilized the earth and the red grass had grown taller. On either side of the road, at irregular intervals, spots of tall grass told the story of a herd that had been shot.

Many of the homeward wanderers from Ladybrand had slept the previous evening under the clear and refreshing star lit heaven of a balmy summer night. Jacob and his party had found hospitality on a farm where they were welcomed. They listened in disbelief to the eyewitness reports of the deliberate destruction, and the slow decimation and genocide of the concentration camps.

Those destined for Ficksburg began the second day of their walk early, hoping to arrive that evening.

They passed farm after farm that had been burned to the ground. In some places the owners had returned and were living in small make-shift quarters, struggling to wrest a livelihood from the soil with barely any implements and means. In some places only tall trees stood lonely sentinels around the ruins as if waiting, while slowly swaying in the breeze, for the return of those who had planted and nurtured them, but in vain.

The closer they came to the town, the more definite the information obtained from farmers about their families. Jacob went straight to his father-in-law's townhouse. He knew by now that he would find Lenie and the children there. The nearer home, the less he realized what was going on around him. The agony of years of separation seems to be compacted into the short time left to reach home—the nagging apprehension about his family's safety that had dragged through the years like an eternity, the uncertainty whether he would ever see them again. Exhausted as he was after two days and thirty miles on foot, his pace quickened and his pulse grew more rapid. The last few miles seemed longer than the entire journey on foot.

Then the house came into view. A few of the children were outside. He hardly noticed how they had grown and changed. Tears came to his eyes as he hastened into the yard.

Lenie got the news, for which she had been waiting for so long, from one of the children. Torn between disbelief and great anticipation, she rushed for the door. Then she saw Jacob. Instinctively she ran the few yards between them. The burden of the years of separation was suddenly lifted. Lenie's attention was always occupied with the daily cares for seven children, mostly in flight in the small wagon, in abject poverty that had suddenly beset them, ill-clad, hungry, and homeless in the veld, seldom certain of the next day's food, or safety. Only at night, when she was awake, crammed in her narrow sleeping quarters, with the wind blowing cold, or the rain spattering on the canvas ever so close to her, and a wild animal howling on a distant hill, did she really have time to think of her hardship, and how much she was missing her husband. But this was also her inspiration. It kept her hopes alive that some day Jacob would return alive and that her life would be different again. Although she knew that many had suffered infinitely more than she did, the death of little Dawie was a great sorrow that she would never forget. There was always the nagging thought that perhaps she could have done something to save him.

Jacob's sudden arrival was like a great illusion of a dream to her. Each step began to feel like a mile. Big swirls began to blur her vision. Her knees buckled under her and she collapsed in a dead faint while Jacob tried to grab her. There was no time for tears of joy and embraces. Anxiously he called her name repeatedly, but there was no response.

Frantically they tried to revive her. They grew quiet as they waited with apprehension at the sudden, strange turn of events. Then she blinked her eyes and looked at Jacob as if she had awakened from a long sleep, and a horrible nightmare.

For the Storm family the bitter war was over at last, but its effects, that had twisted and wrenched their lives, would linger for as long as they would live.

Except for the few head of cattle that were saved with the *kappiekommando*, Jacob had nothing—no implements to begin his farming again, no means of conveyance, except the little old wagon—not even a donkey.

Then early one morning he set out on foot for Helderfontein—three hours on horseback, or about eighteen miles away. Most of the day was spent walking. He found that his father-in-law had already restored his own place a great deal. With bitter resentment he looked over the ruins of what was once his home. He got a few helpers and began to remove the caved in stone and mortar walls that had tumbled to the inside. It was a tedious task that would take many days. Then one day it became unbearably hot as they were digging. Soon smoke began to come from the stones and mortar. It was hard to believe. Where Lenie and the children had stored the wheat the last time they had harvested, a fire was still smoldering. When the house was set to the torch the grain had caught fire as the thatched roof had caved in on it, and began a slow combustion from the top downward, shielded from air and rain by the walls that had collapsed on top. It got so hot they had to abandon the project for a while.

For months Jacob commuted for weekends on foot between the farm and Ficksburg where the family had lived. He began to rebuild his house on the old foundations and started a vegetable garden, which he enclosed with a stone wall to keep animals out. Meanwhile Dawid had made a trip to Basutoland. There was a white man who had an enormous number of cattle that he had hustled from the deserted farms in the Orange Free State. He did not have enough grazing and was glad to let Boers use the oxen and cows, if they would provide grazing. But Dawid had some money that he had saved before the war and he bought cattle.

They could plow some, but they did not have seed to plant. With a great deal of trouble Jacob found about a hundred pounds of maize seed. He had to pay the exorbitant amount of £3 sterling for it. Before the war about one tenth, or about six shillings, would have been a fair price.

When Jacob had three rooms under the roof, he moved his family back to the farm. The five girls had to share one bedroom, Jacob and Lenie had another, while Hennie slept under the kitchen table. Most of the children were still sleeping on the floor. There was no money to buy the needed furniture. Jacob continued to restore the rest of the house so they could live more comfortably.

Lenie, the eldest daughter, ran a little school for her sisters and other children from the neighboring farms.

Then a school was opened on a farm called Kwaggafontein, about eight miles from Helderfontein. But the Storms and many others did not have a quick means of transportation to make daily trips, and there was no money to pay for lodging nearby the school. But an arrangement was made to pay lodging in kind.

Every Monday morning, very early, the Storm children fell in the road on foot to be on time for the opening of the school. They carried their food supplies in bags on their backs—for each one of them a loaf of bread, meat, and some coffee and sugar. A neighbor, Giel du Toit, who had a cart and horses, picked up vegetables from Jacob's garden once a week, and took it to where they were staying as pay in kind.

Clothing was scarce. Each child had only one outfit for the week. To help keep their dresses clean Lenie put aprons on the girls, which they wore until Wednesdays.

Friday afternoons, after school was over for the week, they trudged home again on foot for weekends.

On Monday mornings in the winter the frost was always white on the grass along the dusty road to Kwaggafontein. Little fingers were frozen, red noses ran profusely, and their small bodies shivered under thin clothes without coats. They wore shoes which Jacob had made. It was winter, and it was supposed to be cold.

Other children came from all around, some also on foot and others in donkey carts rolling on old squeaky plow wheels, closely hugging the road. About seventy attended the school.

A Miss Leipoldt supervised those who were lodging at the school as house mother. She was a descendant of a German missionary, Leipoldt, who had chosen to work in the Cape Colony. The teaching was done by two ladies, Mrs. Jan du Preeze (Frieda) and Mrs. Pieter du Preeze (Annie), cousins of Miss Leipoldt.

But the school went only as far as the fourth standard, which a child would normally reach at the age of twelve. Many of the children were older because they had missed several years during the war. So, after a few years, Lenie moved back to Ficksburg again where the children could go through the sixth standard, the end of grammar school. She took in boarders to help supplement their income.

After grammar school, Katerina, Nellie, and Anna went to Bethlehem for further education, including some training as teachers. Then they were sent out to small rural schools where they taught and studied at the same time. Their salaries were only seven pounds, ten shillings per month, or £90 a year, but they were glad to have jobs. They even sent money to their parents. Katerina went to the District of Reitz, Nellie went to the District of Senekal, and Anna went to the District of Bethlehem. Upon completing grammar school, Hennie went to work in a store in Ficksburg. Lenie married Henry J. Storm, who had gone to war although only a teenager, and who was a prisoner of war with Jacob in Ceylon. (They settled down in Ficksburg where they spent the rest of their lives. They are buried in the cemetery in Ficksburg with their daughter Johanna, where the author paused for a while in tribute to these three dear people while looking for the grave of Boy van der Merwe, as earlier reported.)

When the older children had studied as far as they could go in the Ficksburg school, and had gone elsewhere, Lenie moved back to the farm again.

Two more children were born into the family, a girl, Susanna, nicknamed Susie, and a boy, Jacob, who was called Japie.

*　　　*　　　*　　　*　　　*

The war had visited deep trauma on the rural people, and by far the majority were farmers. Materially they were broken, having lost their possessions for which they had worked and saved frugally for generations. Their dire poverty weighed heavily on their already scarred spirits. Those who were landowners before the war had some financial resilience, but those who did not own farms were dealt a setback from which most never recovered. It was usually their aim to save enough and to be sufficiently strong as farmers with an adequate number of livestock to afford their own farms some day. Now these people had to start from the beginning. To make things worse, many had large families which they had to feed, clothe, and educate, if they could afford an education at all, for to go beyond grammar school, usually meant boarding school. This required money which they did not have.

The slow reproducing cycles of nature, with its miscrops, droughts, and other uncertainties of farming, just could not restore them fast enough before many were past their prime years of enterprise and new undertakings. Even landowners could not recover sufficiently to afford their children an adequate start when they had to launch out on their own.

The country was now reduced to colonial status with many of the economic disadvantages of the mercantile system which half a century later would explode to drive the independence movement in India and Pakistan to an unavoidable climax. Raw materials were exported to England, processed, and the finished products returned and retailed where the raw materials came from to swell the coffers of British entrepreneurs. Industrialization of the colonies did not serve the interests of the conqueror. There were few new jobs. Consequently, many of those who moved from the farms to seek a new life in the towns and cities, were doomed to menial employment, if they could find employment at all. For more than a generation the problem of these "poor whites", as sociologists call them, plagued the country.

*   *   *   *   *

The coal burning, steam locomotive had been chugging laboriously for a good part of the day pulling a train that had originated in Cape Town that morning. As the journey progressed northward the train rolled along the valley of the Great Mountain River. At Gouda it turned southeast following the valley of the Broad River into the spectacular Hex River Mountains. The scenery along the way was breathtakingly beautiful for the passenger as the train meandered through the fertile valleys covered as far as the eye could see with vineyards and orchards made famous by the French Huguenots who began to come to the Cape in 1688 and some years later. Rugged mountains with rocky peaks, serrated against a blue sky, stood sentinel over the valleys all along the way.

Danie had boarded the train that afternoon at Wolseley, the junction for the train from Ceres. He was conservatively dressed in a tailored suit A tight waistcoat fitted snugly around his middle. He wore a white starched collar and a narrow tie. A silver pocket watch on a silver chain, looped into a waistcoat buttonhole and looped again into the pocket on the opposite side. His French cuffs were held together with a pair of shiny, silver cuff links. A thick mustache bristled on his upper lip. A bright pair of greenish-gray eyes had a sharp and resolute look. He stood about five feet nine inches tall, strongly built and well developed by taxing work on the farm where he had grown up. On the top bunk in the compartment he had placed his portmanteau, stuffed with all his personal possessions.

The great financial reverse sustained by him and his brother, Pieter, when they were taken in by the butcher who had declared bankruptcy, had finalized his decision to move to the Orange Free State where there was more room. He had shipped his cart and horses before boarding himself.

At De Doorns, meaning "the thorns", an extra locomotive

was added to negotiate the steep ascent into the Hex River Mountains. As the journey resumed, listening to the engines, it was easy to tell that they were laboring near capacity. Then the whistles blew long and ominously, reverberating through the ravines, as if warning of imminent danger. Suddenly amid a deafening roar they were enveloped in darkness, and smoke swirled in through the open windows. It took a while for the unsuspecting and some frightened passengers to realize that they had plunged into the tunnel through the mountains.

On the other side the train emerged into another world—the Karroo, an arid plateau, four to six thousand feet above sea level, stretching for several hundred miles northeastward. It was covered with scrubby growth. Rainfall is very low, but when it does rain, it is transformed into a breath-taking garden within a few weeks, dazzling with wild flowers of all descriptions like various kinds of daisies, portulaca, etc.

The three to four hundred mile journey from the Hex River Mountains to De Aar in the northeastern Cape Province was monotonous, and seemed to take forever. The farmhouses were miles and miles apart. A farmer could not make a living here with a basket full of soil. At intervals a sheepherder's hut would squat among the low shrubs. The sheep were in good condition. They seemed to be constantly nibbling on the great variety of tough, drought resistant vegetation.

A good part of the Karroo was traveled under cover of darkness. At De Aar, an important railway junction, Danie changed trains for Naauwpoort in a southeasterly direction and then almost due north across the Orange River and into the Orange Free State. It was barely a decade ago when the names of these sleepy towns suddenly appeared in headlines of front pages the world over pinpointing the area of important encounters during English War II.

The vastness of the enigmatic Karroo was now far behind. The extra engine had been dropped once through the Hex River Mountain Pass. The train puffed on through richer, grass-covered plains which became more lush with increasing summer rainfall. At various places little groups of black children with potbellies and G-strings as their only clothing, if any at all, would stand in

218

awe of the noisy, fire eating and smoke belching monster as they have done every time a train went by. Homesteads were now closer together, marked by clusters of eucalyptus trees, planted for shade and windbreakers—a peaceful, pastoral plateau, the high veld, rolling on with valleys, meadows and low hills for about four hundred miles, across the Vaal River, into the Transvaal.

Daniel Johannes Jacobus Theron (Jr.). Picture about 1910

These plains would be Danie's new home. His eyes scanned the horizons, seemingly days away. It satisfied his expectations—well suited for livestock and cultivation.

As the train came closer to his final destination in nervous excitement he pulled his watch out of his vest pocket more often. At last the heavy, steel wheels thundered into Lindley Road station, later called Arlington. The train came to a stop and the glistening steam locomotive stood hissing in swirls of smoke and steam, looking very much like an overly exerted animal. He detrained. His cart and horses were there and it was not too long before he rode into an easterly direction in search of a farm to lease.

Hospitality was common among the Afrikaners. At night he would stop at a farm and would be welcomed and invited to overnight. It was a usual courtesy shown to travelers. He soon found that his name was almost a magic asset. Captain Danie Theron was a distant relative, and by now the daring part he had played in the war had made him a legend. Everyone knew how he had risked his life to slip through to Cronje's *laager*, and back at Paardeberg, dealing decisively with a guard, how he had operated with great success against the British railway system, and how he finally had perished in a wild shootout, rather than surrender. The fact that Danie had fought in the Cape Colony and had taken up arms voluntarily at the peril of being shot as a rebel, further helped to establish and cement relationships. In addition he had been on Smuts' staff as a spy. (A picture of Smuts and his officers shows Danie standing at the far left.) He was an entertaining narrator and evenings, spent with strangers, passed by almost unnoticed as they shared their war experiences.

Bitter memories of the war were being pushed aside by great events that were in the offing, which evoked lively discussion, and which would shape the destiny of South Africa.

Eight years had now elapsed since the signing of the peace treaty of Vereniging. Self-government was one of the most cherished clauses of peace for the Afrikaners.

On May 31, 1910 it came to pass. The Cape Colony, Natal, the Orange Free State, and the Transvaal were joined together into the Union of South Africa. Each Province had its own local government with a Union Government, consisting of a House of Representatives and a Senate under a Prime Minister, which bound all together. The Crown of England was represented by a Governor-General. The question of a capital, as mentioned before, was solved by establishing three capitals—Cape Town the legislative, Pretoria the executive, and Bloemfontein the judicial capital.

The birth of political union consisting of four separate entities in South Africa was a direct, beneficial outflow of the English War, although at a price of enormous trauma, far outweighing its value. Had the Boers won the war, it is highly doubtful that unity would have eventuated for many, many decades, if ever.

The flag that waved over the Union of South Africa was the Union Jack, an indignity which many of the Afrikaners in the two former republics suffered in silence, but they took pride in the fact that many of their former leaders sat in their halls of government and ruled them.

General Louis Botha became the first prime Minister of the newly created Union of South Africa.

*   *   *   *   *

Danie had found a farm to his liking near the town of Senekal, about sixty miles northeast of Ficksburg. From the cash that he had raised in partnership with his brother Pieter he could buy livestock and farm implements. He signed a lease for five years. Rainfall was good, grazing was lush, and he prospered.

He soon discovered that his personal involvement in the war would carry him only so far. One day the landowner came to his house. He immediately noticed a change in his usual, friendly attitude. He stood before him, tall and rather heavy set. His blue eyes looked at him only at times, as if avoiding a direct confrontation. His clean-shaven, pinkish face was expressionless. To Danie's amazement his fat fingers were clutching a heavy cane. He never carried a cane before. Attempts to be friendly and pleasant were ignored. Then in arrogant tones he announced that he wanted his farm back. He wanted to break the lease. He needed it for his son. Protests that there was a five-year contract seemed to enrage the old man and he seemed at the point of assaulting him with the cane. The house boy, who also did the cooking, stood in the kitchen, his mouth open and his eyes wide as if expecting violence at any moment. Then the old man got into his cart and drove off. He had given his notice.

A visit to an attorney allayed Danie's fears. "You have a contract," the attorney assured him, "and you cannot be forced from the farm." The attorney advised him to bring the contract to him next time he is in town, which he did. But he made a bad mistake. He did not ask for a receipt.

All seemed peaceful at first. But Danie began to notice that some people were avoiding him and others seemed less friendly. He could sense an uneasiness in the neighborhood. He was bucking a powerful man. Then infringement on his farm began. A herd of cattle would appear in a section he was saving for later grazing. Avoiding personal involvement, he would send his help to drive out the herders and the cattle, but the infringement continued. Under the law he could round up the cattle and demand damages, but he knew that it would precipitate an incident.

Then one day he could take it no longer. He saw the cattle coming and waited until they had spread out in his pasture and the herders had dozed off, as was common. He had his riding horse saddled. He tightened the saddle for a rough ride and dug his heels into the flanks of the horse as soon as he had mounted.

The herders were at peaceful rest until the thumping of hoofs were upon them. He shouted orders to round up, rapidly galloping back and forth laying a heavy sambok unmercifully into cattle and herders alike. In the wild stampede that followed a gatepost was knocked over, but the cattle were driven out. He had served notice that he would not stand for any more harassment. It was no secret whose cattle it was. He fully expected another visit from the landowner, but he did not come.

Subsequently Danie stopped to see his attorney. The attorney appeared embarrassed. He informed him that he had apparently "lost" his contract. A search of his office had proved futile. An uneasy silence fell over the two men as they stood facing each other. The attorney kept on pulling his shoulders up in a helpless gesture, frowning with half-mooned eyebrows under a furrowed forehead while Danie's greenish-gray eyes pierced him with daggers. It took a while to dispel his disbelief. He had no receipt for the contract. "Oh, I see!" he uttered at last, turned around, and left.

With the contract "lost" he had no choice but to vacate the farm on which he had made some improvements in anticipation of a five-year stay. He had made some good friends while in the area. At the end of the harvest season he left Penhoek, as the farm was called, and moved to another farm which he had leased from a certain Coennie Celliers.

It was on the Celliers' farm that Nellie Storm was teaching. It did not take long before she was introduced to the eligible bachelor. Danie was immediately attracted to her. She stood about five feet, seven inches tall. Her jet-black hair, never cut since she was born, was parted in the middle, lightly draped over her ears, and then swept back and rolled into a neat bolla held together with hair pins behind her head. Her slender figure was well accentuated with a high middle and a long skirt nearly touching her shoes. She had a soft white skin, purposely shielded from the sun, which contrasted attractively with her deep-brown eyes, black eyebrows and eyelashes. He began to call on her and on weekends they went for long rides in his two wheel carriage with a tan-colored canopy and two well groomed horses.

He found moving disrupting. He had to learn about the quality and nature of the soil, hire new help, and adjust to a dozen other things before a new routine would be established.

By mid-summer he was well settled with his grain waving in deep green on the fields and his livestock in good condition with a number of new-born calves.

For several days he had not been feeling himself. He had a headache that got worse by the day. His stomach was upset, and his back ached. He spent most of the time lying down and got up only to give orders. He knew his temperature was abnormally high. He had hoped that it was only a passing indisposition, but he developed chills and got worse. He became weaker as no food seemed to agree with him and he felt dizzy when he got up. A rash began to appear on his chest and abdomen.

More than a week had passed since he first began to feel sick. Each day he was getting worse and he had to do something. He had his house boy harness and hitch his horses to his carriage. Ill and weak, he half staggered to the cart and with great difficulty raised himself on the steps into the seat. He took the reins himself. The house boy was not experienced to handle the spirited horses. His head ache was unbearable. It felt as if his head was as large as an anthill on his shoulders. The boy sat with him to open the gates.

He drove to the house of a neighbor, Nicolas Kruger, with whom he had become good friends. He thought that he would ask him to take him to the doctor. When he drove up to the house, Kruger came out. He was a stout, friendly man, with deep blue eyes. He thought the call at mid-morning was unusual. When he noticed Danie's dry lips, ashen color, and eyes dulled by a high fever, he knew immediately that something was radically wrong. He called his wife, Sannie, and they took him to a room off the porch and separate from the house. He was put to bed and Nick, as he was called, immediately sent a messenger on horseback into town to summon a doctor. He came late in the afternoon. His diagnosis was typhoid fever in an advanced stage, the disease that had taken thousands of lives in South Africa.

The Krugers had five children, four girls and a boy. But in spite of the fact that they might contract the dread disease, they decided to let Danie stay where he was. The doctor gave strict orders about precautions to the Krugers to protect themselves against being infected themselves. Flies, always a pest on a farm, were to be kept from the bedroom. Feces and urine had to be buried. Laundry had to be kept separate and sterilized. Hands had to be washed with soap and kept clean at all times, especially after handling the patient, or being in his room. He promised to be back soon, which meant a few days.

That night Danie became delirious with fever. Nick and Sannie began a vigil around the clock that would last for more than a week. Often they sponged him off with cold water and more than once in the course of days they thought that the end had come.

Horrible nightmares haunted him—on torrid plains with hot sand dunes that seared his feet; the sun beating down on him unmercifully; the devil in hot pursuit; a desperate search for shelter, but finding none on the inhospitable dunes; a losing battle with the devil; a temporary escape, and then another exhausting run for his life, falling down and gasping for breath and water. Then the same thing all over—fleeing from a posse of Khakis; trying to raise his gun in self defense, but his arms turning to water; then facing a firing squad as a captured rebel. Nick and Sannie Kruger stood faithfully by his side. They could not see the parched plains, or hear the threatening voices as his tormentors sought his life, but they saw large drops of perspiration rolling off his forehead as he agonized. They sponged him off, trying to lower his fever and to alleviate the anguish which they caught in his groans.

The doctor came several times. He had little hope. The disease had gotten too far and had done vast damage to his intestines. He had a constitution made of steel and, although, eyes closed most of the time, outwardly unaware of his surroundings, his strong will to live subconsciously battled steadily day after day to survive.

The Krugers were worn out. They took turns at night, sleeping a few hours, and then up again. Other neighbors came to relieve them. The minister came to call. The gravity of the situation was more than apparent to all.

As his life hung on a thread for days, a letter was dispatched to the Therons in Ceres. It would ease the shock. They went to Ceres daily for the mail, hoping that there would be none.

*   *   *   *   *

Most of Jacob and Lenie's children were now on their own, providing for themselves and, although their incomes were small and barely enough to live on, they sent some cash home from time to time. The setback of the war had dealt Jacob a blow from which he could not recover. They made their farmhouse on Helderfontein as pleasant as possible for the children who frequently returned to visit for weekends or holidays. Jacob loved music and had a beautiful tenor voice. Their children were musically inclined, inherited from the de Villiers side of the family. The girls could all play the little organ in their grandfather's home. There were necessities that the family needed, but their father saw to it that they got a piano. Often they gathered around the piano in the Storm home and passed an evening singing and playing. The Dutch *Hallelujah Boek* and an English collection called *The Globe* were frequently used for

Hymns. They were a happy family closely knit together by hardship and struggle.

Nellie had fallen in love with a cousin who had planned to study for the ministry. They would probably have been married, had not her parents counseled against it very firmly. They both knew that the advice was sound and broke off their relationship, but Nellie just could not forget. They had been so fond of each other. Danie's visits helped her forget a little how heart-broken she was. As for him he was also thinking back of a girl that he had in Ceres. They too were very fond of each other, but she contracted influenza and died. Then he just did not pay attention to the opposite sex for a long time.

And now Danie was desperately ill. For a few days his condition became somewhat stable, but the doctor cautioned that any slight complication could tip the balance unfavorably, and mean the end.

When Danie opened his eyes one day and looked around the strange room, memories of the harrowing nightmares began to haunt him, and he asked where he was. The Miraculous and the Supernatural had won the battle! Improvement was slow. When he got up again, he had to learn to walk on Nick's arm. More than a month after he had gone to the Krugers that morning, he was able to go home. He owed them a debt that he knew he could never repay, but he thought he would ask anyway. It was the proper thing to do. "You owe us nothing," said Nick, "but take better care of yourself."

He went to see Nellie again. He was about to propose, when one day she told him that she had accepted another position and that she would be leaving for Ficksburg. She would be in charge of a little school for a group of children who lived too far from the regular school in town. A few of them were physically handicapped and could not get around too easily.

Danie was greatly disappointed and could not help wondering whether she wanted to get away from him. Ficksburg was sixty miles away and a long distance to cover by horse carriage. It was a full day's journey.

As the courtship continued long-distance, World War I exploded over Europe. England became mired down in a war

226

from which she could not extricate herself. Indirectly the English War of 1899—1902 in South Africa had hastened the day of reckoning in Europe. Her enemies, especially Germany, had lost their respect for her war capability as demonstrated in South Africa, and rightly so.

To the dismay of many Afrikaners their government entered the war with England. This was too much for thousands whose memories of the war and defeat of 1899-1902 were still raw and vivid. The indomitable spirit of the Afrikaner, who had now been solidified in the Union of South Africa, began to boil in some, and they saw in the circumstances an opportunity to rid themselves of the British yoke for good. De Wet once again swung in the saddle against England. Beyers, Kemp, and others followed. A rebellion broke out.

Smuts, as Secretary of the Interior, had the task of putting down the rebellion. Many of the Afrikaners rallied to the support of their government to help prevent violence and bloodshed. Afrikaner was now pitched against Afrikaner in an ugly confrontation.

Danie had been a rebel against the Crown during English War II. His views and oppositions to the British domination of South Africa were well known where he lived. It was no secret that he, like many a Cape rebel, had little time for Smuts. As a consequence he was suspect from the very beginning, and it would not have surprised anyone had he joined the rebellion. He made the mistake to leave his farm on a Saturday by carriage for Ficksburg. Speculation immediately began that he was in reality on his way to join up with rebel forces. He visited Nellie for the weekend, but while he was in town all movements were restricted. The town was garrisoned by volunteer civilians. He could not get out. Men with white arm bands stood watch for the government and maintained the status quo. It was November 1914, a time of the year when he could ill afford a long absence from his farm. No matter how he pleaded, he could not get permission to leave. He attempted to leave by night, but guards turned him back. He contemplated making a mad dash for it, but he realized the situation was like a tinderbox that could catch fire any moment. His horses would be shot down and he himself

227

might be killed by some trigger happy volunteer. He realized how suspect he was. So he turned back into town. For two long weeks the tense situation dragged on. The only redeeming factor was that he could see Nellie frequently.

During one of the encounters of rebels and government forces a cease fire had gone into effect, but it was not observed by all the rebels. A certain young man, Jopie Fourie, continued to shoot. He was captured, tried, and condemned to face a firing squad. Urgent appeals were lodged with Smuts to commute the sentence. Smuts had already evinced traits of an unbending legalist in the execution of some National Scouts in the Transvaal and in the case of Colyn, a traitor, at Windhoek in the Cape Colony. He was still the somewhat aloof, tough general with limited appreciation for political expedience and the common man. The appeals went unheeded and early one morning, as scheduled, Fourie fell before his executioners. It might have been military justice, but it was a lasting, political blunder of a magnitude that Smuts could not imagine. He could have used the incident to win over, or at least to disarm, many of his opponents among the Afrikaners. Instead it alienated them even more. Fourie almost immediately became a martyr, right or wrong, and the death of this young man furnished Smuts' opponents with a sentimental weapon most appealing to the younger generation for as long as he lived. Even thirty years later Fourie's name would still come up at political meetings.

The summer of 1914-15 was a busy one for Jacob and Lenie Storm. They were preparing for a double wedding. Nellie was to be married to Danie on the same day that her younger sister, Lettie , would be married to a certain Andries Swanepoel.

February 9, 1915 was a bright, sunny day. It was warm. The fullness of summer had spread a lazy quiet over the town of Ficksburg nestled among the hills on the banks of the Caledon River in the shadows of the majestic Malutu Mountains. In the Dutch Reformed church that dominated the town with its massive steeple they solemnly said their vows. The Reverend John Daniel Kestell, local clergyman, a chaplain in the war with the Boers, and one of those entrusted with the minutes of the Vereniging meetings, as stated before, officiated.

A lively reception followed at the house of the two brides' sister, Lenie, who by now had three little girls, Lulu, Kitty, and Johanna. Their sister Katerina, who had recently married a Jan Taljaard in the District of Reitz where she was teaching, also came. There were toasts to the brides and toasts to the bridegrooms, and a lot of merry-making.

When the wedding and reception were over, Jacob and Lenie returned home. The sun had already set when they reached the farm. A song fest of crickets and an assortment of frogs had set the meadows in endless swaying motion of nature's music. Their children, who had miraculously survived the war, were now all on their own. A privation that only parents could appreciate, they had made the education of their children one of their primary goals. Only Susie and young Jacob, named after his father, both born after the war, were still with them. Struggle and hard work had enabled the Storms to recover somewhat from the devastation and setback of the war, but the best years of their lives were already far behind them. They would never be well-off, or own their own farm, as they had planned. The future and hope of the land and of the infant Union of South Africa were now in the hands of a younger generation. The two elder Storms had quietly settled down with a deep sense of contentment as only a peaceful pastoral life could create.

At dawn one morning, after a brief honeymoon, Danie and Nellie boarded their carriage, the same one that had come with him from Ceres some six years earlier. It had been left in Ficksburg. They were setting out on the long journey to their home. As the day slowly broke over the mountains in the east, the two spirited horses were straining at the reins. Animals always know when they are going home. They can't wait. There is no doubt about it. Their hoofs tapped in perfect rhythm on the hard road like sticks on drums in a lively parade. The large wheels of the carriage whirred around and around endlessly with shiny spokes flashing in the early sun, grinding sand into sound—a little band of man, horse, and carriage at the accompaniment of their own music on a swift journey through the veld to a destiny. As far as the eye could see green pastures rolled on and on, wrapped in splendor of summer, and hope of the future.

Neeltje Johanna Elizabeth (Storm) Theron with children
Magdalena Johanna and Daniel Johannes, 1922, wearing black in
mourning of Jacob Storm who had died that year. She had made
all clothes, but shoes.

CHAPTER VIII

THE FLIGHT OF THE PHOENIX

The century since the fateful English War of 1899-1902 has been one of totally unexpected change for Southern Africa.

The formation of the Union of South Africa, including the provinces of the Cape Colony, Natal, the Orange Free State, and the Transvaal, was a most significant development. The Union was to have an elected, Westminster form of self-government (House of Representatives and Senate), headed by a prime minister. The Crown of England was to be represented by a Governor General, mostly a ceremonial position. Because it was difficult to decide on a capital, an ingenious compromise was reached, although in many respects clumsy and costly to maintain. Cape Town in the Cape Province became the legislative capital, Pretoria in the Transvaal the administrative capital, and Bloemfontein in the Orange Free State the judicial capital, seat of the supreme court. It meant that when Parliament was in session in Cape Town a large number of government employees had to journey to Cape Town and be lodged in the city to be at hand when needed.

The first Prime Minister was a Boer general, Louis Botha, who had wide support among the Boers and Boer generals, as well as among the English speaking white population. In reality the Boers, who had lost the war on the battle field, had won it at the ballot box, because they were in the majority, and they would continue to do so increasingly in most of the subsequent elections.

The black population, mostly uneducated, was unfortunately left out of the government as they had been in British Colonies in other parts of Africa. By twenty-twenty hindsight, had they been given at least limited representation in the government with gradual increments leading eventually to full democracy for all, much of the trauma of three quarters of a century later could have been avoided. But such an enlightened vision was not part of the milieu the world over. As a direct result of this omission in 1912 the African National Congress was formed to agitate for political rights of black people, but they would be ineffective for many a decade.

The outbreak of World War I brought a change in the coalition of the Afrikaners, descendants of the Boers, and citizens of British descent, mainly because the Union of South Africa joined England in the war. The rebellion that ensued was fortunately of short duration. However, it unfortunately became a factor in the rending asunder of the political coalition that had been in place. James Barry Munnik Hertzog, also a former Boer general like Botha and Smuts, parted ways with them and formed the National Party, which elected a formidable opposition in Parliament.

Upon the death of Botha, Jan Christiaan Smuts became Prime Minister, but he was defeated in the election of 1924 by the Nationalists with the help of the Labor Party, and Hertzog, leader of the Nationalists, became Prime Minister. The Nationalists pushed for greater independence, and Dominion status was obtained. Other parts of the British Empire, e. g. Canada, Australia, and New Zealand, benefited, and also became dominions. The Union got its own flag, which replaced the Union Jack, although it was retained in the middle of the flag in miniature form along with the flags of the two former republics of the Transvaal and the Orange Free State. Hertzog was reelected in 1929.

In 1933 Hertzog and Smuts joined political forces again, forming the United Party, which combined the Nationalist Party and the South African Party. As leader of the new United Party, Hertzog was reelected Prime Minister in 1934.

Of utmost importance to the country was the influence of Christianity through the centuries. During the apartheid era the Dutch Reformed Church of the Afrikaners sided mostly with the government, although there were those in it who vehemently opposed apartheid. However, the negative results of the support of the Church in the political venture of apartheid were far outweighed by the results of its missionary work which it had been doing for centuries, not only in Southern Africa, but even

234

way beyond its borders in Central Africa. This missionary outreach, supported by a spurt in establishing four new seminaries to train black ministers and church workers as well as white missionaries, eventually resulted in the Dutch Reformed Church in Africa, reaching beyond the borders of the Republic where missionary work had been done years ago. Disappointing is the fact that this Church is unwilling to merge with the branch of the Dutch Reformed Church comprised of what is known as Colored People. This Church is eager for such a union. Nevertheless, regardless of its shortcomings, the various denominations, including communions established by English speaking churches among the black tribes, have had and will continue to have a wide-spread, salutary effect in the country, countering a culture of violence so common to Africa. In addition this missionary effort created a large reservoir of goodwill between black and white people that can not but contribute to bring about political harmony.

Daniel Francios Malan, a member of Parliament, with a doctorate in theology and a former ordained minister of the Dutch Reformed Church, did not go along with the 1933 coalition worked out by Hertzog and Smuts. Instead he became the leader of the remnants of the Nationalist Party, and so of the opposition party. He had entered politics some twenty years earlier at the request of people who felt that he would make a good leader. In order to do this he had to lay down his mantle of ordination as required by the Dutch Reformed Church.

During its term that began in 1934 the Hertzog government initiated the Native Act by which, among others, decreed that large tracts of land had to be bought by the government from white people, and turned over to black people.

1938 was an epoch making year in the Union of South Africa. It was the celebration of the centennial of the Great Trek of the 1830s. For three months several covered, jaw bone wagons, pulled by the best teams of oxen that farmers could provide, moved slowly from the Cape Province to their ultimate destinations in the Orange Free State, Natal, and the Transvaal. Every evening where the wagons encamped, proceedings were broadcast over the radio. (It was long before television replaced radios.) The women all over began to wear fancy costumes of the 1830s, the men grew beards, and dressed up with colorful vests. Folk dancing was revived on a big scale. Never had there been such a revival of Afrikaner nationalism. It all culminated on December 16, 1938 at various places of historical significance, but especially at Voortrekkerkoppie (pioneer hill) near Pretoria. Here a massive monument in honor of the pioneers, and commemorating the Great Trek would be erected. This symbolic trek would have far reaching, political consequences for decades to come.

The thunder clouds of war had ominously been gathering over Europe, and as early as the middle 1930s it had seemed inevitable that war would erupt. Hertzog's position was that in such an event the Union of South Africa should decide in a plebiscite whether to be part of such a war eight thousand miles away. (It would most likely have been a negative vote.) Smuts did not share this view of a plebiscite, and it is even suggested that he and those around him had purposely tried in the election of May 1938 to pack Parliament with representatives who would be in favor of declaring war. It was the constitutional prerogative of Parliament to decide in the matter of a declaration of war. A vote for a plebiscite would not have carried in Parliament anyway.

Thus, with the outbreak of World War II in 1939 Hertzog's government fell when it failed to defeat a motion to join England in a declaration of war on Germany. (*Encyclopaedia Britannica* is grossly in error in stating that the vote was 80 to 6. It was more like 83 to 67) So Smuts once again became Prime Minister. As a result the Hertzog/Smuts coalition party of 1933 in essence fell apart , and Malan, who had not gone along with the coalition in 1933, significantly increased his representation in Parliament from those who had favored a neutral stand in the war. Hertzog had no choice but to return to the Nationalist Party which he had formed some twenty-five years earlier.

In short order a massive meeting was organized at Voortrekkerkoppie. People came from a thousand miles away, and others hundreds of miles away in a show of solidarity and strength against entering a war. When the proceedings had concluded, Malan and Hertzog walked slowly down the hill amid thundering applause—Hertzog with his narrow, steel-rimmed, oval glasses, always characteristic of him, and Malan with his heavy tortoise shell glasses, also always characteristic of him.

Hertzog was a highly respected jurist, an able general during English War II, a man of stature, and of high character. The plight visited on the Boers by that war always weighed heavily on him. He filled a unique need as leader of the Afrikaners, and accomplished a great deal for them during his career. He held a special place in their hearts, and no wonder, he was one of their revered heroes. He was a statesman with his focus on Southern Africa. But the British had little time for him. It is not surprising that the article on him in the *Encyclopaedia Britannica* is slipshod, short, and in addition, full of errors. He died in 1942 at the age of 72.

When World War II was over, Malan had rebuilt the Nationalist Party sufficiently to present a real challenge to Smuts' United Party. Smuts was not a people person. He was not known for diplomacy to win friends and influence people. He had alienated the Afrikaner people in numerous ways. Prominent Afrikaners, who spoke out against being at war, were interned for years. A famous wrestler, Johan van der Walt, was shot in the back while trying to escape arrest to be interned. He was paralyzed for life. Peaceful farmers were compelled to surrender their guns. It did not escape him that he had built up a large reservoir of ill will against him.

The British tried to help Smuts. A tour of South Africa was arranged for the Royal family. This was solid cement for the English speaking South Africans. But Smuts had their support anyway. What he needed was a large percentage of support from the Afrikaners to stay in power. The tour had just the opposite effect on them. It was a colossal, political blunder. Politics in South Africa have invariably been marked by a rancorous rough and tumble. The tour was soon dubbed "the great circus," and cartoonists had a field day with it. Had Smuts invited the Queen of Holland to tour the country, he would have done himself a great political favor.

In the meantime the leaven of the symbolic trek of 1938 had

237

quietly done its work among Afrikaner teenagers who could now vote. The massive monument on Monument Koppie, planned in 1938 to honor the pioneers of the Great Trek, long delayed by World War II, had been under construction for several years since the war had ended, and would be inaugurated with a nation-wide celebration. The new nationalism born in them in 1938 and nourished by the rush to complete and dedicate the monument had decidedly molded their choices at the ballot box.

It was not surprising that when the election results of 1948 came in, Malan had won a majority in Parliament and had defeated Smuts as Prime Minister. As leader of the Nationalist Party he became Prime Minister. Smuts even lost his own, supposedly impregnable seat, the District of Standerton, which had been given to him when he had lost his seat in the Cape Province in the 1924 election.

Smuts, who had originally planned to become a clergyman in the Dutch Reformed Church, instead had entered law. His fame as a daring general of English War II, capped by his epoch making foray into the Cape Colony, will always remain one of the most daring and intriguing phases of the war. He was one of South Africa's most brilliant leaders. He had tried to unite the two factions of English and Afrikaans speaking people. It might have been for this reason that he never penned his memoirs of the war. Unfortunately, the wounds of English War II as well as the British involvement of the 19th century in Southern Africa ran too deep in the memories and hearts of many to bring that about during his life time. Some Afrikaners remained loyal to him, but it was sad that by far the majority, despite his high character, ability, brilliance, scholarship, and international statesmanship, had no time for him. It was not surprising that several times his election victories were with slim margins, and twice he was defeated in a bid for Parliament, as noted above, once in 1924 and the last time in 1948. In both instances he was given a seat in Parliament that some other member of his party had contested and won in the preceding, general election, and was generous enough to relinquish to him. Otherwise the leader of their party would have faced the embarrassing scenario of being out of Parliament. Never did he win a seat "unopposed," as

Encyclopaedia Britannica tries to soothe over his defeats. (*Encyclopaedia Britannica* in its article on Smuts, as compared to its treatment of Hertzog, errs in the opposite direction.) The British needed him. He became the front man for the Empire in Southern Africa. He attended several Imperial Conferences and in 1941 was bestowed the honor of being appointed a field marshal in the British Army. This did not sit well with many of the Afrikaners, and did not help him in the 1948 election. Defeat in 1948 weighed heavily on him, like defeat in Parliament did on Hertzog in 1939. Not only did he lose his seat in Parliament for the second time, but he had lost the reins of government as well. Throughout his life he had seen to it that he was physically fit. He was vigorous, exercised by riding long distances on horseback and walking for miles in the veld studying plants, about which he was an expert. But, in spite of constant exercise and physical fitness, he also, like Hertzog, a few years after his defeat, died in 1950 at the age of 80.

Smuts, apart from his hand in establishing Fort Hare as a college for black people, never seemed to concern himself much about them. The Malan government, in contrast, was greatly concerned about the political implications of black people. It set in motion its apartheid policy, envisioning separate development and separate governments for blacks and whites in the country. The apartheid, as originally conceived, was never intended to suppress black people. And whatever bad might have, and might still be said about it, it was in no way a black hole for non-whites as the world press was quick to brand it, and still does.

There were several factors that hobbled apartheid from the very beginning. It was obviously a mistake to name it apartheid to begin with. It was also a gross mistake to solidify it in statutes. Apartheid had been the order of the day practically all over the world. For example, the United States' armed forces lived in, and fought in apartheid until it was changed after World War II. Apartheid had dominated the major sports, football, baseball, and tennis. And when the Supreme Court decreed that schools in the United States should be integrated, whites fled the inner cities by the millions and built new suburbs with virtually guaranteed segregated schools, for blacks could not afford the suburbs to begin with. It truly aided immensely in turning inner cities into black ghettos. Then bureaucrats and legislating judges got hold of the the Supreme Court ruling and drove it to the ground with the ingenious solution of bussing children, sometimes twenty miles in one direction across a city to effect integration. Fortunately, in the long run, this hopeless situation collapsed under the weight of its own absurdity.

Apartheid had existed in Southern Africa, dating back since the first day in 1652 when whites had set foot permanently on the southern tip of the continent with some Hottentots and Bushmen around, and even more so when the first black people were encountered in the interior in 1779. It existed not only between whites and non-whites, but also between the various tribes that had settled in Southern Africa.

Furthermore, the concept of apartheid in South Africa went against the spirit of reconciliation that began to permeate the world after World War II. In addition, millions of black people were already, and had for more than a century, lived among the whites on the farms and in the cities, integrated into the economic system. But the Afrikaners, being Calvinists, who called a spade a spade, unfortunately, had little aptitude for diplomatic niceties. Had it been given any other name with a positive connotation, it would not have given critics an easy handle to condemn it. As the policy of apartheid developed, bureaucrats got hold of it and drove it to extremes in some cases as they would do anywhere in the world. They ignored the power of history.

History is reality and it moves on inexorably in the world. Attempting to make it stand still or even worse, attempting to reverse it, is folly. History will deal harshly with whose who attempt to do so in politics, religion, or in any other sphere of human existence, and leave them behind encapsuled in cocoons from which there will be no escape without much pain, and suffering.

Yet, apartheid, misconceived as it might have been, had envisioned many laudable goals. Education was to receive a major push among blacks. Housing would be provided to replace the miserable shanty towns of squatters, and definitely was, eventually by the hundreds of thousands of homes. Unemployment would be attacked by aiding the start of industries where most needed. Although universally damned abroad by the press, the apartheid policy of the Nationalists had done more for a third world people within its own borders than probably any government anywhere else on this globe. Eventually, several black tribes, when they so desired, did indeed get self-government with emphasis on democracy, electing representatives who would function along with the tribal system of hereditary chiefs and councilmen, a system which would hopefully be phased out as time went on and be replaced by general democratic elections. A fond dream even to this day.

After World War II communism had become a strong influence in the world. China had succumbed to it, and Africa was fertile ground. The African National Congress became enamored with it, and Russia exploited the opportunity, fanning the winds of discontent by supplying arms and training terrorists. Russia and atheistic communism, with the ANC as a ready tool, galvanized a much more united front of both Afrikaans and English speaking whites. Many English speaking citizens began to vote for the National Party, and its majority in Parliament became progressively overwhelming with successive elections. They were loathe to yield to communism and opposed any attempts by the ANC, which became known as a terrorist organization, to give them representation in the government of the republic. The good will between black and white, which had always been a corner stone of a peaceful country, suffered undue damage as a result of violent agitation.

On May 31, 1961 the Union of South Africa severed its ties with the [British] Commonwealth and became the independent Republic of South Africa, stretching from towering Table Mountain in the south to the Limpopo River in the north. So a dream, envisioned by Paul Kruger and cherished by the National Party for many decades, finally became a reality, in no small part due to the Boer-Afrikaner love of freedom.

Industry in the Republic was booming, so much so, that it became the most highly industrialized country in the southern hemisphere! This booming was in no small part due to sanctions and boycotts imposed upon the country in opposition to its apartheid policies. Therefore, what they could not import anymore, they began to produce themselves, and what is more, began to export to the world in competition with the sanctioners.

As the Republic prospered black people also prospered. The most important objective of apartheid of bringing education to black people was a Herculean task. Boycotts supposedly designed to wreck the country's economy notwithstanding, many schools were built for non-whites. Their standards were lower than schools for whites that had been in existence and developed for centuries. Normal schools by the dozen were built to train teachers for the many new schools for black children. Twenty-six Technical Colleges for black students in twelve urban centers were in operation by 1982, with another fourteen planned by 1987. Universities were built for black students, including a medical school. (Black medical students had been trained before at the University of Cape Town and Witwatersrand, Johannesburg.) The new institutions were of exceptionally high quality. They were staffed by integrated black and white faculties to prepare blacks for more productive careers in society, industry, and in farming.

It was a surprising sight, totally non-existent before, in a much maligned country of apartheid, to see thousands of black children on their way to schools every morning—all over, even in the outlying farming districts, and in the bush veld!

When the Malan government began to institute its program of black education, black children in schools and students in universities totaled barely 400,000. By 1994, when Mandela became president, between four and five million were being educated, not counting the millions whose illiteracy had been wiped out during the intervening decades.

The Nationalist government had been studying constitutional change for decades. It became obvious that apartheid, as originally envisioned, was impractical. This led to advisory representation of Colored People and Indians to the government. It was a mistake not to have extended the same to black people. One of the main reasons for this was probably the communist commitment and loyalty to atheistic Russia as represented by the

ANC, which the whites were loathe to grant any quarters.

Inevitably communism in Russia and eastern Europe had to collapse as a viable economic system. The ANC had lost its sponsorship. This made whites in Southern Africa less fearful and more amenable to deal favorably with blacks seeking participation in governing the country.

The cornerstone, education, absolutely essential for a viable democracy, had been laid many decades before and was bearing fruit. So, one of the greatest and unexpected accomplishments of apartheid was that by educating non-whites on such a large scale, it was inexorably working itself out of a job as a statutory policy.

As education increased and as economic prosperity began to create a strong black middle class, it became inevitable that the franchise be extended to all and that majority rule be instituted. Under the able leadership of F. W. de Klerk, President, as well as Mandela and other representatives, a new constitution was hammered out, and a general election scheduled for the entire country. Thus Nelson Mandela was elected President of the Republic of South Africa in 1994. Mandela had shortly before been released from prison where he had spent some twenty-seven years for terrorist activity in which people were killed. He could likely have drawn the death penalty. Yet, Mandela became a respected president, even among the whites.

The gracious, peaceful, democratic transfer by ballot box of the reins of government from a white minority, which had been in power for centuries, to a black majority took place without even a ripple of violence on election day. It was in itself indeed a miracle, without a revolutionary war as has happened so many times in world history, and is most likely unprecedented in world history.

And as the Republic moves forward into the twenty-first century, a host of problems remain: Birth control continues as a taboo, and spawns uncontrollable, and unmanageable unemployment.

Many of Mandela's followers and his heirs apparent still espouse the communist theory of economics. This is the single most dangerous threat to a highly developed, capitalistic country, for communism presents no lure of capital, foreign or domestic, which would spur economic growth, creation of jobs and prosperity. A confiscatory tax is being levied on capital assets to help support the millions of unemployed. During the first term of ANC rule inflation has skyrocketed. Interest rates have done the same, and as a consequence entrepreneurs can not afford new ventures. Crime has proliferated at an alarming rate. Many living in government housing refuse to pay their rent.

A tell tale warning of economic problems besetting South African is its currency, the rand. It has tumbled to less than half of its value in recent years.

Hopes of a melting pot developing in the Republic of South Africa like in the United States of America is a pipe dream. The USA may still have its little Italys, its little Hollands, its little Polands, but most of these "littles" are made up of people who had long ago said farewell for good, some many generations ago, to a former heritage to seek a new open door, a new land, and a new future. Their ancestors have said goodbye to the blood, sweat, and tears of their own fatherlands to embrace a new world. The further their descendants generate from the original immigrants, the more attractive the comfort of the new haven with its umbrella of economic security and personal safety appeals to new generations. The past becomes a vague mist. What makes America a melting pot was once most succinctly summarized by Franklin D. Roosevelt in an address to the staunchly patriotic Daughters of the American Revolution. He began with the shocking words, "Fellow Immigrants, ..."

In South Africa citizens, white or non-white, have long ago already ceased to regard themselves as descendants of immigrants. The whites, especially the Afrikaners, think of themselves as descendants of South African pioneers mostly going back to some three hundred years. Consequently, blacks as well as whites regard themselves as indigenous with a right won by their ancestors, who had shed their blood for the land on which they live and which they love, black tribes fighting other black tribes, whites and blacks fighting, whites and whites fighting. Instead of the melting pot, or conglomerate of the United States, the population of Southern Africa constitutes a polyglot—parallel columns of tribes written in different languages with home land boundaries fairly clearly defined by history, and cast in cement by the British during the 19th century. There are some six major black tribes, and it has been the custom for centuries, with few exceptions, found mainly in the cities, that there be no intermarriage between different tribes. The same applied to a large extent even to the Afrikaners and the British descendants. Apartheid between tribes, like it or not, has been the ingrained custom for centuries, and it will not be eradicated for centuries.

And now, a century after English War II, what about the Afrikaners whose ancestors had risen from the ashes of that war and what about the English speaking whites whose ancestors were wedded to the Crown and supported England in the war? What does the new century that will be inaugurated on January 1, 2001 bode for them? From time to time these two groups had been able to strike a political accommodation. The first such accommodation came in 1910 with the birth of the Union of South Africa, but is was of short duration and fell apart with the outbreak of World War I when the Boers, now turning Afrikaners, were loathe to be drawn into a war that was England's business. The second came in 1933, but it too was shattered for the same reason in 1939 with the eruption of World War II. But now these two groups have no choice but to adopt the spirit of a frail, dear old lady who used to play the harmonium for the *kappiekommando* for evening vespers while they were fleeing to escape the deadly concentration camps, Sannie de Villiers Fourie. An attitude of reconciliation had come to her when the war was barely over in these simple words spoken in 1977 when she was in her nineties: "We felt so sorry for the poor Tommies. They could not help it." *Nolens volens*, these two groups have to find the only ground that makes sense—reconciliation and cooperation.   And the amazing phenomenon is that they are being joined by all, regardless of color or creed, who have acceded in the intervening years to join the middle class. Once again, unexpectedly, like the Boer pioneers of the nineteenth century, not only the Afrikaners and white English speaking segments of the population, but the middle class of their compatriots of other races as well, are

245

forced jointly into pioneer *laager* status of a different kind in a land which they had long deemed safe and their own. The *laager* begins with the very homes in which they live—behind high fences, a series of locked gates and doors, large watch dogs, and security systems to safeguard them against burglars, and in some cases even against indiscriminate murderers who get away with impunity. The *laager* even extends to their automobiles which have to be safeguarded against highjackings, carried out by the thousands per year. And finally, the *laager* extends to the guarantee of their personal property, which is supposed to have been safeguarded by the new constitution, but which is now being whittled away by taxes on assets to fund entitlements paid out to thousands of unemployed due to overpopulation. Now the disquieting question is, how long will the guarantee of the constitution last to protect personal assets? Other countries in the history of mankind did become alarming examples of what happens when personal property is no longer guaranteed. Such a country will inevitably become an international pariah, shunned by brains and investment capital from abroad, which will inevitably cause it to descend into the abyss of third world nation status.

In *laager* status they are once again proceeding into an uncharted future. Fortunately, their defenses and their means of protection are formidable and of great variety: stamina for survival in adversity as inherited and recorded in their history, intellect, knowledge, expertise, political skill, strong religious convictions, and character, all of which have carried them through trying times of the past. In addition there still exists the valuable reservoir of good will with many non-whites filled through the centuries by kind deeds and mutual respect. These characterize the nature of the assets that will enable them in due time to break out of the *laager* imposed upon them, and once again, this time without the sword, to overcome the seemingly impossible and to help lead the new Republic of South Africa to be a power of liberty and justice for all, undergirded by a loyalty of all segments of its greatly divergent population.

Valuable as these characteristics and assets may be, coupled with its storehouse of natural resources, it will not yield the

246

success to which the Repbulic of South Africa is entitled, unless strict enforcement of law and order is established and maintained, the lack of which has created and made necessary this debilitating circling into a *laager* once again.

And God bless the Republic of South Africa, all its people, and those who rule it!

Here is a tribute to a beautiful country with exceptional promise:

O!   SUID-AFRIKA*

1. Suid-Afrika, met skoonheid toegerus,   (a)
    Met jub'lend see en branderryke kus,   (b)
    Rustig in sonvloed en vlaktes gewieg,   (c)
    Trosts, majesteus, in berge hoog gestyg,   (b)
    Met duif en leeu en storm hef ons die lied,   (c)
    Geliefde Land, om hulde aan te bied.   (d)

2. Toevlug en rusplek en van ons voorgeslag
    Mid graan en vee, fabriek en blomglimlag,
    Ons pioniers en leiers van weleer;
    Ons sing hul lof met dankbaarheid en eer.
    Vryheid en waarheid was hul steeds getrou.
    Op hierdie rotse word ons land gebou.

3. Land met verskeidenheid van volk en taal,
    Veelkleurig saamgestik soos die heelal,
    Met sede van geloof uiteenlopend,
    Tog saamgevleg oor stad en veld en rant,
    Jou kinders soek na eenheid in ons land.
    Ons is as een aan harmonie verpand.

4. O! Land, oorvloedig deur Voorsienigheid,
    Jou bodem so met rykdom toegerus,
    Ons ag dit hoog met diepe dankbaarheid.
    Jou roep tot adel maak ons steeds bewus
    Van broederskap verenig hand aan hand.
    Tesame marsjeer ons vir jou, ons Land!

* Geadapteer op die wysie van "God of our Fathers," George William Warren, a-c; b-d

O! SOUTH AFRICA*

1. O! Land of grandeur, lovely to behold,   (a)
   Guarded by breakers, jubilant and bold,   (b)
   Cradled serenely in sunburst and plain,   (c)
   Mighty in mountains, pride of your domain,   (b)
   With lion, dove, and storm this song we raise (c)
   O! our dear Land, to you we sing our praise.   (d)

2. Land of our birth where now our forebears rest
   Midst maise, and smile of flow'r, and waving wheat,
   Leaders and pioneers of fortitude,
   We sing their praise with joy and gratitude,
   Because on freedom's rock they built our land;
   On truth's foundation you will always stand.

3. O! Land of hope for millions in the past,
   Quilted in customs and beliefs so vast,
   Spraed over city, mountain, plain, and vale
   In unity that friendship may prevail;
   Contrast of all creation's wonderment,
   Our destiny one purpose and one land,

4. O! Land of plenty, blessed by Providence,
   With treasures grand, precious, and so immense,
   We cherish all that you have stored for us;
   We shall obey your call to nobleness.
   In brotherhood we grasp each others hand;
   Together we shall march for you, our Land!

* Music of "God of our Fathers," George William Warren
adapted: vss. a-c; b-d

GLOSSARY

Assegaai............... A long speer used by natives in war

Boeretroos .... Farmer's consolation, a cup of coffee

burg....................... A town or city, often used as a suffix to name a city or town like Johannesburg, or Pittsburgh

Dolos..................... The *astragulus*, an anklebone of sheep, cattle, or goats collected by little boys as toy cattle.

Donga .... A deep, wide ditch created over many years by water carving it out, especially during heavy rains

-dorp .... Town or village, often added to the name of a town or a village, forming one word, like Klerksdorp

-fontein................. Fountain, often used in naming farms, like Leeufontein, meaning fountain of the lion.

Impi...................... A formation of Zulu warriors

Kappiekommando Bonnet commando—Boer women and children fleeing in ox wagons to escape the concentration camps before and after their homes had been torched

Koppie .... A low, free standing hill

Kraal.................... An enclosure for livestock, a corral

Laager.................. A group of wagons drawn in a circle or triangle to fend off an attack

Nek....................... A pass

Olifant.................. Elephant

Pickaninny............ Affectionately used to mean a young black boy

Pt............................ Port

Sambok/Sjambok... A mean whip cut out of hippo skin

Sdng .... Siding, meaning a place where a train stops

-stad .... City, more likely a town or village, like Greylingstad

Stn. .... Station

Veld .... Pasture land, usually undulating or flat and stretching for many miles on end

INDEX
(Partial)

INDEX OF MAPS